SPECTRAL READINGS

Also by Glennis Byron

LETITIA LANDON: The Woman behind LEL

DRACULA: The New Casebook (*editor*)

DRACULA (*editor*)

NINETEENTH-CENTURY STORIES BY WOMEN

REIMAGINING WOMEN: Representations of Women in Culture
(*editor with Shirley Neuman*)

Also by David Punter

THE LITERATURE OF TERROR: A History of Gothic Fictions from
1760 to the Present Day

ROMANTICISM AND IDEOLOGY (*with David Aers and Jon Cook*)

BLAKE, HEGEL AND DIALECTIC

THE HIDDEN SCRIPT: Writing and the Unconscious

THE ROMANTIC UNCONSCIOUS: A Study in Narcissism and
Patriarchy

GOTHIC PATHOLOGIES: The Text, the Body and the Law

INTRODUCTION TO CONTEMPORARY CULTURAL STUDIES
(*editor*)

WILLIAM BLAKE: Selected Poetry and Prose (*editor*)

WILLIAM BLAKE: The New Casebook (*editor*)

Spectral Readings

Towards a Gothic Geography

Edited by

Glennis Byron

and

David Punter

Published by PALGRAVE MACMILLAN
Houndmills, Basingstoke, Hampshire RG21 6XS and
175 Fifth Avenue, New York, N. Y. 10010
Companies and representatives throughout the world

PALGRAVE MACMILLAN is the global academic imprint of the Palgrave
Macmillan division of St. Martin's Press, LLC and of Palgrave Macmillan Ltd.
Macmillan® is a registered trademark in the United States, United Kingdom
and other countries. Palgrave is a registered trademark in the European
Union and other countries.

Outside North America
ISBN 0-333-69909-2

In North America
ISBN 0-312-22223-8

This book is printed on paper suitable for recycling and
made from fully managed and sustained forest sources.

A catalogue record for this book is available from the British Library.

Library of Congress Catalog Card Number: 98-52329

Transferred to digital printing 2002

Contents

List of figures

Notes on contributors

Fred Botting lectures in literary theory, romanticism and Gothic writing at the University of Lancaster. His publications include *Making Monstrous* (Manchester University Press, 1991), *Gothic* (Routledge, 1996), and the *New Casebook* on *Frankenstein* (Macmillan, 1995).

Glennis Byron is Senior Lecturer in English Studies at the University of Stirling. Her publications include *Letitia Landon: The Woman Behind L.E.L.* (Manchester University Press, 1995), an edition of *Dracula* (Broadview, 1998), and the *New Casebook* on *Dracula* (Macmillan, 1999).

Christine Ferguson is currently a doctoral student in English at Tulane University in New Orleans. She has published on Victorian Freak Shows and the Modern Primitivist movement, and has recently completed an MA thesis on the literature of Jack the Ripper at the University of British Columbia.

Jerrold E. Hogle is Professor of English, University Distinguished Professor, and Chair of the Faculty at the University of Arizona. His books include *Shelley's Process* (Oxford University Press) and *Evaluating Shelley* (Edinburgh University Press), and he has served recently as President of the International Gothic Association. He has published many studies of the Gothic and is currently completing a thorough study of *The Phantom of the Opera* as a cultural phenomenon.

Avril Horner is Senior Lecturer in English and Associate Director of the European Studies Research Institute at the University of Salford. Her publications include *Landscapes of Desire: Metaphors in Modern Women's Fiction* (with Sue Zlosnik; Harvester Wheatsheaf, 1990), and she is co-author, with Sue Zlosnik, of *Daphne du Maurier: Writing, Identity and the Gothic Imagination* (Macmillan, 1998).

Jeannette Idiart and **Jennifer Schulz** are at the University of Washington in Seattle, where they are working on topics in early twentieth-century American literature, including moral reform writing; the literature of the Civil War; and the Harlem Renaissance.

Robert Mighall was recently a Research Fellow in English at Merton College, Oxford, and is now a commissioning editor for a major London publisher. He has written articles on various aspects of nineteenth-century literature and history, and has edited a volume of Oscar Wilde's poems. His historicist study of Victorian Gothic fiction is forthcoming with Oxford University Press.

David Punter is Professor of English at the University of Stirling. His publications include *The Literature of Terror* (Longman, 1980; new two-volume edition, 1996); *The Hidden Script* (Routledge, 1985); *The Romantic Unconscious* (Harvester, 1989); and *Gothic Pathologies* (Macmillan, 1998).

Eric Savoy is Professor of American Literature at the University of Calgary. His recent published work has been on Hawthorne and melancholia; on Henry James and queer theory; and on AIDS and poststructuralism. He is co-editor of *American Gothic: New Interventions in a National Narrative* (University of Iowa Press, forthcoming).

David Seed is Reader in English Studies at the University of Liverpool. He has published monographs on Thomas Pynchon, Joseph Heller, Rudolph Wurlitzer and James Joyce. He is general editor of the *Science Fiction Texts and Studies* series (Liverpool University Press).

Helen F. Thompson has recently completed her dissertation, on Edmund Burke, Frances Burney and the bourgeois public sphere, at Duke University. She has been appointed Assistant Professor at Arizona State University.

Barnard Turner teaches modern literature at the National University of Singapore. He has published a monograph on Thoreau, and other work on German and Australian writing. He is currently completing a book on the dramatist Heiner Müller.

William Veeder has lectured and published essays and books on various Anglo-American Gothic writers including Mary and Percy Shelley, Irving, Poe, Hawthorne, Le Fanu, Stevenson, Bierce, Gilman, James, Hardy and Stoker. He is presently working on *The Turn of the Screw* and an historical novel on Bierce.

Alexandra Warwick is Lecturer in English at the University of Westminster. She has published on vampires and the Empire; on nineteenth-century painting; and on aspects of women's studies. *Fashioning the Frame: Dress, the Body and Boundaries* was published in 1997, and *Terminal Conditions*, on the apocalypse in the nineteenth century, appeared in 1998.

Sue Zlosnik is Head of English at Liverpool Hope University College. She has published *Landscapes of Desire: Metaphors in Modern Women's Fiction* (with Avril Horner, Harvester, 1990), and *Daphne du Maurier: Writing, Identity and the Gothic Imagination* (with Avril Horner, Macmillan, 1998).

Introduction: of apparitions

David Punter

As the millennium approaches, at least in the terms laid down by the most economically, ideologically and theologically dominant of the world's communities, it seems at the same time as though we live increasingly in a world peopled by ghosts, phantoms, spectres. There are, Derrida assures us from within a long tradition, spectres haunting Europe, or haunting the West; there are, Abraham and Torok affirm, phantoms haunting and distorting the process of psychological transmission down the generations. There are, the theorists of post-modernism assert, perhaps *only* simulacra; entranced by the flickering glow of the new technologies, our bodies vanish from our apprehension, leaving only media constructs, apparitions of desire, hungry *revenants* whose appetite is matched only by their impotence.

Seen from one side, this looks very like a process of psychological disavowal. For the bodies, which, as so much contemporary science fiction tells us, may become increasingly unnecessary as we fare forward into the labyrinths of a prosthetic universe, are none the less not absent from our screens: they are, indeed, there in their starving, battling millions, but conveniently placed, as Freud would have it, 'on another scene'; or, in Julia Kristeva's resonant term, 'ab-jected', thrown violently away from us and below so that we shall not need to confront the unacceptable abjections of our own psychic and social processes.

Seen from another angle, this landscape looks like a world in ruins, a world where the exquisite lines and super-powered machineries of the present future are gratingly grafted onto the wreckage of older systems, and where the breaks and fractures between these incompatible realms threaten at all points to open onto an abyss; or where the circular perfections of currency exchange and information orbitals place only an insecure mask over the ob-scene face of poverty. It is under these circumstances, then, that it continues to be essential to think and imagine the future, to escape from the soft trap of conceiving ourselves to be at the end of history, to attempt new construals of the landscape around us, to map its geographies and to interpret the symbolism of its remains.

Such a rhetoric inevitably reminds us of the phenomenon of the Gothic; for the rise of the Gothic as a cultural code in the late eighteenth century provides us with a benchmark against which to test our accommodation with the ruins, a language in which to address our ghosts. It also looks increasingly probable that the Gothic has come to have, or is coming to have, something quite specific to do with the turns of centuries, as though the very attempt to turn over a new leaf unavoidably involves conjuring the shadow of the past, watching its curious shapes fall over the attempted purities of the future.

Certainly recent years have seen an efflorescence of Gothic phenomena, from the apparently trivial through to the catastrophic. More horror fiction is being written than before, and it is evolving its own set of registers for addressing ever younger clienteles. Film and video developments currently seem set to provoke a new crisis in the crisis-ridden history of state censorship, in Britain at least. Issues of the articulation between cultural texts that are explicit about violence and terror and criminal behaviour, especially on the part of the young, are investigated with increasing intensity and, it has to be said, decreasingly convincing results. Over and above these matters hang other, more cloudy ones: a radical questioning of memory, for example, which has arisen in the spectrally linked loci of psychoanalysis and the law, connected to the appalling ghosts generated by child abuse, and which challenges us to look again at the inevitability of historical and chronological distortion which has always been the cornerstone of the Gothic perspective.

A very great deal of Gothic is being 'written', in the widest sense of that term; simultaneously, a very great deal *about* the Gothic is being written, and this collection of essays attempts to explore some of the crucial current critical themes and approaches. The essays arise from a conference held at the University of Stirling in 1995, the second conference of the International Gothic Association. Papers from the first conference, held at the University of East Anglia in 1991, have already appeared as *Gothick Origins and Innovations* (ed. Allan Lloyd Smith and Victor Sage, 1994); the third conference will be held in Halifax, Nova Scotia, in 1999. The essays in this volume are different in many ways, but they do seek to address some of these issues of the terrain of

Gothic, the Gothic perspective, and in doing so they necessarily address the question: What *is* Gothic?

The answers offered – or perhaps it would be better to describe them as 'takes' on the question – are manifold, and that seems entirely apposite. It is apposite because any genre surviving over several centuries will undergo change and development; but it is also apposite because of the peculiar nature of the Gothic as a para-site. I mean by this to suggest that Gothic exists in relation to mainstream culture in the same way as a parasite does to its host, and that Gothic writing can often be seen as a *perversion* of other forms, albeit a perversion which, as perversions do, serves to demonstrate precisely the inescapability of the perverse in the very ground of being. But I also mean to suggest that it is, in fact, impossible to see this relation as merely one-way: the parasite supports the host as much as vice versa, as the pragmatic daylight world survives only in its infolding of the spectral world of desire.

Gothic represents, then, a cultural knot: entirely unsusceptible to purgation, it constantly demands that we reject the narrative of cultural cleansing and engage instead with a textual and psychic *chiaroscuro* where plain sight is continually menaced by flickerings from other worlds. This is not, contemporary Gothic also and quite specifically tells us, a phenomenon which is going to go away or radically mutate as technology goes about its apparent work of deleting uncertainties, producing monsters of accuracy and detail; on the contrary, the ghost is already in the machine, there would be no machine without a ghost, and the question of quite *whose* powers – or perhaps one should say the powers of *what* – technology is extending remains central to our imaginings and our fears.

The essays are set out under five headings. Part I, 'Theory: Regions of the Gothic', contains three essays which address general issues about the location and structure of the Gothic; they attempt, we might say, a general geography. In Part II, 'Heartlands: The British Nineteenth Century', are three essays which all in different ways look at the Gothic as a specific historical phenomenon, and all link it with specific aspects of British (late) nineteenth-century society. Part III, 'America: States of Instability', takes the argument across the Atlantic where, of course, the original fiction of writers such as Charles Brockden Brown has been through a series of mutations in many ways closely parallel to the evolution of Gothic in Britain. Part IV, 'Europe: Dimensions of the Body', reminds us that in any case Gothic was, and is, by no means an English-language phenomenon; in its origins, of course, there was a close intertwining of British texts with European and especially German ones, and the Gothic continues to cross national and linguistic boundaries. Part V, 'Contemporary (Re)Versions', contains two suggestive essays on aspects of Gothic writing during recent decades.

By referring in the book's subtitle to a 'Gothic geography' we are, of course, speaking as always in a metaphor; perhaps one of the main subtexts of this specific metaphor is to suggest that a unified Gothic geography is an impossibility. Just as Gothic castles from Udolpho to Gormenghast exist in a world where there are no maps, where halls, corridors and stairways go on for ever, where rooms that were there in the night have vanished by morning, so Gothic itself challenges that very process of map-making by means of which we might hope to reduce the world to manageable proportions; while, of course, it remains constantly fascinated by the very impossibility which it so convincingly propounds.

The first essay in the volume, Fred Botting's 'The Gothic Production of the Unconscious', addresses the problem of the *site* of the Gothic directly, placing Gothic at the heart of the development of fiction and enquiring into its fluctuating relations with scientific 'progress'. In calling for a new form of Gothic criticism, Botting also argues that by thinking of Gothic in terms of repression and transgression we ignore the ways in which it serves too a function of ideological stabilisation; 'fear and ghosts', Botting reminds us, 'are defence mechanisms', protections against death, guardians against the onrush of psychosis.

The second essay, 'Ceremonial Gothic', sees Gothic from a parallel perspective, questioning the limits of its transgressions and using, as it happens, some of the same material from Lacan to enquire into issues of stability and perversion. The essay also attempts to read various examples of the genre, from *Melmoth the Wanderer* through to Anne Rice and to William Gibson's *Neuromancer*, against the background of Freud's collocation of obsession and religious ritual.

William Veeder, in 'The Nurture of the Gothic, or, How Can a Text be Both Popular and Subversive?', adds a further strand to the argument, basing his observations about the *healing* power of Gothic on the psychological ideas of D.W. Winnicott and asserting that 'Anglo-American culture develops Gothic in order to help heal the damage caused by our embrace of modernity'. Putting into play ideas from Foucault, the anthropologist Michael Taussig, Ross Chambers, and Stallybrass and White, he concedes that there may be a sense in which Gothic texts affirm orthodoxy, but does this in the context of the essentially *doubled* structures that Gothic enacts.

Moving to more detailed textual workings, Alexandra Warwick, in 'Lost Cities: London's Apocalypse', identifies a particular moment of

Gothic's history with a notion of the 'popular secular' strain of apocalyptic. 'The narrative of apocalypse', she says, 'is a sado-masochistic rehearsal', and she amasses a considerable amount of evidence to demonstrate the ways in which 'imperial urban Gothic', typical of the closing decades of the nineteenth century, is inevitably bound up with apocalyptic themes.

In the process, she alludes to James Thomson's *City of Dreadful Night*, which is also the subject of David Seed's essay, 'Hell is a City: Symbolic Systems and Epistemological Scepticism in *The City of Dreadful Night*'. Seed sees faith itself as a Gothic image in the poem; he speaks also of Thomson's terminology of the gulf and the abyss, and supplies us with some lines from Thomson which could well be envisaged as an epigraph to Gothic in general: 'can words make foul things fair?/Our life's a cheat, our death a black abyss:/Hush and be mute envisaging despair.'

Robert Mighall, in ' "A pestilence which walketh in darkness": Diagnosing the Victorian Vampire', moves us on to another of the major Gothic images of the nineteenth century, Dracula, and shows us in great detail how the image of the vampire altered over time in such ways as to bring it into line with the despised or abjected figure of the masturbator, both being, as one might say, 'those who prefer darkness and solitude ...'. Mighall concludes with a powerful reading of one of the most intriguing of vampire stories, Sheridan LeFanu's 'Carmilla'.

Jeannette Idiart and Jennifer Schulz move us to America, and specifically, in 'American Gothic Landscapes: The New World to Vietnam', to the American Constitution and the structure of *exclusions* around which it is built. The essay involves three examples of texts that threaten to remanifest these exclusions – Brockden Brown's *Edgar Huntly*, Melville's *Benito Cereno* and Coppola's film *Apocalypse Now* – concluding by suggesting to us that 'American Gothic is not simply an aesthetic or psychoanalytic category but an unofficial political history and a methodology for hearing the voices of dissent that interrupt narratives of national consensus'.

Helen F. Thompson's 'Gothic Numbers in the New Republic: *The Federalist* No. 10 and its Spectral Factions' sees the operations of the Gothic in a different area of American political life, namely in the spectralisation produced through the various definitions of democracy that attended the birth of the new republic, which she extends to a more general description of the ghostliness of political relationship: 'a Gothic mathematics', she suggests to us, 'can never quite count all of its members', and must instead find itself enmeshed in the operations of virtualisation, surely a resonant thought also for the end of the twentieth century.

In 'Spectres of Abjection: The Queer Subject of James's "The Jolly Corner"', Eric Savoy continues this discourse of the spectre, partly through a discussion in the Jamesian context of prosopopeia, the 'trope of haunting', partly through a concentration on abjection, melancholia and loss, but principally through the Gothic as a crucial figure for dealings with a (sexually) inadmissible other, representative in this case, perhaps, of a traumatic haunting by an 'effeminate' childhood.

Jerrold E. Hogle, in 'The Gothic and the "Otherings" of Ascendant Culture: the Original *Phantom of the Opera*', takes up precisely this point in the context of a detailed reading of the original text, now obscured by processes of acculturation and sentimentalisation, of *The Phantom of the Opera*. Beginning from a Kristevan/analytic reading, he then proceeds to a far more historically complex assessment of the phantom as a crosser of boundaries of all types, taking up like Veeder the point that Stallybrass and White make in *The Politics and Poetics of Transgression* about the connection between carnival and hysteria, and suggesting a further 'socialisation' of the notion of the phantom as found in Abraham and Torok.

Barnard Turner's essay on Heiner Müller, 'Heiner Müller's Medea: Towards a Paradigm for the Contemporary Gothic Anatomy', takes up the work of this central avant-garde dramatist in the context of Derrida's *Spectres of Marx*, looking also at the various Gothic 'returns' that characterise Müller's work, and suggests that, like Gothic, Müller confronts us with the inescapable questions, 'When is now?' and 'Where is here?' Turner's further remark on the core of a Gothic geography is worth quoting at greater length; it involves, he says, 'the sense of living in premises guarded by spirits and enveloped in laws that, as a newcomer, one finds bewildering and intimidating, and against which one's struggle can appear to take only the form of madness'.

Such madness is much in evidence in Avril Horner and Sue Zlosnik's 'Deaths in Venice: Daphne du Maurier's "Don't Look Now"', partly because it is the hero's very grip on rationality in this fable of terror that is seen as rendering him ripe for an all too literal deconstruction. Again, Gothic here is seen to have close connections with the world of masquerade and carnival; again we find ourselves in a world of grotesque, abjected bodies; again an exploration of the social construction of identity, as the authors aptly describe the story, turns out to have a dark underside, in this case a disgust with the ageing (female) body that the text cannot repress, but by which it remains fascinated.

The fascination of Patrick McGrath, according to Christine Ferguson in the final essay, 'Dr McGrath's Disease: Radical Pathology in Patrick McGrath's Neo-Gothicism', is with pathology and mental dissolution, and yet perhaps also more precise than that; for what Ferguson highlights for us is the way in which the real focus in McGrath's work is quite explicitly on the bizarre displays of reason to be found from time to time in those who are psychologically the most damaged. Thus, we might again say, the delusions and distortions of an internal Gothic geography, just as we might also have experienced them in the shape of so many villains and monsters from the original Gothic whose very protestations of rationality and goodwill emerge as cover stories for exploitation, unreason and violence.

Without damaging the vitality and variety of these individual essays, it would be possible to suggest that two particular questions emerge from them. The first, and perhaps the more obvious, is about the relation in the Gothic between the force of transgression and the force that returns us to the status quo. Put in that way, it is perhaps not so very different a question from the more general one of catharsis; but then, perhaps, we should turn that on its head and say that it is precisely in Gothic that the whole issue of catharsis becomes focused to its most intense point, where the possibility of being 'healed' by surviving atrocious experience is perpetually challenged by the alternative possibility of being overwhelmed by that experience and swept off, like so many Gothic heroes, into the abyss, far away from any available map or compass.

The second question is related to this, and it concerns what one might call 'the ethics of Gothic'. What does it mean, for example, to be involved in the transmission and interpretation of materials that threaten the boundaries of the human – for this is, among other things, what Gothic does, and another reason why its maps are never stable or finite. We could put the question in other terms. We could ask, for example, what kind of knowledge is being produced here, and where responsibility might lie for the ways in which that knowledge might be used. We could ask about the nature of the imagination, about what happens to images of violence and monstrosity when they are introjected into an internal landscape – or, to use the alternative formulation of Abraham and Torok, if they are violently and cannibalistically *incorporated* into an area of the psyche.

And these two questions, the question of cathartic return and the question of the ethical, produce for us immediately the most central question of textual criticism at the present time, which one might frame as follows: in what *sense* is there, as Derrida has proclaimed and as many critics now appear to accept, 'nothing outside the text'? How can we arrange our convictions about the constitutive power of the world of words over against, on the one hand, our everyday, if contradictory or at best equivocal, experience of the inner world, and on the other our irresistible immersion in the processes of death, sickness, the inhumane?

The study of the Gothic has a part to play in the development of these issues; to claim that the spectre, the ghost, the phantom comes as a figure of terror is to oversimplify. It may equally be that in a world that seeks to banish the supernatural, then the very resistance of the revenant to a final expulsion may also be a figure for our own resistance, our refusal to be written out of history, or, perhaps more importantly, to allow others to be thus written out. Certainly the reduction of life to that which can be programmed and assessed by machine, as Gothic has always known, is a process of the monstrous; the discernment of our own inner monstrosities, and thus of those of which we attempt to rid ourselves through abjection, then becomes an essential task and a significant alternative to the doomed myths of intellectual and psychic purification that constitute a major danger of Western culture.

Part I
Theory: regions of the Gothic

Chapter 1

The Gothic production of the unconscious

Fred Botting

Unconscious cerebration

In *Dracula* a new theory of unconscious mental activity called 'unconscious cerebration' is mentioned twice. Unlike other modern theories of the mind which the novel makes a point of citing, unconscious cerebration is referred to only in passing and in connection with the madman Renfield and his psychiatrist Dr Seward rather than the eponymous villain of the text. Where psychologists and criminologists, Jean Charcot, Max Nordau and Cesare Lombroso in particular, are named and their theories employed in the classification and exorcism of the vampiric threat, unconscious cerebration remains in the background, contemporary scientific furniture in a novel obsessed with the limits of *fin-de-siècle* modernity. Unremarkable, it is as if the unconscious has always been there.

When Dr Seward is busy pondering Renfield's behaviour, he speculates: 'there is a method in his madness, and the rudimentary idea in my mind is growing. It will be a whole idea soon, and then, oh unconscious cerebration! you will have to give the wall to your conscious brother' (Stoker, 1897: 94).[1] The psychiatrist, it seems, has kept up with recent psychological literature and practises what he preaches as he exclaims his faith in the mysterious powers of the brain. His description of the mental process through which an idea takes shape without the intervention of consciousness is drawn directly from the initial pages of the work of Frances Power Cobbe. In her 'Unconscious Cerebration. A Psychological Study', she describes as an 'important phase' the way that mental work like calculation or artistic composition can 'arrange itself in order during an interval either of sleep or wakefulness, during which we had not consciously thought of it at all'

(Cobbe, 1870: 25). Here, again, it seems as if there is little to remark upon: *Dracula's* concerns with modernity's human sciences are informed by more researchers than are cited in the text. However, an examination of Cobbe's two essays on the subject raises questions that complicate the assumption that the scientific ideas of a materialistic culture merely inform its literature. Like the 1831 Introduction to *Frankenstein*, which places ghost stories alongside the electrical theories of Galvani and Volta, Cobbe's frame of reference suggests that the relationship between literature and scientific enquiry is more inter-implicated than an imaginative rendering of the latter by the former. With the psychological rather than physical sciences, literature, it seems, in a broader cultural history, reverses the conventional direction of influence and bears upon the structure of scientific narration. With regard to the unconscious, then, truth involves an 'economy of fiction'.[2]

Cobbe begins her discussion of unconscious cerebration by calling up the oracular teraphim of Hebrew necromancers, a decapitated child's head that, when placed on a pedestal and addressed by a sorcerer, magically answers his questions. Supposing a factual basis for enchantments or magic of this kind and, moreover, comparing it to the effects of galvanism which may make a corpse speak, Cobbe advances her case for the automatism of mental operations and relegates the conscious self to the sum of a living brain's activity. Her scientific materialism, deferring to the physiological work of W. B. Carpenter, offers numerous empirical examples from everyday life, dreaming, memory and habitual activities receiving particular attention.[3] In this context mental activities involving words come to prominence and draw the discussion of unconscious cerebration into the realm of the creative arts and writing. The example of the interval in which ideas are arranged in order lists a range of creative and plastic arts and concludes that 'it is as if a "Fairy Order" had come in the night and unravelled the tangled skeins of thought and laid them all neatly on the table' (Cobbe, 1870: 25). In sleep, 'when our unconsciousness of it is most complete', the work of the 'Fairy Order' seems most effective. More than somnambulism, Cobbe insists, it is as if a 'Familiar' is at work in the mechanical, habituated operations of the unconscious mind. But this Familiar, she goes on, 'is a great deal more than a walking dictionary, a housemaid, a *valet de place*, or a barrel-organ man': 'he is a novelist who can spin more romances than Dumas' (27). Though such artistic accomplishment is limited to the powers of reproducing, developing and combining actual experiences, the creative Familiar, Cobbe contends, is also at work in the versatility and profusion of dreams, a natural inventiveness discussed, she notes, by Addison. Absorbed by questions of words and writing, the essay never casts off the literary frame: from dreams, ghosts are seen as *'home-made'* examples of unconscious cerebration (30); and then ghost stories provide more examples for Cobbe's thesis. In her subsequent paper, 'Dreams as Illustrations of Unconscious Cerebration', Cobbe again uneasily calibrates scientific materialism and examples of dreams from poetry, myth and fiction. De Quincey's *Confessions of an English Opium Eater* affords 'amazing evidence of what leaps the Pegasus of fancy is capable under the spur of such stimuli on the brain' (Cobbe, 1871: 519). Activating the unconscious brain to poetic heights, narcotic stimulants release the 'mysterious power' in all minds (520). Cobbe remains in a Romantic vein and returns to the text of another opium eater, a text already cited in her first paper. She rehearses the story of Coleridge's 'Kubla Khan' to note how, from prosaic sentences, opium dreams stimulate the unconscious to attain paradisiacal visions. Not dwelling on the poetic disappointments mentioned by Coleridge in his prefatory remarks, Cobbe instead waxes lyrical about the potential of unconscious cerebration: 'Consider all this, and that the poem of which this is the fragment reached at least the length of three hundred lines, and then say what limits shall be placed on the powers which lie hidden within our mortal coil?' (520). These remarks conclude her discussion of Coleridge but lead on to further examples from the poetry of a friend.

Literature, it seems, has much to say in Cobbe's psychological discussion of the unconscious mind. Her examples of dreams, moreover, are significant not only because they come from Romantic literature: they are dreams that, recounted in literary texts, acknowledge prior textual origins. With de Quincey dreams depend as much on the dreamer's reading as his/her actual experiences. Early in the *Confessions* he compares the dull dreams of a labourer to the more interesting flights of oneiric imagination enjoyed by the cultivated man. Later on he describes the particularly Gothic shape of his 'architectural dreams': recalling the images of Piranesi, de Quincey cites a passage from Wordsworth's *Excursion*, which 'might have been copied from my architectural dreams' (de Quincey, 1986: 107). It is literary images, however, that inform the dreaming mind, rather than an unconscious imagination concocting the source of its own outpourings. In 'Kubla Khan', a history book, as Cobbe notes, provides the raw material for the visionary elaborations of unconscious cerebration. But the mysterious mental process also shortcircuits conscious creativity, and leaves the Romantic imagination in close proximity to the fairy fancies of Gothic romance. Coleridge's prefatory comments on the composition of 'Kubla Khan' acknowledge an almost physical and mechanical process: as he falls into his reverie 'all the images rose up before me as *things*'; as he wakes they 'passed away like the images on the surface of a stream into which a stone has been cast'. Though Coleridge insists on the idea and wholeness of imaginative vision that was only fragmentarily present in the poem, there are echoes of what is, for him, a lesser faculty associated with Gothic romances.[4] In *Biographia Literaria*, he describes the products of circulating libraries as idle wastes of time rather than valued reading, 'beggarly day dreaming' in which

> the whole *materiel* and imagery of the doze is supplied *ab extra* by a sort of mental *camera obscura* manufactured at the printing office, which *pro tempore* fixes, reflects and transmits the moving fantasms of one man's delirium, so as to people the barrenness of an hundred other brains afflicted with the same trance of suspension of all common sense and all definite purpose.
>
> (Coleridge, 1975: 28, n. 1)

Romance reading induces a kind of waking dream that operates mechanically. Automatic, it bypasses the will and displays the febrile and delusional effects of an infectious brain disorder. In Coleridge's criticism, despite the unacknowledged similarity to the composition of 'Kubla Khan', there is little to recommend romances. His position follows conventional eighteenth-century attacks on fiction as a corrupting, sensational and disordered mode of representation.

None the less, the form of imagination deplored as 'beggarly day dreaming' enables the production of the Romantic imagination. Later in the *Biographia Literaria* he states:

> For even as truth is its own light and evidence, discovering at once itself and falsehood, so it is the prerogative of poetic genius to distinguish by parental instinct its proper offspring from the changelings which the gnomes of vanity or the fairies of fashion may have laid in its cradle or called by its names. (218)

What separates the gnomes and fairies of romance imaginings from the self-evident light and truth of the Romantic imagination is the undoubtedly paternal power of that parental instinct called poetic genius. Imagination is distinguished from Gothic fancy by a paternal enunciation of poetic self-affirmation. A problem remains, however, as to the very difference that is asserted. If it is difficult to discern the qualitative difference which separates 'Kubla Khan' and imaginative vision from the automatism of Gothic fancy and romance delirium in Coleridge's own descriptions, it is harder still when Cobbe approaches unconscious cerebration in a more materialistic manner. Even as she retains Romantic assumptions in her reliance on poetry she also discloses another, Gothic and mechanical, chain of significance which exists just below the hallowed and visionary plane of poetry's proper offspring. Indeed, Cobbe's work looks to a 'fairy order' of familiars and ghosts.

The science of the unconscious mind draws on fiction as much as on fact. In *Dracula*, however, 'unconscious cerebration' circulates, without attribution or author, in a way that suggests that it is well within the public sphere. The term, and all that it implies, appears almost natural in requiring no comment or explanation. It certainly demands none of the medical or parapsychological arguments which other putative powers of the mind receive. The notion of thought-reading, for instance, unlike hypnotism that had been proved by Charcot, is rejected by Dr Seward in the course of a long discussion with Professor Van Helsing: the latter, advancing the idea of the existence of vampires, comments on how certain wonders at certain times – electricity provides his example – seem to be beyond the pale of the physical sciences. 'There are always mysteries in life,' the Professor observes (Stoker, 1897: 247). Like the 'mysterious power' of unconscious cerebration for Cobbe, these mysterious outer limits constitute a challenge to scientific explanation rather than a straightforward valorisation of all things spiritual. Indeed, they demand an extended and open idea of the physical universe. From this position, the same can be said of Dracula himself. To explain the vampire phenomenon, Van Helsing speculates that the resting-place of the undead is connected to certain geological and chemical anomalies, arguing that 'there is something magnetic or electric in some of these combination of occult forces which work for physical life in strange way' (411). With this kind of science to invoke, it is a short step to see Dracula as an anomaly of nature rather than an unnatural phantasm, a monstrosity antipathetic to 'human nature' perhaps, but resolutely of nature none the less. The separation and link between the 'human' and 'nature', of course, is what is at stake. Strangely naturalised, Dracula still has to be expelled: here, deviance, the deviance established by normative disciplines like criminology, comes into play to distinguish between a natural but regressive type and a fully humanised subject of bourgeois culture. Fiction, in the shape of the scientific theory utilised in fiction, becomes fact. Deviance is given terrible form and legitimately expelled. At the same time, deviance is naturalised and repressed at a stroke.

So, too, and perhaps more fully, with the unconscious of unconscious cerebration. Like the mysterious natural energies associated with the undead, the unconscious is naturalised and repressed even as it seems to circulate freely in the narratives of scientific enquiry and Gothic fiction. An association between the unconscious and the energies of an unavowable nature is sedimented. Given form, function and, in part, explanation, the unconscious can be credited as a natural and mysterious element of the human psyche, a reservoir of primal energies buried deep but continually at work in the unknowing mind. In Cobbe's postulations, empirical observation and literary reference remain tentative, despite the odd visionary speculation; in *Dracula*'s unacknowledged citation 26 years later, 'unconscious cerebration' is employed as though it were an acceptable part of psychiatry's fabric. While *Dracula* almost renders visible the proximity between nature, unconscious and sexuality in the mirror of late Victorian self-presentation, the shock wave of Freud's sexualisation of the unconscious had still to reverberate through Western bourgeois culture. The unconscious, however, is already there, but not in the sense of a natural faculty waiting to be discovered by the penetrating gaze of science: it lies, waiting to be glimpsed amongst the condensed associations produced in the un-black continent of modernity's literature.

The invention of literature

If *Dracula* manifests part of the process whereby the unconscious, as it is popularly imagined, is made visible and naturalised by literature, the success of this naturalisation is evinced in the manner that psychological science subsequently assumes sole responsibility for its management and explanation. With literature's role in the production of the unconscious occluded, to the extent that it becomes a practically natural mental phenomenon, literary criticism in the twentieth century can authorise itself and its readings with the knowledge provided by sciences of the mind. Retrospectively, the unconscious is (re)discovered everywhere, and Gothic fiction becomes one of its best illustrations. For example, in a discussion of the symbolic prisons and dark spaces of Gothic fiction, Max Byrd glimpses 'the deepest recesses of the human mind in which unreason still clings to life' (Byrd, 1977: 273). These deep recesses, moreover, contain threatening, libidinal energies that must be explosively released. Psychoanalysis, moreover, provides literary criticism with access to a truth buried in deep mental recesses. For Mary Fawcett, discussing *The Mysteries of Udolpho*,

> Mrs Radcliffe hints at a truth, at a scene to be re-animated; Emily St Aubert, her main character, looks repeatedly at scenes which remind us of obsessional neurotic dreams, dreams which a psycho-analytic patient might have in order to screen the primal scene, the child's vision of the sexual act between the parents, proleptically that act at which the child was engendered.
>
> (Fawcett, 1983: 481)

Childhood, sexuality and a screened, unconscious scene cohere as a truth too readily recognised in the mirror of vulgar psychoanalysis as an uncanny return of repressed unconscious wishes and desires. The move-ment, however, may be otherwise: rather than psychoanalysis revealing the eternally buried and universal unconscious of repressed human nature through the parapraxes of a literary imagination interpreted by eager critics, the unconscious may take its bearings from fictional fig-ures. For Terry Castle, Freud is as 'suffused with crypto-supernaturalism' as Ann Radcliffe, so that the concern with mental apparitions and daemonic energies is itself a 'product of late eighteenth-century roman-tic sensibility'. Radcliffe's ghosts become 'our own' in a way quite dif-ferent from common assumptions about unchanging human nature and its repressed and darker side: they are 'the symptomatic projections of modern psychic life', an effect of the images pervading the culture, subject and history of modernity (Castle, 1987: 237).

While the repressed sexual secrets of the unconscious seem newly discovered by the perceptive criticism of twentieth-century Freudians, the sexual implications of Gothic romances were all too evident to eighteenth-century critics, who complained of the superficiality and corruption of the genre's indulgently licentious and lewd tendencies. Twentieth-century criticism, in contrast, seems a little too eager to plunge into unavowable depths and unmentionable desires to notice the resistance that the easy acquiescence of Gothic fiction occludes – a resistance that, mysterious in a superficial way, stares criticism in the face. J. M. S. Tompkins comments very simply and incisively on psycho-analytic criticism of Gothic fiction:

> The Gothic Romance, particularly, has received an enhanced signifi-cance, seen in the light of Freudian and Jungian conceptions. The repressed erotic and sadistic impulses of respectable society – but

were they really so repressed? – break out and shape themselves myths in the Gothic castle and the dungeons of the Inquisition; and the neo-classical façade of accepted literature is fissured in all directions by the subterranean ferment.

(Tompkins, 1969, xiii)

Tompkins sketches familiar territory for Gothic critics, employing distinctions of surface and depth, respectability and repressed desire. Indeed, it is hard not to recognise the opposition of ego and id already in place, psychoanalysis already subsumed within a framework that reconstitutes the obvious – and oft-repeated – dualism of a humanist, ego-centred mode of criticism. The dualism, moreover, is repeatedly replayed in the stock elements and locations of Gothic writing that Tompkins cites: respectable society and subterranean ferment, castle and dungeon, prefigure the oppositions that so-called psychoanalytic criticism readily applies.

The 'discovery' that recognises psychoanalytic 'truths' in Gothic figures, finding unconscious repression in labyrinths and dungeons, castrating fathers in villains and castles or ids among doubles, only reiterates a Gothic *chiaroscuro* of light and dark, good and evil, morality and sexuality to claim the secret depths of the human psyche and its primal, instinctual nature. These reiterations enact the mania Lacan observes among ego psychologists 'which consists in turning the unconscious into another ego, a bad ego, a double' (Lacan, 1993: 240). They also misconstrue psychoanalysis for two reasons: first, because Freudian psychoanalysis generally employs tripartite, not antithetical, schema (ego, id and superego; conscious, preconscious and unconscious), and second, as Tompkins suggests in the interrogative aside 'but were they really so repressed?', repression and taboos seem very close to the surface of Gothic texts: trauma, hysteria, eroticism and the family romance with all its fantasies of origins, castration anxieties and incest themes are far from hidden, buried or repressed. These images, foregrounded as they are, seem a little too obvious to be read as manifestations of latent unconscious impulses. Freud repeatedly comments on the inaccessibility of repressed material to all but the most careful and painstaking analysis: 'unknown' as the unconscious is in *The Interpretation of Dreams*, it, in *The Ego and the Id*, also remains incapable of becoming conscious. As Lacan emphasises the difference between the popular and the Freudian unconscious:

Freud's unconscious is not at all the romantic unconscious of imaginative creation. It is not the locus of the divinities of the night. This locus is no doubt not entirely unrelated to the locus towards which Freud turns his gaze – but the fact that Jung, who provides a link with the terms of the romantic unconscious, should have been repudiated by Freud, is sufficient indication that psycho-analysis is introducing something other.

(Lacan, 1977c: 24)

For Lacan, this something other is the 'discourse of the Other' (Lacan, 1977b: 172), the structure of language and the laws of metaphor and metonymy imprinted from outside: 'the unconscious is neither primordial nor instinctual; what it knows about the elementary is no more than the elements of the signifier' (Lacan, 1977b: 170).

It seems a little glib, then, to find unconscious depths in Gothic surfaces, a little too easy to discover secret meanings originating in the hidden machinations of human nature. In the manner of the chief of police in Poe's *The Purloined Letter*, what tends to be overlooked in the search for concealed meaning and hidden truth is the very economy of fiction that inscribes significance as an effect of textual surfaces and topographical relations. The depths of Gothic fiction were remarkable for their shallowness. Contemporary reviewers regularly complained of the artificial, formulaic and superficial nature of 'gothic machinery', of absurdity, improbability and impossibility, of flights of fancy and ungrounded imagination. In the twentieth century, Eve Sedgwick's study of veil metaphors has demonstrated the irrelevance of applying depth and psychological models to fiction that foregrounds surfaces.[5] Elizabeth Napier, too, agrees, observing that 'the superficial and the formulaic thus, paradoxically, form the very heart of the Gothic...' (Napier, 1987: 29).

Gothic writing displays a curious depthlessness, a depthlessness that emerges with modernity according to Michel Foucault. Discussing the discursive shift that transformed notions of language and literature in the eighteenth century, Foucault identifies the writings of Sade and tales of terror as indices of the new form of literature which 'only speaks as a supplement starting from a displacement' and, shedding 'all ontological weight', leads to language reproducing itself in the 'virtual space of the mirror', to the birth of 'an obscure but dominant figure where death, the mirror and the double, and the wavelike succession of words to infinity enact their roles' (Foucault, 1977: 65–6). The virtual space of language – a space that, like the mirror, positions subjects where they are not – is a heterotopia, a counter-site, 'a kind of effectively enacted utopia in which the real sites, all the other real sites that can be found within the culture, are simultaneously represented, contested and inverted' (Foucault, 1986: 24). Gothic romances are formed as virtual, other spaces: for Walpole the modern romance tries to make its 'mortal agents' 'think, speak and act, as it might be supposed mere men and women would do in extraordinary situations' (Walpole, 1764: 7–8); for critics romances 'transport the reader unprofitably into the clouds, or into those wilds of fancy, which go for ever out of the way of human paths' (in Williams, 1970: 151), a dangerous separation of the reality cultivated in the language of the Enlightenment and the literature that multiplies itself to infinity.

In *The Order of Things* Foucault analyses the shift from Classical epistemology, based on a 'reciprocal kinship between knowledge and language' to a new relationship established by modernity: 'the nineteenth century was to dissolve that link, and to leave behind it, in confrontation, a knowledge closed up to itself and a pure language that had become, in nature and function, enigmatic – something that has been called, since that time, *Literature*' (Foucault, 1970: 89). Language, demoted to the status of an object, was neutralised and polished in scientific usage so that 'it could become the exact reflection, the perfect double, the unmisted mirror of a non-verbal knowledge', and hence transparent to thought (Foucault, 1970: 296–7). In compensation for the demotion of language, literature appears, reconstituted 'in an independent form, difficult of access, folded back upon the enigma of its own origin and existing wholly in reference to the pure act of writing'. Another significant compensation, Foucault argues, is the 'critical elevation' of language as something closer 'both to an act of knowing, pure of all words, and to the unconscious element in our discourse'. A double process was at work in this reconstitution of language:

> it had to be either made transparent to the forms of knowledge, or thrust down into the contents of the unconscious. This certainly explains the nineteenth century's double advance, on the one hand, towards formalism in thought and on the other towards the discovery of the unconscious – towards Russell and Freud.
>
> (Foucault, 1970: 299)

In the depthlessness, the virtual spaces and divisions of literary figures, the unconscious begins to assume its recognisable shape. As a heterotopia emerging within the heterotopia of literature, the unconscious begins to display the 'radical heteronymy' that Lacan's return to Freud discloses: 'since Freud the unconscious has been a chain of signifiers that somewhere (on another stage, in another scene, he wrote) is repeated, and insists on interfering in the breaks offered it by the effective discourse and the cogitation it informs' (Lacan, 1977b: 172, 297). In Derrida's terms, writing on Freud's discussion of the unconscious as a 'mystic writing pad', the textual form of the unconscious emerges as a 'depth without bottom, an infinite allusion, and a perfectly superficial exteriority: a stratification of surfaces each of whose relation to itself, each of whose interior, is but the implication of another similarly exposed surface.' Depthlessness opens onto the tracery of difference:

> the unconscious text is already a weave of pure traces, differences in which meaning and force are united – a text nowhere present, consisting of archives which are *always already* transcriptions. Originary prints. Everything begins with reproduction. Always already: repositories of a meaning which was never present, whose signified presence is always reconstituted by deferral, *nachträglich*, belatedly, *supplementarily*: for the *nachträglich* also means *supplementary*.
>
> (Derrida, 1978: 224)

In Gothic fiction, with all its artificiality, its reproduction of a fantasised, never-present Gothic past, its suspenseful detours, presence and meaning – which is always the restitution of moral and providential law – are repeatedly deferred in the fabulously textual nature of narrative composition. Gothic is an originary print, a fabricated history, a fantasy of cultural and familial origins that belatedly – supplementarily – inscribes itself with morality and significance.

Fakes, however, both have effects and reproduce themselves, as Walpole's fabricated prefatory origins to *The Castle of Otranto* attest (see Hogle, 1994). That these effects are real is demonstrated by the numerous terrified misreaders of fiction, Radcliffe's heroines among them: Emily's horror at seeing the waxen image of the bloody corpse in Udolpho is, despite its artificial cause, real enough a trauma to require the exorcism of many pages of narrative.[6] Indeed, Gothic sites of anxiety are repeatedly, insistently artificial and textual in origin. Earlier in *The Mysteries of Udolpho* when Emily transgresses her father's injunction and reads fragments of his letters, she is more severely traumatised: the cause of horror remains unexplained throughout the novel, though her credulous imagination interprets it as an unspeakable truth. It functions as a primal textual trauma in that it involves paternal impropriety and renders suspect his version of Emily's origins and the identity of her lost mother. As trauma, it haunts the entire novel before being belatedly explained. In *The Romance of the Forest* textual truth is similarly misread: the fragmented manuscript Adeline discovers in the ruined abbey evokes appropriately Gothic literary responses, leaving her unable to discriminate between supernatural and rational worlds. Strangely, in a twist of novelistic reality and fiction only explained at the close of the tale, the manuscript calls for justice from beyond the grave: it turns out to be the story of her real father's sufferings at the hand of a fratricidal brother.

These textual origins are not only repressed within the narrative layers of Gothic fictions. They offer a model of the unconscious that eschews naturalised depths in favour of narrative surfaces. In Lacanian terms, the unconscious is 'the censored chapter' whose truth is written elsewhere, in monuments, archival documents, semantic evolution, traditions, legends and in relation to other chapters. Textual metaphors imprint the subject, corresponding to the body and its symptoms, childhood memories and the acquisition of language (Lacan, 1977b: 50). By means of metaphor, moreover, repression works to produce the unconscious as a layering of symbolic chains. In their careful elaboration of Lacan's formula of the unconscious, Jean Laplanche and Serge Leclaire present it as 'a thesaurus of past metaphors, for it is always a metaphor, a substitution of signifiers that is found at the root of the creation of new meanings' (Laplanche, 1972: 157).[7] Different layers or chains of signifiers, one latent and one manifest, form the basis of this model of the unconscious: meaning is produced by the metaphor which, in the manner of Lacan's *point de capiton* (anchoring point or upholstery button), joins the two chains by arresting the metonymic sliding of signification and thereby producing meaning (see Lacan, 1977b: 46–78; 1993: 258–70).

The name of the father

In eighteenth-century criticism the chain of signifiers producing the unconscious was meshed together from Gothic metaphors, reconstructed from the literary leftovers and physical remnants of a past, medieval culture lingering like shadows in the light of the neoclassical present. Ruins, labyrinths, castles, romantic fragments, found or forged by antiquarians, constituted the principal objects of fascination, fantasy and anxiety, heterotopias occupying the gaps of cultural history as points of continuity or discontinuity with the past. Two modes of narration dominate the period, one emphasising discontinuity, the other foregrounding continuity: the Enlightenment, taking its bearings from classical precepts of order, rationality and civic virtue, represented its cultivation and propriety in opposition to the barbaric, superstitious and tyrannical feudal age; the Gothic revival, in contrast, found inspiration in the ruins of the past and the wilds of native scenery, aestheticising untamed nature to support an idea of indigenous culture and elevate national and personal character over imported Roman forms. Romances and Gothic architecture became a significant part of the aesthetic and cultural reconstruction taking place in the course of the eighteenth century, a reconstruction whose arena was the narratives by which society represented itself.

In the process of eighteenth-century cultural change, literature takes on a recognisable form, as does the unconscious, becoming associated with a darker nature, infantile wishes and sexuality, female desire in particular. Joseph Addison's account of romances, stories and spirits, early in the century, locates what can be described as the uncanny in a textual realm: the 'pleasing kind of horror' and sensations of 'strangeness and novelty' produced by romances arises from the return of familiar but forgotten fears engendered by childhood stories: 'they bring up into our memory the stories we have heard in our childhood, and favour those secret terrors and apprehensions to which the mind of man is naturally subject.' The strange naturalness is underlined a little later as he discusses the supernatural moments of Shakespeare to identify 'something so wild and solemn in the speeches of his ghosts, fairies, witches... that we cannot forbear thinking them natural' (Addison, 1970: 200–1). While noting that there is nothing by which to judge the naturalness of ghosts, Addison's account of what Dryden called 'the fairy way of writing' makes certain important links between reading stories, the supernatural and nature. Associating individual and cultural development to account for the uncanniness, he links Gothic superstition and cultural primitivism to the immaturity and credulity of childhood. The sense of naturalness serves to naturalise a connection sustained purely at the level of superstition-inducing stories and credulous readers.

The concern about individual and cultural maturity reappears in romance criticism throughout the century, as does the question of nature. Romances, like the past they recall, are associated with everything Gothic (barbarity, superstition, wildness and immorality) to signify the absolute inversion – and the antithesis that defined its superiority – of all that patriarchal neoclassical culture valued. As the production and popularity of romances increased, a propagation associated with excessive appetitive indulgence and base sexual reproduction, critics complained more virulently about the corrupting effects of depraved, sensational and feminised fiction. Romances and Gothic fiction were also represented as unnatural, that is, alien to the cultivated, rational nature advocated by neoclassical culture. What emerges in romance writing is a zone lying 'below nature', a lower, baser nature which, many critics demanded, ought to be suppressed for the good of society as a whole (in Williams, 1970: 207). The criticism of fiction's deleterious social effects steadily increased in the course of the century, along with its association with immaturity, sexuality and femininity. Novels and romances encouraged sensuality and obscenity and appealed to the baser appetites, and were 'devoured by every ear' with a 'greediness' born of the 'irresistible desire of satisfying curiosity' (in Williams, 1970: 283–4). An insatiable aural gratification hinders the development of reason or moral understanding necessary to the social and domestic order. Romances perverted, with 'the chimerical ideas of romantic love', young ladies' minds from the proper course of becoming good wives and mothers: females were more at risk because 'the magic power of a lady's fancy' was able to create 'chimera much faster than nature can produce realities' (in Williams, 1970: 214–15). Though novels 'circulated chiefly among the giddy and licentious of both sexes', the weaker sex is more often invoked in the incitement of moral indignation (in Williams, 1970: 240). Another critic claimed that sentimental compositions weaken the mind, rendering it 'unable to resist the slightest impulse of libidinous passion' (in Williams, 1970: 306). James Beattie goes further: unskilfully written romances 'tend to corrupt the heart, and stimulate the passions'. Worse still, fiction 'fills the mind with extravagant thoughts, and too often with criminal propensities' (in Williams, 1970: 309).

Women, as writers and readers, are positioned more and more at the centre of critical concern: 'the general effect of novel-reading on the gentler sex is too obvious to be doubted; it excites and inflames the passion which is the principal subject of the tale, and the susceptibility of the female votary of circulating library, is proverbial' (in Williams, 1970: 337). Novels, 'whose preposterous sentiments our young females imbibe with avidity', cause readers to be 'acquainted with the worst part of the female sex' (in Williams, 1970: 355, 367). Fiction is feminised to the extent that George Canning readily describes novel-writing as the 'younger sister' of romance (in Williams, 1970: 341). It is a danger-ous sexuality, however, that appears, a sexuality in excess of the propri-eties of polite culture and virtuous femininity in which women, as readers, become active as writers. Hannah More asks,

Who are those ever multiplying authors, that with unparalleled fecundity are overstocking the world with their quick-succeeding

progeny? They are NOVEL-WRITERS; the easiness of whose productions is at once the cause of their own fruitfulness, and of the almost
infinitely numerous race of imitators to whom they give birth.

(in de Bolla, 1989: 264)

Fecundity, progeny and metaphors of birth leave no doubt as to the sex
of this multiplying band of writers. The sexed, or sexualised, propagation of fiction is underlined in other accounts of the continually multiplying romances flooding the book market: T. J. Mathias, for instance,
is appalled at the way that 'Walpole's Ghosts' have 'propagated their
species with unequalled fecundity' (Mathias, 1805: 242). Writing in
the 1790s when panic about the moral, domestic and social effects
of female romances became confounded with revolutionary fears,
Mathias is horrified at how 'our *unsexed* female writers' are able to 'turn
us wild with Gallic frenzy' (244). Gallic, in a political context, is closely
linked to Gothic in a fictional one.

Literature, for Mathias, is of paramount concern. Its labyrinths are as
dangerous, gloomy and horrifying as anything in Gothic fiction. While
setting out to lead readers safely through the sexual and political dangers of the labyrinths of fiction and revolutionary philosophy, Mathias
acknowledges an ambivalence at the heart of literature: it is 'the great
engine' by which 'all civilized states must ultimately be supported or
overthrown' (162). In this light, the increasing sexualisation of fiction
in the course of the eighteenth century is situated within a critical
attempt to define, discriminate between and police certain types of fiction. Seen to corrupt children and women with seductive tales and
lewd ideas, romances were thought to undermine the authority of the
prevailing social and domestic values. Indeed, as fiction multiplies its
construction as feminine and sexual in origin turns into the breeding
of monsters whose unregulated passions will engulf any properly
ordered society. The threat becomes sublime and works according to
Burke's theory as an imaginary terror which thrills the subject with the
intense emotion of self-preservation: the excess of desire, the flood of
fiction presents a spectre of social disintegration which requires a stern
and authoritative response. In the process, the metaphors which make
the threat visible also become literal. No one at the time doubted that
reading and writing Gothic romances was a feminine and 'unmanly'
activity, though evidence suggests that as many men read the work as
did women (see de Bolla, 1989: 271). None the less, metaphors of the
sexualised or unsexing threat of novels become literal to the point that
empirical evidence is cited with consummate ease: one critic writes,

'I have actually seen mothers, in miserable garrets, *crying for the imaginary distress of an heroine*, while their children were *crying for bread*' (in de Bolla, 1989: 260). The unspecific plural sits uneasily with the claim to direct visual evidence in this pathetic example of the dangerous disjunction between fancy and reality caused by fiction. However, made visible, identified and brought to light as a barbarous, childish, feminine threat to paternalistic society, romances can be suppressed and their effects and associations repressed.

Legitimated by the threat to society and family, critics repeatedly expressed paternal concerns. One reviewer of *The Monk* observed that a father would pale if he saw his daughter reading such a lewd and corrupting text (Anon., 1797: 451). The concern with daughters' reading practices, sexual virtue and moral well-being is a matter for the father's intervention. In the name of paternal authority criticism can morally justify its condemnations as righteous. The name of the father is also, of course, the paternal No, the enunciation of law and statement of prohibition. Without law there can be no illegitimate space, no other site of transgression, desire and prohibition: in this sense, the paternal law requires an other whose very excess, and the transgression it demands of subjects, legitimates its necessity and reinforces its limits. The law introduces the arbitrary divisions and differences that articulate the desires of its subjects:

> Consequently the father separates, that is, he is the one who protects when, in his proclamation of the Law, he links space, rules, and language within a single and major experience. At a stroke, he creates the distance along which will develop the scansion of presences and absences, the speech whose initial form is based on constraints and finally, gives rise to the structure of language but also to the exclusion and symbolic transformation of repressed material.
>
> (Foucault, 1977: 81)

Desire takes its bearings from this structure of differentiation and exclusion, just as, in eighteenth-century criticism proper, texts and improper romances are discriminated in the paternal eyes of the law as it identifies and expels its other. Sex, nature, passion are driven literally, that is by the word of law, into the suppressed chain of signifiers, the gloomy, underground subtexts, into the vaults, labyrinths and darkened spaces of illegitimate, Gothicised desire. And these spaces, steadily filled with Gothic images and anti-social passions, take their place in a network of power, its limit and definitive antithesis.

The proper language of criticism does not simply cast out those objects, figures and energies that it cannot tolerate; it absorbs and constructs them and then excludes within itself the objects that mark its interior limit: 'Rather, since Sade and the death of God, the universe of language has absorbed our sexuality, denatured it, placed it in a void where it establishes its sovereignty and where it incessantly sets up as the Law the limits it transgresses' (Foucault, 1977: 50). While Gothic fictions are presented as shamelessly indulging illicit desires and excessive passions, they simultaneously serve the interests of a system of power, reinvigorating its surveillance, bolstering its discipline, reinforcing its vigilant attention to limits. And in representing, with a seemingly relentless vigour, the labyrinthine contours and torturous alleyways of libidinous passion, Gothic fiction alerts the laws of rationality and adverts readers to the monstrosity of lawlessness.

In Foucault's early essays on language, literature, transgression and sexuality the model of the repressive hypothesis already manifests itself. Gothic fiction, it seems, is part of the 'discursive explosion' of sexuality over three centuries on which Foucault's *History of Sexuality* looks back (Foucault, 1984: 17). Foucault argues that 'the idea of a rebellious energy that must be throttled has appeared ... inadequate for deciphering the manner in which power and desire are to one another.' The link is 'more complex and primary' than

> the interplay of a primitive natural, and living energy welling up from below, and a higher order seeking to stand in its way; thus one should not think that desire is repressed, for the simple reason that the law is what constitutes both desire and the lack on which it is predicated. Where there is desire, the power relation is already present: an illusion, then, to denounce this relation for a repression exerted after the event.
>
> (Foucault, 1984: 81)

From this position, Gothic criticism and fiction can be seen to interrelate in more complex ways than the simple condemnation of one by the other, or, inversely, as the rebellion of the other against the one. The concern with sex, young readers and an ungovernable female desire is situated in a network of relations and operates in a similar manner to the policing of children's masturbation in the nineteenth century:

> The child's 'vice' was not so much an enemy as a support; it may have been designated as the evil to be eliminated, but the extraordinary

effort that went into the task that was bound to fail leads one to suspect that what was demanded of it was to persevere, to proliferate to
the limits of the visible and the invisible, rather than to disappear
for good. Always relying on this support, power advanced, multiplied its relays and its effects, while its target expanded, subdivided
and branched out, penetrating further into reality at the same pace.
In appearance we are dealing with a barrier system: but in fact, all
around the child, indefinite *lines of penetration* were disposed.

(Foucault, 1984: 42)

In criticism, and in the fiction that takes critical morality seriously, the
boundaries between vigilant vision and invisibility constitute the sites
for the disclosure of the lines of force linking desire and power. Indeed,
in giving criticism cause and objects to condemn, fiction becomes
inextricably linked to its desire to lay down the law. Power and desire,
law and transgression, produce, and repress, complex webs of relations
rather than forge absolute and inviolable limits.

Webs of fiction

Gothic fiction, despite the efforts of its critics, does not lie outside
polite, rational and moral culture as a threatening locus of the unre-
served expression of immoral desire and passionate transgression. On
the contrary, novels, like those by Radcliffe, share the same anxieties
about the limits of reason and morality; they remain preoccupied by
the laws regulating society and domesticity and, in narratives which
insistently turn on the absence or failings or tyrannical impostures of
the paternal figure, return to the necessity of a moral resolution with
a Providential guarantee. At the end of *Udolpho* a divine Father is
invoked to preside over the heroine's wedding and emphasise the law
that rewards virtue and punishes vice. *Dracula*, a novel in which no
natural father is in evidence, ends with the birth of a son, the literal
manifestation of the restored symbolic order of bourgeois domesticity.
The absence of fathers only underscores the symbolic need for them
since, like the terrors of superstition and unanchored imagination that
are rationally explained, any other closure is utterly unsanctionable.
The name of the father thus constitutes the primary symbolic issue in
Gothic novels of the late eighteenth and nineteenth centuries as they
replay critical concerns about romances. In *Udolpho*, the superstitious
and curious heroine repeatedly disobeys rational paternal injunctions
against excess. In *The Romance of the Forest* the heroine, at one point,

believes the villain to be her father. Only with the legal proceedings at the end do readers discover the proper paternal lineage and its remunerative legacy. Similarly, Maria Roche's *Clermont* is structured around the mysterious and very suspicious family past of the paternal figure. A guilty secret has caused him, erroneously, to conceal his true identity. The interwoven narratives mislead further, until, of course, the father is finally restored to his true name and title.

Narratives continually attempt to discriminate between good fathers and bad. Gothic heterotopias – castles and labyrinths in particular – are part of this process of discrimination: they are the locus where orphans, those without proper paternal protection, are subjected to vicious, illegitimate and tyrannical authority. In the vaults of *The Monk* Ambrosio commits his act of incest: inscribed as a dark and hidden psychogeographical locus, the labyrinth and the act of incestuous gratification signal the horrifying dissolution of familial bonds, a cautionary, paternal lesson on the dangers of excessive passion. Like labyrinths, castles also signify a space for the sovereign exercise of selfish, vicious and illegitimate desires: remote, inaccessible and gloomy, their malevolence impersonates that of the villain. The absence of symbolic and legal restraints in these zones outside the bounds of a paternalistic order confers absolute freedom and complete sovereignty, a return to the power of feudal lordship. In *The Romance of the Forest*, Montalt explains the criminal advantages of desolate locations: 'the abbey well suits my purposes; it is shut up from the eye of observation; any transaction may be concealed within its walls' (Radcliffe, 1791: 223). Hidden from the eye of observation Gothic labyrinths, abbeys and castles are, like the Panopticon, an effect of the Enlightenment 'fear of darkened spaces' and an attempt to render it visible and legible (Foucault, 1980: 153). Gothic fiction penetrates, makes visible and demystifies the darkness of these other spaces, giving them form and function as the absolute inversion of proper social relations. Differentiated, legible, these metaphoric heterotopias can be repressed, expelled to the wilds, beyond the pale of home, heart and nation.

To fabricate these absolute distinctions, to enact its warning against Gothic, the fiction must work against fiction itself, demonstrating the dangerously disturbing effects of Gothic figures in the process of defining their negative nature. Hence the endless Gothic mis-readings of events, signs and texts. The labyrinth becomes the metaphor identifying the locus of danger in networks of evil, and the place and effects of reading. A metaphor for the bewildering complexity of Gothic narratives, the 'labyrinth of literature' has to be penetrated, rendered legible

and its effects dispelled. The labyrinth is thus as artificial as it is superficial, a network of signifiers of desire and power. Fiction does not simply represent darkened space: it is one itself: as reading, in the course
of the eighteenth century, increasingly occurs in the privacy and solitude of the home, the question of the supervision of readers, of how
they will discriminate and understand the duplicitous texts in their
hands, is bound up with the moral panic about Gothic romances (see
de Bolla, 1989: 266). Without the presence of a parent or governess,
children are left to their own devices and superstitious imaginings,
prey to the corrupting effects of romance. Hence the need to inter-
nalise the paternal figure, to introduce into the private scene the super-
egoic figure of law and discrimination.

The paternal figure thus emerges from the spaces of darkness inaccessible to law since absence allows law to appear, to fill in the gap that
was previously unregulated. It involves a process of unravelling the
dense, labyrinthine network of corrupting narrative and retying the
threads with the paternal knot separating proper fiction from its credulous other. At the end of *Clermont* the father states, 'the web of deceit is
at length unravelled ... and the ways of Providence are justified to man'
(Roche, 1798: 366): the symbolic order is reconstructed in the process
of unravelling fictional deceits. At the end of Charlotte Dacre's *The
Libertine*, a tale recounting the evils caused by paternal corruption, the
final crime, suicide, provides the occasion for conventional moral over-
coming of 'labyrinthian confusion':

> Thus ended the career of the once gay Libertine, an awful example
> *'that the sins of the father shall be visited on the children'*. Dreadful
> decree, yet intended by an all-wise Being to serve the great cause of
> society, and impress upon the mind of man the crime of which he is
> guilty in the subversion of a *moral duty*.
>   The wisdom of past ages perceived the necessity of decreeing holy
> ties – subsequent ages found it necessary to abide by the law. mar-
> riage became the bond of society – strong, though imperceptible
> chain which linked mankind together. From it sprang the dear and
> tender affinities of husband, father, wife, mother, brother, and sister.
> To outrage the sacred institution, entails misery and ruin upon
> unborn myriads, sinks and loses in labyrinthian confusion every tie
> of consanguinity, causes an unknown offspring to wander through
> the world unclaimed, and plunges them into a vortex of misfortune
> and crime.
>   (Dacre, 1807: 224)

Paternal failings, absence and transgression establish the occasion for an authoritative inscription of 'a system so glorious, rational and indispensable' (Dacre, 1807: 224). The father, as a figure or a name, is erected over the object causing social and familiar ruin and dissolution, the metaphor that arises precisely at the juncture of two narratives, in the gap between them, the point that differentiates 'labyrinthian confusion' or, in Roche's terms, 'webs of deceit', from 'holy ties', 'the bond of society', a 'strong, imperceptible chain' linking 'mankind' together. The external metaphor of complexity and deceit, the labyrinth also relates to a state of mind, a confusion to be overcome by retying the symbolic fabric uniting social and domestic spheres: it establishes, to use Lacan's description of the unconscious, a 'symbolic construction' which 'covers all human lived experience like a web'. 'The unconscious', he states a few pages later, 'is fundamentally structured, woven, chained, meshed by language' (Lacan, 1993: 112, 119).

The unconscious, however, is not reducible to language. A space of metaphoric substitution, it lies in excess of the final paternal word. It is 'a concept founded by the trail [*trace*] left by that which operates to constitute the subject' (Lacan, 1995: 260). Split by the introduction of the signifier from the real being of the undifferentiated body, subjectivity is organised around an object, a kernel or remainder of the Real. This object, or Thing, exists as the locus articulating the signifier with the real and, in the system of signifiers, takes the form of a 'vacuole', a gap, an absence, a point where meaning is both distinguished from and dissolves in non-meaning (Lacan, 1992: 150). Between the chains of signification through which signifier is hooked onto signified there remains a gap which metaphor occupies but never completely closes, a hoop net of signification into which meaning is sucked. In the two narratives articulated by the name of the father, the one that is presented as the proper symbolic form and the other, its Gothic and repressed counterpart, the gap of the Thing still remains, a leftover like the ruins and castles of the romantic landscape. Beyond the darkness and gloom that discloses the need for Reason and Enlightenment, there lies a space that is 'un-black', the gap between consciousness and its other. For Freud, using the example of *sacer*, meaning both sacred and profane, the unconscious confounds straightforward symbolic opposition. Prior to Freud, Lacan argues, the unconscious '*is not* purely and simply': 'that is because it names nothing that counts anymore as an object – nor warrants being granted any more existence – than what would be defined by situating it in the "un-black" [*l'in-noir*]' (Lacan, 1995: 260). The un-black lies beyond the darkness populated by Gothic images and metaphors, the very space of the Thing, the absence inimical to discourse and constitutive of its reproduction after the fact.

The un-black darkness remains to be illuminated and resists all light; it is repeatedly filled by images and yet returns no knowledge. The metaphors around which the double narratives of Gothic fiction are knotted emerge in the un-black but never conceal it. Indeed, the proximity of two chains of signification in Gothic novels, entwining law and transgression, power and desire, disclose a gap that narrative cannot close. As an effect of Gothic literariness, a different and less visible scene of writing is encountered. A 'schism of the symbolic system', the unconscious is encountered in gaps, fissures, ruptures (Lacan, 1977c: 25–8, 153). The repeated attempts of Gothic writing to narrate past, present and future, and thus repair the symbolic network, do so by unravelling and repressing the webs of artifice in fictional labyrinths of their own making. This not only stages their own artificiality but insistently revolves around the gaps that cause the anxiety, entwining things more inescapably in language. The encounter repeats an unspeakably traumatic disclosure: the labyrinth of fiction offers no other ground, no ultimate reality, no depth and no origin. Hence the significant absence of mothers in Gothic enactments of the traumatic splitting of the subject caused by symbolic law, a loss that testifies to the absence of any final signified and the imposture that is the paternal metaphor.

The un-blackness of the Thing, however, is continually screened. Colonised by collective imaginary schemes in which objects of terror give form to and assuage anxiety, the place of the Thing is where fears and fantasies are projected, metaphors substituted in the gap of representation (Lacan, 1992: 99). This is why fear and ghosts are defence mechanisms, 'protection against something that is beyond, and which is precisely something that is unknown to us' (Lacan, 1992: 232). It is also why Gothic figures of terror and horror change their shape over centuries. Repressed – expelled and internalised – by the institution of the proper paternal metaphor, the chain of Gothic figures and the absence at their core insists as a literary unconscious throughout the nineteenth century. The labyrinthine darkness of city comes to be seen as the breeding ground of depravity and decadence: it is primitive, regressive, a 'house-forest' in *The Woman in White*, a site of lascivious violence for Hyde and a hunting ground for Dracula. Informing the pathological characteristics of regression identified by nascent criminology, internalised Gothic metaphors become symptomatic of deranged and pathological mental states. Egotism signalled by Dracula's 'child brain' and linked to his feudal castle, signifies the irruption of primitive unreason. Underlying these transformations in cultural figures of fear is a space of apprehension. Marie-Christine Leps, in her Foucauldian account of literature and criminology in the nineteenth century, notes the shift from 'dark German dungeons' to 'dark English or French criminal ghettos' (Leps, 1992: 84). Literary, as much as scientific, discourse serves to 'apprehend' social dangers: making them visible, it enables them to be understood, categorised, arrested and excluded. But apprehension, as a mental and physical seizure of the object of fear by means of metaphors and signs, emanates from a space of nothing, a space of generalised apprehension linked to the resistance of the Thing and the un-black unconscious. Dracula signifies an inapprehensible object and free-floating anxiety, his in-visibility in the mirror and the non-presence of his undeath making him unknowable, unarrestable, a gaping hole in the symbolic order of western bourgeois culture. Only when the fragmentary texts composing the fiction are pieced together is the threat of Dracula made visible: only then can the absence he represents be countered and overcome by the good metaphorical father, Van Helsing.

Repressed and returning as an insistent chain of associations, the Gothic unconscious is not reducible to the figures and terms in which it is represented, but, in excess of the figures it generates with such fecundity, it remains a space of inscription and dissolution. The unconscious, Lacan notes, *'will have been'*; the repressed returns, not from the past, but from the future: a symptom, a trace that receives its value and significance in a process of symbolic realisation (Lacan, 1988: 158–9). This is why 'the notion that the unconscious is merely the seat of the instincts will have to be rethought' (Lacan, 1977b: 147). Moreover, the uncanny return of the repressed identified with these instincts and seen to be endlessly expressed in the figures of Gothic fiction will also have to be rethought. As Hélène Cixous suggests in 'Fiction and its Phantoms', her reading of Freud's essay on the uncanny, literature is never expunged from his texts but returns to undermine claims of scientific authority. The return of the repressed, she argues, is associated, not with any *thing* unconscious, but with the movement of signifiers. The ghost, crossing boundaries and disturbing the supposedly fixed states of symbolic reality, manifests the signifier, 'death', which has no signified and thus inscribes an internal errancy in the language of the living. For Derrida, too, the uncanny manifests the mobility of meaning and the operations of metaphorical substitution unanchored by any final ground or meaning (Derrida, 1981: 286n). The movement, the play of metaphors, like the artifices of Gothic fiction, suggests that the uncanny is more than an objectified wish returning from an unconscious identified as a seat of instincts. Instead, in Lacan's terms, the uncanny marks the decomposition of the fantasy underpinning imaginary subjective integrity and the assumption of symbolic consistency: its apprehension discloses, in horror, nothing but a void (Lacan, 1977a). Which is why, furthermore, that even as the evident artifices of Gothic fictions raise the question of meaning they do so in respect of the signifier: as Gothic metaphors produce a recognisable form of the unconscious, making its darkness visible and literal, they also disclose something quite Other. Their link to the unconscious is a matter of writing, of a general text of marks and traces. As a counter-history to the 'history of literary forms' that, Derrida notes, 'was destined precisely to authorize this disdain of the signifier', Gothic writing can be understood to be bound up with a *'becoming literary of the literal'* and demands 'a psychoanalysis of literature respectful of the *originality of the literary signifier'* (Derrida, 1978: 230).

Notes

1 Later, in another interview with Renfield, Seward comments, 'unconscious cerebration was doing its work, even with the lunatic' (348).
2 In his 'Seminar on "The Purloined Letter"' (1972), Jacques Lacan discusses the importance of the signifier in the constitution of subjectivity to comment, 'it is that truth, let us note, which makes the very existence of fiction possible' (40). Later he observes of the tale 'that truth here reveals its fictive arrangement' (46). Jacques Derrida's response, in 'The Purveyor of Truth' (1975), complicates the relationship between truth and fiction, science and literature, through the (un)veiling play of metaphors: ' "Truth inhabits fiction" should not be understood in the somewhat perverse sense of a fiction which is more powerful than the truth which inhabits it and is inscribed in it. In truth, truth inhabits fiction as the master of the house, as the law of the house and as the economy of fiction. Truth brings about the economy of fiction. It directs, organizes and renders fiction possible. "It is that truth, let us note, which makes the very existence of fiction possible". The question is thus to ground fiction in truth to guarantee it within truth and to do so without stressing, as is the case of *Das Unheimlich*, this resistance, always renewed, of literary fiction to the general law of psychoanalytical knowledge' (46–7).
3 In chapter 13 of the third edition of his *Principles of Mental Physiology* (London, 1875), Carpenter refers to Cobbe's work.
4 For a discussion of Romantic subjectivity, Gothic writing and psychoanalysis, see Belsey, 1982.
5 For an account of the textual surfaces of Gothic labyrinths, see Hogle, 1980.
6 For a discussion of readers and misreading in Radcliffe, see Botting, 1994.
7 Lacan's formula for the relation of metaphor and the unconscious can be found in *Four Fundamental Concepts*, 1977c: 248.

Works cited

Addison, Joseph. 1970. *Critical Essays From the Spectator*. Ed. Donald F. Bond. London: Oxford University Press.

Anon. 1797. Review of *The Monk*. *Monthly Review* (New Series) 23, 451.

Belsey, Catherine. 1982. 'The Romantic Construction of the Unconscious'. In *1789: Reading, Writing, Revolution*. Ed. Francis Barker et al. Colchester: University of Essex, 67–80.

Botting, Fred. 1993. 'Power in the Darkness: Heterotopias, Literature and Gothic Labyrinths'. *Genre* 26, 253–82.

Botting, Fred. 1994. '*Dracula*, Romance and Radcliffean Gothic'. *Women's Writing* 1.2, 181–201.

Byrd, Max. 1977. 'The Madhouse, The Whorehouse, and the Convent'. *Partisan Review* 44.2, 268–78.

Carpenter, William. 1875. *Principles of Mental Physiology*. London: King.

Castle, Terry. 1987. 'The Spectralization of the Other in *The Mysteries of Udolpho*'. In *The New Eighteenth Century*. Ed. Laura Brown and Felicity Nussbaum. London: Methuen, 231–53.

Cixous, Hélène. 1976. 'Fiction and its Phantoms: A Reading of Freud's *Das Unheimliche* (The "uncanny")'. *New Literary History* 7, 525–48.

Clery, E. J. 1994. 'Against Gothic'. In *Gothick Origins and Innovations*. Ed. Allan Lloyd Smith and Victor Sage. Amsterdam: Rodopi, 34–43.

Cobbe, Frances Power. 1870. 'Unconscious Cerebration: A Psychological Study'. *Macmillan's Magazine* 23, 24–37.

Cobbe, Frances Power. 1871. 'Dreams as Illustrations of Unconscious Cerebration'. *Macmillan's Magazine* 23, 512–23.

Coleridge, Samuel Taylor. 1975. *Biographia Literaria*. Ed. George Watson. London: Dent.

Dacre, Charlotte. 1807. *The Libertine*. 4 vols. New York: Arno, 1974, Vol. 4.

De Bolla, Peter. 1989. *The Discourse of the Sublime*. Oxford: Oxford University Press.

de Quincey, Thomas. 1986. *Confessions of an English Opium Eater*. Ed. Alethea Hayter. London: Penguin.

Derrida, Jacques. 1975. 'The Purveyor of Truth'. *Yale French Studies* 52, 31–113.

Derrida, Jacques. 1978. 'Freud and the Scene of Writing'. In *Writing and Difference*. Trans. Alan Bass. London: Routledge, 196–231.

Derrida, Jacques. 1981. *Dissemination*. Trans. Barbara Johnson. London: Athlone.

Fawcett, Mary Laughlin. 1983. '*Udolpho*'s Primal Mystery'. *Studies in English Literature 1500–1900* 23.3, 481–94.

Foucault, Michel. 1970. *The Order of Things: An Archaeology of the Human Sciences*. Unidentified collective translation. London: Tavistock.

Foucault, Michel. 1977. *Language, Counter-Memory, Practice: Selected Essays and Interviews by Michel Foucault*. Ed. and Intro. Donald F. Bouchard. Trans. Donald F. Bouchard and Sherry Simon. Oxford: Blackwell.

Foucault, Michel. 1980. 'The Eye of Power'. In *Power/Knowledge: Selected Interviews and Other Writings, 1972–1977*. Ed. Colin Gordon. Brighton: Harvester.

Foucault, Michel. 1984. *The History of Sexuality, Volume I: An Introduction*. Trans. Robert Hurley. Harmondsworth: Penguin.

Foucault, Michel. 1986. 'Of Other Spaces'. *diacritics* 16.1, 22–7.

Hogle, Jerrold E. 1980. 'The Restless Labyrinth: Cryptonomy in the Gothic Novel'. *Arizona Quarterly* 36, 330–58.

Hogle, Jerrold E. 1994. 'The Ghost of the Counterfeit in the Genesis of the Gothic'. In *Gothick Origins and Innovations*. Ed. Allan Lloyd Smith and Victor Sage. Amsterdam: Rodopi, 23–33.

Lacan, Jacques. 1972. 'Seminar on "The Purloined Letter"'. *Yale French Studies* 48, 38–72.

Lacan, Jacques. 1977a. 'Desire and the Interpretation of Desire in *Hamlet*'. *Yale French Studies* 55/6, 11–52.

Lacan, Jacques. 1977b. *Écrits*. Trans. Alan Sheridan. London: Tavistock.

Lacan, Jacques. 1977c. *The Four Fundamental Concepts of Psychoanalysis*. Trans. Alan Sheridan. London: Hogarth.

Lacan, Jacques. 1988. *The Seminar of Jacques Lacan: Book I*. Trans. John Forrester. Cambridge: Cambridge University Press.

Lacan, Jacques. 1992. *The Ethics of Psychoanalysis*. Trans. Dennis Porter. London: Routledge.

Lacan, Jacques. 1993. *The Psychoses*. Trans. Russell Grigg. London: Routledge.

Lacan, Jacques. 1995. 'Position of the Unconscious'. In *Reading Seminar XI*. Ed. Richard Feldstein, Bruce Fink, Maire Jaanus. New York: SUNY, 259–82.

Laplanche, Jean and Serge Leclaire. 1972. 'The Unconscious: a Psychoanalytic Study'. *Yale French Studies* 48, 118–78.

Leps, Marie-Christine. 1992. *Apprehending the Criminal*. Durham, NC: Duke University Press.

Mathias, T. J. 1805. *The Pursuits of Literature*. 13th edn. London: n.p.

Napier, Elizabeth. 1987. *The Failure of Gothic*. Oxford: Clarendon.

Radcliffe, Ann. 1791. *The Romance of the Forest*. Ed. Chloe Chard. Oxford: Oxford University Press, 1986.

Roche, Maria Regina. 1798. *Clermont*. London: Folio, 1968.

Sedgwick, Eve Kosofsky. 1986. *The Coherence of Gothic Conventions*. London: Methuen.

Stoker, Bram. 1897. *Dracula*. Ed. Maurice Hindle. London: Penguin, 1993.

Tompkins, J. M. S. 1969. *The Popular Novel in England 1770–1800*, 2nd edn. London: Methuen.

Walpole, Horace. 1764. *The Castle of Otranto*. Ed. W.S. Lewis. Oxford: Oxford University Press.

Williams, Ioan. 1970. *Novel and Romance 1700–1800*. London: Routledge.

Chapter 2

Ceremonial Gothic

David Punter

I mean in this essay to try to place Gothic in a different light; under, we might say, a different shadow. It has become a truism to say that Gothic is transgressive. Against, or behind, the daylight images of the realist tradition, Gothic throws up a parodic, difficult array; things which might seem regular are revealed in their grandiose, shocking asymmetry; history passes through a series of distortions; perversions surface and are given concrete form.

What would it be like, I want to ask, if we were to see Gothic differently from this; if, instead of the moment of transgression, we were to focus on the moment of stabilisation? I am not speaking here of a political argument about conservatism and subversion; the shape of my argument has perhaps more to do with a logic of parasitism, as described by Derrida; with a logic whereby Gothic might be seen to function as a 'foreign body' within the institution of literature.[1]

This logic, as we might expound it, would focus on the curious, essential co-necessity of parasite and host, and therefore on the moment at which we can no longer clearly see what is the bearer and what is being borne; we might wish to see – or we might come to see, despite our overt wishes – stability from the viewpoint of the parasite rather than of the host. Gothic, then, not as an irruption through an otherwise smooth surface, as a disruption of what Deleuze and Guattari refer to as the plane of consistency;[2] but rather in the manner in which, as I shall go on to describe, Lacan refers to the perversions, the site – the para-site – only on which, and by means of which, such a smoothness can be attained.

In order to help me to focus on this view, I have adopted the standpoint of ceremonial. I have in mind a view of Gothic as a panoply of ceremonies, and we can begin by listing some of them: the ceremony of the expulsion of the vampire, precisely of the foreign body; magical ceremonies and exorcisms; ceremonial feasts and banquets, at which a ghost is inevitably present; religious services, in places appropriate and inappropriate; funerals and other ceremonies of mourning; Black Sabbaths and ceremonies of all souls; ceremonious robings and disrobings; the list, like the struggle, continues.

What is ceremonial? The *Oxford English Dictionary* offers us some beginnings. Ceremonial can be equated with ritual, and this is a connection to which I shall be returning, particularly through Freud's short paper of 1907 on 'Obsessive Actions and Religious Practices', which draws tight the link between these three terms: ceremonial, ritual, obsession. Ceremonial, we learn, also means 'addicted to ceremony or ritual'; and thus we could begin also to trace the force of an addiction through these compulsive ceremonies. But ceremonial strikes in two ways. It strikes towards the unearthly, the hieratic, the sense of the beyond and signs which might be directed towards or might emanate from the beyond: 'a ceremonial and superstitious man', the Dictionary suggests to us, a constellation in which ceremonial stands in for signs and portents much in the way that superstitions do.

But ceremonial also stands in for the conventional, the quotidian, that which is reduced to 'mere ceremony', that which is drained of meaning; 'it is *non ens,* a meer flash, a ceremony, a toy, a thing of nought'. Ceremonial, then, as a surplus of meaning or as an absence of meaning; the term begins to deconstruct itself. At all events, what can be said is that ceremonial relates closely to what Derrida speaks of when he embarks on his analyses of ruins and remains (Derrida, 1992: 36–7). The ceremony always points past and beyond, behind itself; it signifies, even in its superflux of meaning, the absence of whatever it was that preceded the ceremonial. Similarly, ceremonial speaks of repetition: a repetition without which the ceremony is not a ceremony, a repetition which also serves through the very force of its stability to invoke a past which has always already vanished. Ceremonial as reminder, as a gesture towards what is absent, as a site that is perennially haunted by all that it is not.

Literature has its masters of ceremonies. One of them would be Crashaw, with his stagings of impossible dances, his insistence on perverted theological ritual, his own nameless sinking amid the ornate weight of his imagery. Another would be Christopher Smart, master of the unending invocation, of the poem as litany.[3] Shakespeare has much to say about ceremony. In *Macbeth* we learn that 'To Feed were best at Home; / From thence, the Sauce to Meat is Ceremony; / Meeting were bare without it' (*Macbeth*, III.4. 35–7). Ceremony, then, is a public matter, a conversion of the merely domestic ('feeding', which is what one merely does at home) into something altogether more stately, which is none the less permissive of a sly pun, 'meat' and 'meeting', for ceremonial is impressive and laughable, pompous and ridiculous, sacred and the butt of the joke, as Polonius elsewhere came to know.

'O, the sacrifice, / How ceremonious, solemn, and unearthly / It was i' th'off'ring!', Dion reports in *The Winter's Tale* (III.1. 6–8); 'solemn' and 'unearthly', so that ceremony becomes a mediating force, an assertion of meaning which in the very act of assertion relegates that meaning to another place, another 'scene', and thus plunges us into an abyss where the only thing of which we can be sure is that the ceremonial is not what it purports to be, it is a coagulation around a secret, and no matter how hard we probe the ceremony we shall not be permitted to discover the truth behind it; for such a manifestation of presence would at once dismantle the ceremony, rob us of the need for an intercessor; which is not ever the need for an intercessor as such but the need for the secret to be withheld, the need for the crypt to remain unopened, for the remains, the ruins, never to be fully exhibited, like the sacred relic, to the light of day, before which they would crumble, like the remains of the vampire, into a thing of dust. This might indeed be the fate which is alluded to in *Julius Caesar* when Flavius adjures his companions to 'Disrobe the Images,/If you do find them deck'd with Ceremonies' (I.1. 69–70); for the ultimate consequence of this disrobing is a disappearance, a catastrophe, a disaster which these 'ceremonies', like others, are designed to avert.

A ceremony, then, we might also see as a portent, an omen, and the omen concerned here is the downfall of Caesar, the revelation of the nakedness of the emperor who can survive only so long as he upholds the ceremonies, but, more, so long as the ceremonies uphold him. These ceremonies, though, are ambiguous, and they have to do also with the night world, and we know Caesar is on skid row when Cassius couples these ceremonies with other omens and portents: 'For he is Superstitious grown of late', he observes,

> Quite from the main Opinion he held once
> Of Fantasy, of Dreams and Ceremonies.
> It may be these apparent Prodigies,
> The unaccustomed Terror of this Night…

> (*Julius Caesar* II.1. 193–7)

And so it goes as Cassius seeks to explain how it can be that the once master is now suffering from doubt, how those very ceremonies which should sustain the imperial ego can rise up against it and figure forth the inexpressible terror of the night.

Calpurnia comes to feel the same way: 'Caesar, I never stood on Ceremonies, /Yet now they fright me' (*Julius Caesar* II.2. 13–14), she says, before she launches into her catalogue of portents of doom; and here too we can see the trajectory of debasement of the term 'ceremony' itself through the shift in the trope of 'standing on ceremony'; Calpurnia means to say that she never believed in these curious and ornate absences, yet that meaning has been drained from the contemporary use of the phrase in a redoubled debasement or ruination in which we can again see the shadow of the duplicity of ceremony itself, which is always suspect, always double, always superseded yet potent, always ridiculed and feared.

These Gothic visions, such as Calpurnia's, do not transgress; they come to shore up a sense of the world in ruins, they come, if you like, to defend the soul against worse realisations. In so far as ceremonies are ritual namings, they come to protect us against namelessness, against anonymity; they are, to allude to Derrida again, to do with monumentalisation, with the inescapable possibility that the name will supersede the body and will provide its epitaph.[4]

We could then see Gothic texts as monuments, and as a certain signal of the monumentalisation of all writing, which is haunted by the deferral of its own supersession and what its future fate will be. The novels of Ann Radcliffe, for example, are monuments: largely unreadable, frequently unread, they bear a limiting position in regard to the tradition; their importance lies not in themselves but in the kind of thing they are, and yet the kind of thing they are cannot be reduced or paraphrased, parasited: they have a ceremonial texture which cannot be shortcircuited or cut off, like a piece from a roll. Each chapter has its epigraph, which, as is the way with epigraphs, slide into epitaphs, for dead writers, whose names are both obliterated and preserved by their problematic absorption into Radcliffe's texts. Sometimes these epigraphs are attributed, for example, to Shakespeare, sometimes to particular plays, *Julius Caesar* as it might be, without distinction (Radcliffe, 1794: 182): there is no difference here between the mortality of the writer and the mortality of the titular character, there is an anonymity to Gothic which provides its strength and its weakness, its survival and its decay.

Let us, in ceremonial fashion, turn to Freud.

I am certainly not the first person to have been struck by the resemblance between what are called obsessive actions in sufferers from nervous affections and the observances by means of which believers give expression to their piety. The term 'ceremonial', which has been applied to some of these obsessive actions, is evidence of this. The resemblance, however, seems to me to be more than a superficial one, so that an insight into the origin of neurotic ceremonial may embolden us to draw inferences by analogy about the psychological processes of religious life.

(Freud, 1907: 117)

Freud proceeds to an analysis of obsessional actions in respect of which he observes that 'a ceremonial represents the sum of the conditions subject to which something that is not yet absolutely forbidden is permitted, just as the Church's marriage ceremony signifies for the believer a sanctioning of sexual enjoyment which would otherwise be sinful' (Freud, 1907: 124–5).

A ceremonial, therefore, is the Other of transgression. What would 'otherwise' have been transgression is now allowed; ceremony supersedes the law, permits a breach through which things may flow. We see here again the motif of stabilisation: a threatened irruption can be stabilised by surrounding it with, embedding it in, a sequence of actions. Freud's analysis is geared towards probing through the meaninglessness of these actions to demonstrate their causal connections with events in his patients' lives; but perhaps we should stay a while a little closer to the surface, up against, as it were, the meaninglessness.

'I am certainly not the first person', says Freud, and now we paraphrase, to notice the similarity between neurotic ritual behaviour and the ways in which we deal with matters of the supernatural. What Freud verges upon here, but never broaches, is the connection between the neurotic and the supernatural, or as we might put it in terms offered earlier, the ceremonial and the superstitious. How may we best phrase this connection, even if, like Freud, we admit that we are not the first people to have thought of it? An invocation of the law of repetition, the alternative law, as it were, would clearly take us one step further. The connection can be expressed in terms of a rage against meaning. The obsessional neurotic squirms in the grip of a world where meanings are all too pressing, all too proximate; they obscure, like a net, Blake's net or Iris Murdoch's, the beyond, the inexpressible. But something of this inexpressible can be brought into the world, even if at the cost of continuing nagging pain: some small hollow can be opened, especially in the most petty of daily actions, by seizing these actions and rending them, so that their meaning is lost, subsumed, in a parodic replication of the noumenal sense of what lies beyond.

The thrust of Freud's analysis is to suggest, with the utmost politeness, the psychological roots of religious observance; for our purposes, perhaps a more important trajectory would be to note the sanctification of the petty, its translation to a higher realm precisely through a draining of meaning. One of the examples he quotes hinges on the idea that the key lies in a phrase, a proverb, a magic word: 'Don't throw away dirty water till you have clean' (Freud, 1907: 120). Gothic; ceremonial; the magic word. We can see all of these at play in a passage from William Gibson's *Neuromancer*.

The monstrous Artificial Intelligence Wintermute, in human guise, brings us to the centre, the heart, of the Villa Straylight, where there is a jewelled head on a pedestal. The head begins to speak, or rather, as it turns out, to recite: 'The Villa Straylight', it says,

> is a body grown in upon itself, a Gothic folly. Each space in Straylight is in some way secret, this endless series of chambers linked by passages, by stairwells vaulted like intestines, where the eye is trapped in narrow curves, carried past ornate screens, empty alcoves.
>
> (Gibson, 1984: 206)

We have been here before; we were here, for example, last year, at Marienbad; we were here two centuries ago in Otranto or Udolpho; we visit here, of course, each night in a series of acts of folly, in a series of obsessional repetitions, repeating dreams. We may not have been the first people to have known this; indeed, we shall never know the origin of this scenario, nor how it is that we seem to have managed to penetrate the crypt; nor shall we ever know whose voice this is speaking to us, for we are here, now, in a ceremony.

The essay that the head is recounting was written by 3Jane on a semiotics course; but what is this head? Wintermute (in human form as the 'Finn', the end, the end of all things, the end of the labyrinth) tells us: 'This thing's a ceremonial terminal, sort of' (Gibson, 1984: 207). Sort of? What sort of? Or is it a terminal ceremonial, another Finn, another end? At all events, in this central space, protected (but never sufficiently) from intrusion (obsessional acts are almost always performed in private, and thus it is, Freud tells us wistfully, that they usually escape the analyst's attention), a ceremony is taking place. Or would take place, save for one lack. Wintermute has here almost all he needs for the completion of his design; one thing is missing. 'I need Molly in here', he says, 'with the right word at the right time. That's the catch. Doesn't mean shit, how deep you and the Flatline ride that Chinese virus, if this thing doesn't hear the magic word' (Gibson, 1984: 207).

And so the crypt is not (yet) penetrated. The magic word – and I do not have to spell out here Abraham and Torok's work in this area – is not (yet) available, and so the head's recitation remains what it is, a recitation, an endless repetition, without enlivening force (see Abraham and Torok, 1986: 79–83). I shall return to this question of repetition and vitality later in one or two remarks on autism and its treatment; for the moment, what we need to bear in mind is that 'Gothic folly' is centred on ceremonial, but this ceremony cannot be brought to life. Ceremonial is that which resists being brought to life, that which stands in for the absence of life, that set of ornate coverings, modelled, we are told in this case, upon the microchip, which repels the intrusion of life in the name of stabilisation, a monumentalisation after death, here in the ruins, the remains of the Villa Straylight, where light has not been captured.

What is lacking here, then, is vitality, a certain richness which could only be facilitated by the tearing, the ripping, of this beautiful jewelled fabric by the force of something inalienably other. This is something of what Lacan has to say about perversion:

> In adults, we are aware of the palpable richness of perversion. Perversion, in sum, is the privileged exploration of an existential possibility of human nature – its internal tearing apart, its gap, through which the supra-natural world of the symbolic was able to make its entry.
>
> (Lacan, 1988: 218)

Note the reference to the supernatural. And again, referring us back to Freud:

> in obsessional neurosis, the object with relation to which the fundamental experience, the experience of pleasure, is organised, is an object which literally gives too much pleasure. ... What in its various advances and many byways the behaviour of the obsessional reveals and signifies is that he regulates his behaviour so as to avoid

what the subject often sees quite clearly as the goal and end of his desire. The motivation of this avoidance is often extraordinarily radical, since the pleasure principle is presented to us as possessing a mode of operation which is precisely to avoid excess, too much pleasure.

(Lacan, 1992: 54)

Lacan on perversion, Lacan on obsession; and finally, to connect the two:

By what deep attachments is it that a certain relationship to the Other, that we call Sadistic, reveals its true connection to the psychology of the obsessional? – the obsessional, whose defences take the form of an iron frame, of a rigid mould, a corset, in which he remains and locks himself up, so as to stop himself having access to that which Freud somewhere calls a horror he himself doesn't know.

(Lacan, 1992: 203)

Here, indeed, are our Gothic castles, our torture racks, even a certain hysteria marked in the hesitancy about the location of the Freud quotation, but more so in the context of this last sentence, which ends abruptly and is broken off by a quite different text, with the astounding title, 'The Death Drive according to Bernfeld'. Further than this barrier of horror, then, one cannot go; one is leaving words behind.

The 'richness' of perversion I shall take up later in connection with Anne Rice's *Interview with the Vampire*. The excess of potential pleasure, the revelling in a drive which would here seem to be inseparable from the thanatic, to which Lacan points in the second quotation, would seem to have much to do with the Gothic, with the idea of the castle not as a site of fear but as the para-site of an enjoyment whose sources are unknown, whose limits are figured, like Gormenghast, as unbounded; what Gothic itself would figure, on this interpretation, is the place, not behind the arras, but rather where we pause before the arras and where we may play before confronting, or as an evasion of confronting, the threatened lifting of the veil, the occupant, or the site, of a curious limbo, what we might call a psychic departure lounge where we have lost our nationality, our citizenship, our passport, and yet have not yet crossed over the edge into the other world, even if the price of this hesitation be the unending repetition of a set of meaningless gestures whose richness is perceived not even, or especially not, by our selves.

Perhaps we can examine further these 'deep attachments' and their relation to ceremonial by looking at a passage from *Melmoth the Wanderer.* We encounter Melmoth and Isidora before their promised marriage, Isidora hiding amid the gravestones while Melmoth goes to fetch the 'hermit' who, he says, will unite them in a chapel 'attached to the ruins, but not like them in decay, where sacred ceremonies were still performed' (Maturin, 1820: 393). Here all is remains, the 'remains', for example, 'of an altar and crucifix'; there is 'also a marble vessel, that seemed designed to contain holy water, but it was empty'. In pitch darkness, Melmoth clasps her hand and whispers 'He is here – ready to unite us.'

> The long-protracted terrors of this bridal left her not a breath to utter a word withal, and she leaned on the arm that she felt, not in confidence, but for support. The place, the hour, the objects, all were hid in darkness. She heard a faint rustling as of the approach of another person, – she tried to catch certain words, but she knew not what they were, – she attempted also to speak, but she knew not what she said. All was mist and darkness with her, – she knew not what was muttered, – she felt not that the hand of Melmoth grasped hers, – but she felt that the hand that united them, and clasped their palms within his own, was as *cold as that of death.*
>
> (Maturin, 1820: 394)

This is, we might say, the dream of ceremony. It has the air of something remembered, repeated under the repetition compulsion; it has no recognisable content and is recognised as a ceremony as such only by virtue of a generalised apparatus which continues to operate even after its meaning has drained away. We may speak here properly of perversion, of a pleasure which has renounced pleasure, signified in the sliding of the marriage ceremony, through the graveyard and the ruined chapel, into a ceremony of death, into a foreshadowed funeral.

This is a ceremony which permits the flow of what is forbidden, but the action of this permission is redoubled. What will follow from this marriage is not a liberation but a consignment to death, so that the pleasurable and the thanatic are intimately intertwined, signified in the triple clasp of the hands, two living, one dead. This is ceremony at the limit of the impossible, and the text signifies as such by breaking off; we do not return to this scene, or rather to its aftermath, for a further hundred-odd pages. Lacan's text breaks on the point of 'horror he himself doesn't know' – textually attributed, but hazily, in darkness, to

Freud; here we have a text that breaks on the hand as 'cold as that of death', in the midst of inexpressibilities, uncertainties.

We find ourselves, then, in the realm of ceremonial up against a barrier; we can see this barrier as the altar-rail beyond which lies the mystery of transubstantiation, or in magical terms as the barrier of incomprehension signified in our unknowingness as to what spirits might be invoked, liberated, by the repeated actions of the drawing of pentagram, the placing of cup, book and candle. 'What is beyond this barrier?', Lacan asks in an apposite context:

> Don't forget that if we know there is a barrier and that there is a beyond, we know nothing about what lies beyond. It is a false beginning to say... that it is the world of fear. To centre our life, even our religion, on fear as a final term is an error. Fear with its ghosts is a localisable defence, a protection against something that is beyond, and which is precisely something which is unknown to us.
>
> (Lacan, 1992: 232)

If we can find this barrier, its attempted propitiation through ceremonial, and the invocation of a world of fear which functions ambiguously as a 'localisable defence', throughout Gothic – if, indeed, we might be tempted to see in this collocation of objects and actions placed over against the barrier the very hallmark of the Gothic – then we can see it at its most emblematic in Stephen King's *Pet Sematary*. Here, as you may recall, the place which stands over against the barrier, which can be visited, like Melmoth's chapel, only under conditions of night and secrecy, is the pet cemetery itself, where animals have been placed in a symbolic spiral which signifies to the initiated the possibility of their return, but in a hideously transmuted form; at the far end of this 'clearing', this neurotic hollow in the quotidian, lies what King describes as a 'deadfall', a vast tangle of broken and whitened trees and branches which can figure also as a tangle of bleached bones. The dying boy who comes to warn our hero tells him not to go past that 'deadfall', for to do so will entail his own destruction and the destruction of all he loves (King, 1983: 46, 126ff).

What is found on the other side (and it would be a very short novel if our hapless hero heeded this injunction) is something altogether less nameable, a place where a parallel human resurrection is possible, a place of ceremonial transubstantiation which nevertheless supplies us with images of horror as the hero's son is brought back from the dead a murderous travesty of the small boy he was when he was first killed;

the book ends on the point of a similar resurrection of the hero's wife. 'One doesn't have to read very far for this collection of horrors', writes Lacan, in connection with De Sade, but the translation to King is effortless, 'to engender incredulity and disgust in us, and it is only fleetingly, in a brief flash, that such images may cause something strange to vibrate in us which we can call perverse desire' (Lacan, 1992: 232). This perverse desire is obvious in *Pet Sematary*, but characteristically displaced; when you cross the barrier it is as though, as with so many crossings of the threshold, you have changed, your subjectivity has been taken in thrall – a similar thing happens in King's *The Sun Dog* – and the obsession, for which the ceremonial was merely a cover-story, emerges in full force. The ceremonial protects and beckons, forbids and invites; in a parasitic formation it confuses host with that which is borne, and engenders a reversal of terms, that reversal of terms in perversion which, Lacan says, is constitutive of psyche.

Taking as his starting-point, like Lacan, the Freud, and the 'beyond', of *Beyond the Pleasure Principle*, Derrida says that in the

> fate neuroses... repetition has the characteristics of the demonic. ... Coming back (*revenant*) – subject to a rhythm [and thus we might say to a ceremonial] – this phantom deserves an analysis of the passages and the procedure, of everything that both makes him come back and conjures him up cadentially. The very procedure of the text itself [of *Beyond the Pleasure Principle*] is diabolical. It mimes walking, does not cease walking without advancing, regularly sketching out one step more without gaining an inch of ground. A limping devil... without ever permitting the conclusion of a last step.
>
> (Derrida, 1987: 269)

And again, in speaking of the *Gerusalemme Liberata*, what is most moving, according to Derrida,

> is not only the twice repeated unconscious murder of the beloved disguised as a man (in the armour of an enemy knight, the trees of the fantastic forest full of spirits and revenants...); not only the return of Clorinda's ghostly voice; not only the *unheimlich* repetition, beyond the pleasure principle, of the murder of the beloved. No, what is '*most* moving'... is the repetition (call it 'literary' if you will, a kind of fiction which in any event no longer derives from the imaginary), of these *unheimlich* repetitions of repetitions.
>
> (Derrida, 1987: 343)

We might suggest on this basis that the very condition of the 'literary' might be what is exposed in these fictions of *revenants*, of what comes back from the beyond to play the role of present absence in the ceremonial, of what can be captured, in however distorted a form, from the world beyond the barrier, of the means by which we can telepathically reach out and find some answering call beyond the deadfall, beyond the ruination of the chapel. When we conceive of Gothic solely in terms of transgression, we incline to view it in figures of motion, pursuit and flight; what might emerge from these dealings with the *revenant* is more a series of frozen tableaux: the bite, with the gaze beyond the shoulder; the stand-off between Frankenstein and the monster; the magical scenarios of the pentagram and the laboratory, from which there is no escape as the various realms of soul are held in stasis.

Gothic, then, we might say – and here it harks back precisely to its own older, specifically ruined but charismatic foundations in architecture, stained glass, the whole panoply of remains – attempts the impossible task of stabilising the world through ceremonial and ritual, and in doing so necessarily involves itself in a structure of perversion which can alone give force to that stability, which can shore up our shifting perceptions of the 'natural'. But there is also a sense in which this move towards stability, towards an invocation which is perpetually frozen, petrified with fear, can be seen only as a waiting, as a waiting for the telepathic link to the beyond to come into being. 'What', Lacan asks, 'is the obsessional waiting for? The death of the master. What use does this waiting have for him? It is interposed between him and death. When the master is dead, everything will begin' (Lacan, 1988: 286). This, of course, we may say as an aside, is the plot of *Caleb Williams*, where all the journeyings, all the trajectories of flight, remain in the end bound in one position, where the postponement of death and the longing for an end, a *fin*, become inseparable and undecidable.[5]

In the passage from Maturin, as in the one from William Gibson, it is clear that the ceremonial functions around that which has been encrypted. The jewelled head at the centre of the labyrinth waits, waits for the magic word which will release it from a world of recitation and repetition. In the *Melmoth* scene, much is made of who is waiting for whom, of whether Melmoth and his bride or the darkened figure as cold as death will be the first to reach the scene. We would therefore perhaps be correct to see the most typical enactment of the ceremonial as the funerary, for it is here that we encounter the full difficulty of establishing a moment of stasis and that we see that this is only possible in the mode of the thanatic.

In *The Wolf Man's Magic Word*, Abraham and Torok, in their discourse of the magic word and of that which has been encrypted, show us also the difficulties of dealing with these moments of stasis. For example:

> The present and the past merge. Behind the show of obedience to the mother, a cryptic identification with the policelike nurse (who had raised little Sergei to the rank of witness) continues to be active. ...The increasing desire to speak out mobilises the forces of countercathexis. They hark back to the period when the mother tried to use religious training to calm the temper tantrums of the 'broken' witness. The analysis thus opens the way to regression.
>
> (Abraham and Torok, 1986: 64)

In the curiously redoubled ceremonial of a psychoanalysis of a psycho-analysis (and you will recall that Freud's own 'crypt' is at stake here, and perhaps also the ceremonial final words of this chapter: 'The pros-ecution is about to reach its climax'), present and past merge and are superimposed; or rather, their superimposition is revealed as some-thing stirs and shows signs of wishing to return across the barrier. Yet at that point, it seems to me, the rhetoric of the text tries to speak in two different directions: on the one hand, to reassert the stabilisation achieved by the encounter with the forces of countercathexis, on the other, to proceed anyway, despite these difficulties and prohibitions, with the unlocking of the crypt through the (post-funerary) use of the magic word. The wolf man is dead; yet something can, *must*, be brought back if his ghost is to be laid to rest; the fictional, metaphori-cal structure of the magic word is in danger of being lost amid the ter-rors of what would ensue if the crypt were to remain buried, in a hysteria which demands manifestation.

The dialectic of ceremonial and vitality can be seen in another way. The dictionary speaks also of ceremonialism and ritualism, close to the substance of Freud's analysis; beyond, or behind, the anthropological, or dramatic, fields in which we might closely situate ritual there still lies the realm of obsessive action. What then might we make of these connections between ceremonial; the funerary; the structure of infant ritualism; and the obsessional neuroses which serve to stave off death? The name of Beckett comes to mind, and with it the impossibility, self-proclaimed, of Derrida's ever approaching Beckett's work (see Derrida, 1992: 61), but we can also situate these dealings in a more practical psychiatric field which will underline the ambiguity of trying to use the magic word, trying to unlock the castle.

The condition of autism has often been metaphorically referred to in terms of the empty fortress, as a state in which so much energy is directed into maintaining psychic defences that nothing is left inside.[6] In an essay on the reality systems of disordered children, Arnold Miller and Eileen Eller describe a method by which autistic children were encouraged to break out of their patterns of ritualistic behaviour using a specific game construct which allowed them to move free of their usual physical co-ordinates and to appear, for a time, to be taking vital choices. But 'the children, after a number of repetitive sequences, seemed to turn their vital involvement into sterile, unthinking rituals very much like their meaningless rocking or twiddling rituals. True, they continued to perform the various problem tasks in response to signs and words, but they did so automatically – without the alertness apparent originally' (Miller, 1989: 24).

What are we hearing here, in this text? The impotence, certainly, of the magic word; the collapse of a fantasy of liberation from stasis. More widely, we might ask, who speaks here, and with what authority? What is the meaning of the 'automatic', and what is the 'origin' here spoken of? Also, what can we see here of the way in which such a diagnosis of psychopathology, which tends to turn everything, through addiction, into poor repetition, or replicas (like fictions) of the 'past' or the 'real', turns into a kind of version of life itself, as we cascade down the falls of repetition and things which have once been vital become 'ceremonious'?

Let us be clear here. A world of extreme stasis, a world in which all energy is frozen in a ceremony which permits no intrusion, in which nothing is present but the hauntings of a violence to the self which must be forever postponed, forever suspended, no matter what the cost to the self, a world where vitality is replaced by obsession, such a world opens us to the extremes of perversion, manifested in this textual reminder of the perpetual temptation towards a kind of paternal care which will somehow liberate 'repressed forces'. Perversion as the *père-version*, as Lacan puts it, as the version of the father, in which:

> The only way for him to be a model of the function is by fulfilling its type. It matters little that he has symptoms provided he adds to them that of paternal perversion (*père-version*), meaning that its cause should be a woman, secured to him in order to bear children, and that, of these children, whether he wishes to or not, he takes paternal care.
>
> (in Mitchell and Rose, 1982: 167)

So it would be with the magic word, the penetrative unlocking of the crypt; so it might be with the history of Gothic fictions as we look back on what may now appear before us as a series of accounts of the paternal version, the persecutions of a Manfred repeating themselves down through Lewis, Dickens, Collins, and so on to the present day; a series of avatars of that darkest and most gleeful of masters of ceremonies, Freddy Krueger, endlessly and from beyond death, from another scene, revisiting the history and scenario of abuse which reduces us to ritual action, which continues to reverberate down through the generations.

Lest it seem as though I have nevertheless veered away from the Gothic, let me conclude with a few remarks on Anne Rice's *Interview with the Vampire*, which I will preface with a final brief passage from Lacan:

> What is perversion? It is not simply an aberration in relation to social criteria, an anomaly contrary to good morals, although this register is not absent, nor is it an atypicality according to natural criteria ... It is something else in its very structure.
>
> A certain number of perverse inclinations have not without reason been said to arise out of a desire which dare not speak its name. Perversion in fact is to be placed at the limit of the register of recognition, and that is what fixes it, stigmatises it as such ...
>
> Perversion is an experience which allows one to enter more deeply into what one might call, in the full sense, the human passion ...
>
> (Lacan, 1988: 221)

Anne Rice's vampires are creatures of ceremony, they are beings who are shot through and through with an ultimate fixity of lifestyle; we see this emblematically in the scene in the Théâtre des Vampires, where we witness an enactment of an enactment, a performance, a staging, a ceremony which is no longer distinguishable from the life which lies behind it, ceremonial collapsed in upon itself (Rice, 1976: 232ff). Yet there can be no doubt that it is precisely within this fixity of structure, this neurotic stabilisation from which, in one sense, the vital has fled, that we witness a flower of passion blooming, in the loving depictions of the dark nights in which the vampire, here so obviously an extension of Walter Benjamin's Parisian *flâneur*, walks; in the exacerbated senses which are the vampire's curious gift; in the asexual yet passionate purity of the vampires' feelings for each other; in the extraordinarily liminal state of Claudia the child-vampire. What would appear sentimental were it to occur in a context other than that of perversion is here freed to allow us to enter the ceremonial whereby true passion may be discovered.

Claudia is a *revenant*; she comes back from a history of abuse, but transformed, like Gage in *Pet Sematary*, into something different, something which has moved beyond the pleasure principle, or, seen from the other side, as something which can be brought back nightly from that very beyond itself. If *Interview with the Vampire* is an emblematic Gothic text, then this centrality lies not in its transgressive quality, I would argue, but in its intimate depiction of a ritual from which human subjectivity has been largely drained.

Ceremonials, perhaps, are of only two kinds: they exist to welcome or expel the phantom. In so far as they are themselves always already ruined, they constitute also our strongest commitment to that which will appear in fantasy to withstand ruin, the obsessive activity which will stave off death. Yet at root, what is also revealed is that these two devices, the welcome and the expulsion, are perhaps one and the same, held in a stasis in which we see wild eyes beyond the firelight; we know the *revenant* is coming, but we do not know what it is; we know the invocation has worked, but there is still a moment in which to wait, in which perhaps to play or merely to expect, frozen in hope and terror, before the impossible appearance which would break the ceremony and in which our innocence would be finally drowned.

Notes

1 See Derrida, 1990: 18, and Foreword to Abraham and Torok, 1986: xxv.
2 See Deleuze and Guattari, 1988: 39–74.
3 On these examples, see my *Writing the Passions*, 1998.
4 See Derrida, 1984: e.g. 26, 50.
5 See my *The Literature of Terror*, Vol I: *The Gothic Tradition*: 118–24.
6 The classic reference is to Bettelheim, 1967.

Works cited

Abraham, Nicolas and Maria Torok. 1986. *The Wolf Man's Magic Word: A Cryptonoymy*. Trans. Nicholas Rand. Minneapolis: University of Minnesota Press.
Bettelheim, Bruno. 1967. *The Empty Fortress: Infantile Autism and the Birth of the Self*. New York: Collier-Macmillan.
Deleuze, Gilles and Felix Guattari. 1988. *A Thousand Plateaus: Capitalism and Schizophrenia*. Trans. Brian Massumi. London: Athlone.

Derrida, Jacques. 1984. *Signéponge/Signsponge*. Trans. Richard Rand. New York: Columbia University Press.
Derrida, Jacques. 1987. *The Post Card: From Socrates to Freud and Beyond*. Trans. Alan Bass. Chicago: University of Chicago Press.
Derrida, Jacques. 1990. 'Theory of the Parasite: Bootleg Jacques Derrida'. *Blast 2*, 16–21.
Derrida, Jacques. 1992. 'This Strange Institution Called Literature'. Trans. Geoffrey Bennington and Rachel Bowlby. In *Acts of Literature*. Ed. Derek Attridge. London: Routledge, 33–75.
Freud, Sigmund. 1907. 'Obsessive Actions and Religious Practices'. In *Standard Edition of the Complete Psychological Works of Sigmund Freud*. Trans. James Strachey et al. 24 vols. London: Hogarth, 1953–74, Volume 9.
Gibson, William. 1984. *Neuromancer*. London: Gollancz.
King, Stephen. 1983. *Pet Sematary*. London: Hodder and Stoughton.
Lacan, Jacques. 1988. *The Seminar of Jacques Lacan*. Ed. Jacques-Alain Miller, Book I: *Freud's Papers on Technique, 1953–1954*. Trans. John Forrester. Cambridge: Cambridge University Press.
Lacan, Jacques. 1992. *The Seminar of Jacques Lacan*. Book VIII: *The Ethics of Psychoanalysis, 1959–1960*. Trans. Dennis Porter. London: Routledge.
Maturin, C.R. 1820. *Melmoth the Wanderer*. Ed. Douglas Grant. London: Oxford University Press, 1968.
Miller, Arnold and Eileen Eller-Miller. 1989. *From Ritual to Repertoire: A Cognitive-Developmental Systems Approach with Behaviour-Disordered Children*. New York: Wiley.
Mitchell, Juliet and Jacqueline Rose, eds. 1982. *Feminine Sexuality: Jacques Lacan and the 'École Freudienne'*. London: Macmillan.
Punter, David. 1996. *The Literature of Terror*. Volume I: *The Gothic Tradition*. London: Longman.
Radcliffe, Ann. 1794. *The Mysteries of Udolpho*. Ed. Bonamy Dobrée. London: Oxford University Press, 1970.
Rice, Anne. 1976. *Interview with the Vampire*. New York: Macdonald.

Chapter 3

The nurture of the Gothic; or, how can a text be both popular and subversive?

William Veeder

The question I want to begin with is impossibly overdetermined – it is the question of why we are so afraid.

The particular answer I will trace out derives from my increasing belief that Gothic literature in the nineteenth and twentieth centuries is more than a phenomenon of Anglo-American life. It is a project. To explain and explore this notion, I want to offer a contribution to one of the longest on-going enterprises in fiction studies – the attempt to define the nature of the Gothic in literature. Nearly two hundred years ago, vexed reviewers struggled to explain the amazing, perverse, inescapable, loathsome, irresistible phenomenon of *The Monk*, by contrasting the narrative strategies of Matthew Gregory Lewis and Ann Radcliffe. From the controversy over the *Monk* came the first tools for defining Gothic fiction: the distinction between terror and horror. The inadequacy of these useful terms has driven students of the Gothic for the past two centuries to offer other terms, to devise other distinctions.

A distinction common in recent Gothic studies is my starting point. Critics frequently create a binary opposition between inside and outside, between Gothic as an exploration of the unconscious and Gothic as a concern for and even an intervention in social reality. In refusing this bogus binary of Freud versus Marx, I want to define a Gothic praxis that involves – necessarily – the interplay of psychological and social forces. This interplay has determined both the title and the subtitle of my essay.

My title, the nurture of the Gothic, plays obviously on the phrase already old by John Ruskin's time – the nature of the Gothic – because I believe the nature of the Gothic is to nurture. This belief derives from what I take to be a basic fact of communal life: that societies inflict terrible wounds upon themselves *and at the same time* develop mechanisms that can help heal these wounds. Gothic fiction from the later eighteenth century to the present is one such mechanism. Not consciously and yet purposively, Anglo-American culture develops Gothic in order to help heal the damage caused by our embrace of modernity. Thus my title: Gothic's nature is the psycho-social function of nurture; its project is to heal and transform.

To define this healing process, I will begin with the work of a physician, the British paediatrician and psychoanalyst, D.W. Winnicott. His notions of potential space, transitional objects and play will help me produce a general definition of Gothic that I can then historicise and contextualise, drawing upon such thinkers as Michel Foucault, Michael Taussig, Ross Chambers, and Peter Stallybrass and Allon White. This will bring me to the question posed in my subtitle – how can a text be both popular and subversive? Why do we hug closest that which threatens us most? This is another way of asking, how does Gothic nurture? Which is another way of asking, why are we so afraid?

A model for Gothic

D.W. Winnicott's view of human function enabled him to discuss both infant development and cultural life in *Playing and Reality*. Essential to his view are three concepts: potential space, transitional objects and play. Potential space is what Winnicott calls 'the third space' (Winnicott, 1971: 102). It is not the internal psychological, nor the external social; it is the space between, where we are 'when we are … enjoying ourselves' (106). Our need for this third space begins soon after birth. 'The baby has maximally intense experiences *in the potential space between the subjective object* [the maternal introject] *and the object objectively perceived* [the mother]' (100).

What occurs in this third space between the psychological and the social is, for Winnicott, the paramount human action – play. For play to occur, the child abiding in the space between psyche and society must be in touch with an object which is also characterised as in-between. 'I have introduced the terms "transitional objects" and "transitional phenomena" for designation of the intermediate area of experience between the thumb and the teddy bear, between the oral erotism and the true object-relationship' (2). Winnicott is careful to establish precisely the peculiar ontology of the transitional object. It 'is related both to the external object (mother's breast) and to internal objects (magically introjected breast), but is distinct from each … it is a possession. Yet it is not (for the infant) an external object' (14, 9).

Practically speaking, the transitional object is something soft, the edging of a blanket, a strip of flannel from pyjamas, even a string. But we must not let any particular object obscure the ontological peculiarity that Winnicott specifies for all such objects. Paradoxically, the 'baby creates the object, but the object was there waiting to be created' (89).

Creativity is play of a momentous type. It is 'in playing, and perhaps only in playing, [that] the child or adult is free to be creative' (53). Winnicott's belief that play is constitutive of human being means that he sees us continuing to play our whole lives. What adult play produces is nothing less than culture itself. 'Health here is closely bound up with the capacity of the individual to live in an area that is intermediate between the dream and the reality, that which is called the cultural life' (150). Many theorists of play posit, of course, a continuity between childhood and adulthood; what attracts me to Winnicott is that he defines play in a way that confirms our life-long continuity as creatures in-between.

All three notions of Winnicott – potential space, transitional objects, play – are useful in defining how Gothic may be experienced by readers and how it is positioned in culture. What I cannot proceed immediately to do, however, is to map Winnicott directly onto Gothic. Such a mapping would fail to engage the historical specificity of Gothic, its temporality, the fact that Anglo-American culture produced it at a moment of specific needs. I will, therefore, begin with Winnicott's first concept, potential space, and proceed historically.

What makes Gothic fiction a potential space is its commitment to the simultaneous exploration of inner and outer, the psychological and the social. Now I am fully aware that the same thing can be said for other modes and for the various genres of fiction. I make no claim for absolute uniqueness, for any rigid opposition between Gothic and, say, the novel of manners. All fiction engages some psychological factors and social forces. Granted, however, that any difference will be a matter of degree, not of kind, I believe Gothic is, of all fiction's genres, the one most intensely concerned with foreclosed social issues, since Gothic presents most aggressively the range of *outré* emotions conventionally considered beyond the pale – incest, patricide, familial dysfunction, archaic rage, homoerotic eros.

The psychological orientation of this fiction is evident to any reader, but Gothic's association with the political and social conditions of Anglo-American life is no less substantive. We find questions of race, for instance, in Poe's *Gordon Pym*, Melville's *Benito Cereno*, Crane's *The Monster*, Faulkner's *Absalom, Absalom!* and Morrison's *Beloved*; questions of professionalism in Shelley's *Frankenstein*, Stevenson's *Jekyll and Hyde*, James's *The Turn of the Screw*, Barnes's *Nightwood*, Prager's 'The Lincoln-Pruitt Anti-Rape Device'. Rather than extending the list, I want to become still more historically specific and to argue that Gothic is part of that textual proliferation which Foucault defines as a salient trait of Western life from the later eighteenth century onwards.

Historical context

Why did Gothic not *flower* at the time of its inception in 1764, why did all the major Gothic texts – with the exception of *Otranto* – appear *after* the French Revolution? Answers of an expressly political nature have been offered by Paulson and others for British Gothic and by various students of Brockden Brown in America. Enlightening as this political approach is at its best, it can neither account for non-political features of the texts in question nor, more importantly, explain the *ongoing* force of Gothic, the endurance of the tradition after the issues of revolutionary politics had ceased to enflame and frighten. Likewise, a too-exclusive focus on the specific social issues dramatised in post-revolutionary Gothic texts – economic exploitation, racial and gender discrimination, religious intolerance – makes it difficult to achieve a coherent, overall perspective on the diverse social issues and the different decades in which each issue produced particular upheaval. What I propose is a contextualisation of my earlier theory about social healing. Granted that societies simultaneously inflict terrible injuries upon themselves *and* develop ways of healing those injuries: the severest injury suffered by the Anglo-American middle-class readership in the later eighteenth and nineteenth centuries was, I believe, inflicted by a force that drew strength as never before from every site of conflict in every decade of the period. This force of injury is repression.

Repression and pleasure

The very mention of repression re-evokes the figure of Michel Foucault, whose attack on the 'repression hypothesis' in the introductory volume of his *History of Sexuality* constitutes one of the influential arguments of our time. What Foucault establishes beyond question is that the nineteenth century was *not* an era when sexuality was unilaterally silenced; the period was characterised, in fact, by what Foucault famously calls the 'multiplication of discourse'.

What I want to go on to say is that Foucault's book-long argument functions finally to *confirm*, rather than *refute*, the repression hypothesis, once we understand 'repression' to mean the identifying and policing of sexuality. To view Foucault this way allows us a purchase on the question of how Gothic heals through pleasure.

My discussion of repression has three parts. First, in the process of demonstrating beyond question that the nineteenth century spoke about sexuality obsessively, compulsively, Foucault acknowledges again and again what is simply true – that silencing was prevalent and intimidating. 'Without question, new rules of propriety screened out some words: there was a policing of statements' (1978: 17–18). Thus, Foucault attempts to rebut the 'repression hypothesis', not by denying that the nineteenth century engaged in silencing, but by insisting that the nineteenth century did *more* than silence. Concomitant with silence was a great deal of talk.

Second, these discourses were – by Foucault's own admission – dualistic. As silencing coexisted with the multiplying of discourses, so discursive formations themselves had two functions. They policed society and they produced pleasure. Before focusing on this phenomenon of pleasure – difficult to define in Foucault and absolutely essential to my view of Gothic – I must indicate how the policing function of discourses damaged persons by damaging language.

The taxonomic regimes of medicine, law, anthropology, ethics, criminology, demography, pedagogy and psychology were all agents of repression, in so far as they all functioned to control the sexuality they helped produce. I will take as an example of medical discourse Dr William Acton's book *The Functions and Disorders of the Reproductive System* which appeared in 14 editions (eight in Britain, six in America) between 1857 and 1897. Acton uses language to police sexuality, both thematically and rhetorically. Thematically his purpose is to deny that 'normal' women experience sexual desire. 'Any susceptible boy is easily led to believe, whether he is entirely overcome by the syren or not, that she, and therefore all women, must have at least as strong passions as himself. Such women, however, give a very false idea of the conditions of female sexual feeling in general' (Acton, 1857: 62). Notice the binary oppositions here. Susceptible boys versus knowledgeable professionals like Acton; a few promiscuous sirens versus the majority of sexless ladies. These judgemental oppositions rigorously foreclose the intricate complications of human desire and the diverse social forces that encourage 'female sexlessness'. Functional and dysfunctional; healthy and diseased; ultimately, good and bad. These binaries are, in turn, constitutive of both Acton's class and his profession. As the bourgeoisie defined themselves by means of denial – neither dirty, ignorant and noisy like the lower orders, nor effete, irresponsible, and arrogant like the aristocracy – so nineteenth-century medicine founded its emergent but still precarious status upon difference. Doctors were well trained, unlike midwives; responsible, unlike quacks; scientific, unlike faith healers. By deploying in their syntax the judgemental oppositions foundational for society, the discourses of sexual science functioned to police both desires and self-understanding.

Denial is also at work rhetorically – in the implicit contract between Acton and his readers. There is an obvious erotic charge to Acton's materials, particularly the numerous case studies in which patients confess sexual secrets. We readers are repeatedly made privy, for instance, to anxieties that early contamination by masturbation has had or will have dire consequences for the marriage bed. Readers' affective involvements in these intimate materials Acton cannot acknowledge. Here and throughout the nineteenth-century discourses on sexuality, what tantalises must be mediated through its opposite, through scientific objectivity, social concern, even disgust and indignation. The result is prurience. Only by lying to oneself – only by denying one's desire and thus one's place in the community of desiring and desirable creatures – can the reader experience desire.

In claiming that Gothic fiction works differently, I want to avoid any easy polarisation. Mediation operates in fiction as well as in discourses, but in fiction the mediation is effected not through denial but through displacement. In *The Monk*, for instance, it is indispensable that Ambrosio is Italian, not English, and Catholic rather than Protestant. In *The Scarlet Letter*, issues of female sexuality and independence that are volatile with Hawthorne's Victorian readers are projected back upon early American history. Without the mediation of these or other types of distancing, readers could not engage in that empathic relationship with literary characters which is the ground and precondition of novelistic art in the nineteenth century. Given such distancing, however, readerly desire can operate through – rather than in denial of – the desires represented in the text. Reading Hawthorne is not a prurient experience; reading Acton is.

This brings me back to the question of pleasure, and my third point about repression. Foucault defines two types of pleasure produced by the discourses of sexuality. One is the polarised pleasures experienced by the powerful and the disempowered: 'The pleasure that comes of exercising a power that questions, monitors, watches, spies, searches out, palpates, brings to light; and on the other hand, the pleasure that kindles at having to evade this power, flee from it, fool it, or travesty it' (Foucault, 1978: 45). Among several intriguing lines of speculation, which I have no time now to pursue, is whether Foucault is actually championing these pleasures, espousing them as compensation for the damage done by repression. It is impossible to tell for sure. What is unquestionable – and here is my focus – is that Foucault nowhere in *The History of Sexuality* explores the negative consequences of a discursive situation that restricts people to the pleasures of spying and hiding. Granted that in the Victorian period spying and hiding did yield some pleasure – to those affiliating with the dominant position by writing and reading hegemonic tracts like Acton's and to those submissives who enjoyed their abjection. What is crucial is how these pleasures of spying and hiding relate to the damage done by repression itself. The polar enterprises of spying and fooling leave both the powerful and the disempowered caught in a dialectic of slavery that infantilises. The pattern of punishing parent and guilty devious child is never matured beyond. In turn, since infantilisation is another type of silencing, the discursive pleasures of spying and hiding function to exacerbate rather than to heal the wounds caused by repression.

Foucault defines a second type of pleasure by contrasting the *ars erotica* of India and China with the *scientia sensualis* of modern western culture. In the *ars erotica*, pleasure produces truth; in the *scientia sensualis*, truth produces pleasure. Focusing on the *scientia sensualis*, Foucault maintains that we have 'invented a different kind of pleasure: pleasure in the truth of pleasure, the pleasure of knowing that truth ... a pleasure that comes of knowing pleasure, a knowledge-pleasure' (Foucault, 1978: 71, 77). Since Foucault is discussing the *scientia sensualis* in terms of its pleasure-producing truths, we can fairly ask to what extent nineteenth-century Anglo-American readers did indeed experience as pleasurable the 'truths' of scientific discourse.

Consider, briefly, two 'scientific proofs' of women's intellectual inferiority. One was that the female brain is smaller than the male. When someone inconveniently noted that since women's bodies were, on average, smaller than men's, their brains would of course be smaller proportionally, many of the scientists engaged in weighing and measuring switched to other body parts, especially the thigh bone, compared femurs from each sex, and concluded resoundingly that, even proportionally, female thigh bones were smaller. Women were indeed inferior intellectually. A second controversy involved menstruation. Assuming that the amount of blood allotted to the reproductive system during the catamial period meant that only a dangerously small amount of blood remained in the brain, scientists argued that sustained intellectual work at this time of the month could seriously threaten young women's health. College was not for them.

My point in foregrounding the menstruation and brain-weight controversies is not of course to deny that serious men and women throughout the nineteenth century devoted estimable effort to seeking the truth about our gendered selves. These scientists' methods of research and modes of argument were, however, anything but 'disinterested' and 'objective'. As for the femur measurers, since the effect (and maybe the intent) of their experiment was to confirm conventional biases, we can surely inquire whether most of the victims of bias experience pleasure. Women denied admission to college because of discursive systems that judged their brain power in terms of their thigh bones and utterly misunderstood their cardiovascular system – these women and their partisans were made to suffer, both practically and psychologically, as a result of the policing function of discourse.

Foucault thus enables us to establish three things about Anglo-American society in the nineteenth century. Repression in the form of direct silencing was a powerful force; discursive structures exacerbated repression by policing desire rigorously; and the pleasures generated by scientistic discourses made things still worse.

How Gothic fiction produced a quite different type of pleasure in this same historical epoch, pleasure that could potentially heal, I will now try to explain. Gothic can help heal the wounds of repression by putting into play what silencing, denial and infantilisation tried to police. Through its thematic and representational insistence upon *outré* desires, Gothic acts as a counter-discursive formation which fosters pleasure in terms of both psyche and society by the release of repressed affects and by the exploration of foreclosed topics. As counter-discursive, Gothic works in a manner quite opposite from the *scientia sensualis* and much more like the *ars erotica*. In Gothic, it is not truth that produces pleasure, but rather pleasure that produces truth.

How this truth-producing pleasure is generated is suggested by the opening sentence of Poe's 'The Cask of Amontillado': 'The thousand injuries of Fortunato I had borne as best I could; but when he ventured upon insult, I vowed revenge' (Poe, 1846: 116). My guess is that most readers of this sentence's first clauses would agree that Montresor intends to say: 'the thousand injuries inflicted by Fortunato I had endured as best I could'. Montresor, in other words, defines himself as the victim of Fortunato's malice. In the process of making this point, however, Montresor's initial eleven words generate three puns. 'The injuries of Fortunato', for instance, deploys the genitive in a way which suggests not only the injuries *by* Fortunato, but also the injuries *of* Fortunato, *to* Fortunato. 'I had born' suggests 'I had birthed, I had produced', as the obvious alternative phrasing, 'endured' does not. And then there is 'as I best could' rather than 'as best I could, as long as I could'. Montresor is justifying his counter-attack by insisting that he retaliates only after he has held out to the limits of his endurance. 'As I best could' does not *say* this, however. 'As I best could' says that no one could have suffered as well as Montresor.

What do these three plays on words add up to? The puns, I believe, create a latent level to Montresor's sentence, a subtext that dramatically opposes the manifest meaning. At this subtextual level, Montresor is the victimiser, and Fortunato the victim. 'Injuries were inflicted upon Fortunato as only Montresor can.' This is precisely what the story goes on to dramatise, of course. Fortunato, who imagines himself dominant, is reduced to the submissive position, while lowly Montresor reigns untouchable. What Poe's puns provide us readers with is an experience like that of the *ars erotica*. We move from pleasure to truth. From the pleasure of engaging with verbal artistry so elegant, we come to insight into human motivation. We see how conveniently an aggressive will to power can mask itself as victimisation. We see how suspect an emotion socially sanctioned indignation is.

To be clear: my point is not simply that the initial three puns enable us to see in advance what the narrative goes on to make plain; we see in fact a moral/psychological truth that never finds articulation in the text because Montresor never comes to recognise it. He never learns that converting from victim to victimiser – and thus simply reversing a binary – does not undo wrong and produce happiness. The story's initial puns cue us to the underlying truth of Montresor's situation, so that we can be alive to the myriad other pleasure-producing revelations that abide at the latent level of the text.

In focusing on puns I may seem to be praising in Gothic what I have faulted in Acton: a bi-levelled textuality which produces contradictory perspectives. What comparing Acton and Poe reveals, in fact, is a basic difference of procedure, a difference which highlights the pleasure-producing capacities of Gothic fiction. In both Acton and Poe, denial operates to repress unwelcome affect and awareness from the manifest level of the text. At issue is, unwelcome to whom? Unwelcome to Acton and unwelcome to…Montresor. In Poe's story, denial proceeds from the narrator, not from the author. Poe's text allows us to see through what Acton's text wants to restrict us to. In effect, Poe's text thematises nineteenth-century discursive procedures, even as it offers an alternative to them.

In addition to language play and unreliable narrators, Gothic fiction fosters its pleasure through its handling of dénouements – in ways particularly important to the engagement of readerly desire. I believe it can be shown that all major Gothic novels are open-ended to an extent unmatched in other genres and that this mobility is fundamental to the pleasure-producing capability. Immediately, however, I must make a qualification: most Gothic texts allow us to read them as Acton's text insists on being read: as an indictment of *outré* behaviour and an affirmation of orthodoxy. Victor Frankenstein, the younger Wieland, Captain Ahab, Carmilla, Dr Jekyll, Dorian Gray, Count Dracula, Thomas Sutpen – all are exterminated. To take pleasure in stopping here, however, to enjoy a unilateral satisfaction in the defeat of evil and madness, is to refuse many of the pleasures of reading. Everything about great Gothic texts encourages us to see their characters – and thus human desire – as more implicating and pleasure producing. My belief is this: Gothic texts provide us readers with pleasures as multiple and intense as our desires. The pleasure of Gothic involves therefore the adaptation of textual materials to readerly needs. Gothic allows each individual reader to discover the quality and intensity of pleasure most useful at the particular moment of this reader's life.

Take as an example *Dr Jekyll and Mr Hyde*. In addition to seeing it as a righteously resolved tract that exposes the dangers of transgressive medicine, we can also find diverse affects and issues for which Stevenson's dénouement provides no comparably orthodox resolution. We can, for instance, find a novel about compulsion, about how difficult it is to desist from whatever passionate pursuit we are driven to by desire. We can go further and see compulsion as a dilemma of professionalism – or of the difficulties of the medical and legal caste that had joined with the House of Commons to control British society in the later nineteenth century. Going on we can see in professionalism a drama of male sociability – there are *no* major women in the story. And further still, we can see that beneath this homosocial conviviality rage homicidal urges. Killing, in turn, shows itself to be both patricidal and fratricidal. Looked at differently, the homosocial reveals ties to the homoerotic world of night stalking and 'unspeakable' desire.

How much each individual reader participates in the desires loosed by Stevenson's plot depends upon that reader's particular relationship with those desires. One reader may focus on the homicidal and worry that England is destroying itself from within, since the murder of the MP is perpetrated not by a foreigner or a proletarian but by an eminent London physician. This worry, in turn, may or may not be associated by the reader with the increasing anxiety about Britain's fate that was surfacing throughout the culture, an anxiety that Rider Haggard had already dramatised in *She* and that Bram Stoker would soon mobilise in *Dracula*. This same reader might not, however, engage the text's homoerotic elements. Details such as 'Queer Street', 'by-street', 'favourite', and rear entry (Stevenson, 1886: 33, 30, 48) might not receive from this reader the attention necessary to engage with their connotations and to link them to other details such as Utterson's dream of Hyde entering Jekyll's bedroom and the fact that Utterson's relation with Edward Hyde is called 'bondage' (38).

Gothic texts thus do in hyper-intense fashion what all literary art does to some extent: provide individual readers with diverse materials that can be experienced according to the individual's desires. No genre of fiction goes so far as Gothic, however, in encouraging each reader to produce an understanding that gives this reader the quantity and quality of *outré* pleasure appropriate to immediate needs. For myself, I saw fairly early in my work on *Jekyll and Hyde* the operation of patricidal rage, 'that damned old business of the war in the members' (Stevenson, 1901: 323) that Stevenson referred to. It was not for several years, however, that I realised there was a pun here on 'members', that sexuality was also at stake in the homoerotic features of the novel. Last came my recognition that the word 'members' in its familial sense was not restricted to fathers and sons, and that fratricidal rage, the story of Esau against Jacob, was also being enacted. Why did I 'see' some things early and some much later? I was a close reader throughout my work on Stevenson, but only quite late did I notice the 'hairy hands' (88) of Edward Hyde and thence his connection with Esau and Jacob.

What I am offering for your consideration is a general phenomenon of reading that has special relevance for Gothic: why we see some things and not others at any one time, and why we see various things at various times. I believe that as literary critics we tend to be strikingly incurious about our commitments – why we specialise in a particular author, genre, period, and why we 'see' different things at different stages of a project and a life. Obviously, diverse factors will contribute to so overdetermined a phenomenon as scholarly 'seeing'. But one of these factors, a crucial factor I believe, is the way pleasure relates to repressed desire. Gothic fiction aggressively encourages what all art allows: that we build our own artefact out of the materials provided by the object.

This brings me back to D.W. Winnicott and the relevance to Gothic fiction of his concepts of potential space, transitional object and play. A Gothic text positions its reader in a potential space where the psyche's repressed desires and the society's foreclosed issues can be engaged and thus where healing may occur. The Gothic text itself functions as a transitional object. It is created by the reader, yet it is already there. We produce a novel that has never before existed, though a century old. By engaging in the creative play of reading, the individual experiences the pleasure that indicates the extent to which he or she has experienced desire. Desire is in fact what is produced by the reader's healing play with the text.

Healing

Winnicott is not very clear about how healing actually occurs – in the psyche and in society. While no one (including Freud) has ever managed to define this process precisely, I have found helpful the work of the anthropologist Michael Taussig, literary critic Ross Chambers and the cultural analysts Stallybrass and White.

Healing psychic wounds has been and remains in many cultures the responsibility of the shaman. Michael Taussig's book *Shamanism, Colonialism, and the Wildman* is subtitled 'A Study in Terror and Healing'. How terror heals is his theme. Like Winnicott, Taussig recognises the importance of space, in this case 'the space of death' (Taussig, 1987: 4) where coloniser and colonised have killed for centuries. While the death space is not identical to Winnicott's potential space, Taussig is defining a place in-between, 'a threshold that allows for illumination as well as extinction' (4). The shaman in turn functions more like a transitional object than like a western physician, since healing is produced not by him but through him. The shaman with his chanting and powerful *yage* drink enables a creative play through which the patient cures himself – in ways that help explain the play of Gothic healing.

Today in Guatemala, white people can go for healing to Indian shamans whose power is presumed by the whites to be indigenous, a consequence of the Indian essence as dark Other. What Taussig establishes, however, is that the shaman's demonic power derives from the white Spanish missionaries who came to Guatemala in the sixteenth century and 'believed firmly in the efficacy of sorcery, which they supposed Indians to be especially prone to practice on account of their having been seduced by the devil... the magic of the Indian is a colonial creation' (142–3, 145). Taussig is not simply recycling here the banality that conquerors project their fears onto the lowly, who then come back to terrorise them. What occurs with the Guatemalan shaman is not the return of the repressed to haunt but the return of the projected to heal. The healing is self-healing, for what the whites encounter in the shaman is white magic, not black; not his power, but theirs, displaced. The colonisers had been injured by projecting onto the colonised a puissant part of their own being, those desires that were unacceptable to the European orthodoxy of their time. The wound that lingers in the Guatemalan whites today is self-division. They can therefore be healed only by regaining contact with their own puissant desires through the mediation of the terrifying Other. They can be healed only by themselves.

This is what Gothic does – self-healing through terror – though with a difference which I must specify immediately. That white Guatemalans receive great benefit from shamans is inadvertent, and largely undeserved. Projection of terrifying desires onto the dark Other was originally a tactic of imperialist conquest, 'facilitating the legalities of enslavement and the use of military force...the colonizers provided the colonized with the left-handed gift of the image of the wild man – a gift whose powers the colonizers would be blind to' (Taussig, 1987: 142). What was inadvertent with colonialism is constitutive of Gothic. In reading, we avoid that denial of the terrible which repressive culture enacts. Reading Gothic fiction parodies these repressive processes, displacing onto characters and scenes those terrifying desires which are thereby positioned so that we can call them back to us in creative play. What Taussig makes clear is that engagement with the projective Other means re-engagement with our own *power*, our own *magic*. Repression enfeebles. In the projective Other of shamanism and the displaced Other of Gothic we regain contact not simply with forbidden desires but with desires forbidden because of their terrifying – and thus potentially therapeutic – power.

How re-engagement with our desires can help heal the wounds of society is the next question. Ross Chambers in *Room for Maneuver* states with brilliant simplicity that a change in desire can cause a desire for change. Reading, for Chambers, involves 'the possibility of a conversion in the reader from a form of desire assumed to be consonant with the structures of power to an "other" form, more congenial to textual oppositionality and simultaneously constituting the shift that is a *conversio ad se'* (Chambers, 1991: 243). Although a 'conversion' model seems to me too oppositional and manipulative to represent how most fiction – and particularly Gothic – fosters self-healing, I do agree with Chambers's view of the social aspects of changes in individuals' desires. 'What I am influenced by does not change "me" (for what is "me"?); but it changes "my" sense of the desirable, and to that extent…my "production" of the real' (236). Since social reality is not natural and essential but constructed and thereby contingent, cultural forms are forms of desire, and thus are subject to changes in desires.

Chambers's ahistorical, rather abstract discussion leaves unanswered the question of how social change could occur in the specific context of Gothic's heyday, nineteenth-century Anglo-American culture. An answer can be developed through Stallybrass and White.

My starting point here is a fact of cultural history; during the nineteenth century, carnival was increasingly suppressed. Concurrently, there appeared three phenomena – hysteria, psychoanalysis and the ghost story revival – which exemplify in a European context the general cultural mechanism I have posited: society's wounding itself and then developing ways to heal the wounds. In the later nineteenth century, the wound of choice was hysteria. Stallybrass and White relate the outbreak of hysteria to an aspect of cultural life that Bakhtin emphasises: 'post-romantic culture is, to a considerable extent, subjectivised and interiorized and on this account frequently related to private terrors, isolation and insanity rather than to robust kinds of social celebration and critique' (Stallybrass and White, 1986: 180). Stallybrass and White demonstrate that a carnival confined to the private theatre of the psyche is hell on earth:

> It is striking how the thematics of carnival pleasure – eating, inversion, mess, dirt, sex and stylized body movements – find their neurasthenic, unstable and mimicked counterparts in the discourse of hysteria.…It is as if the hysteric has no mechanism for coping with the *mediation* of the grotesque body in everyday life except by violent acts of exclusion. (184)

Where mediated self-recognition can occur for hysterics is in a space provided by an institution which appeared as carnival was disappearing: psychoanalysis.

Freud uses the resonant term 'agencies of disgust' to describe the forces arrayed against him in the struggle to cure hysterics. Those 'agencies of disgust' are the same agencies which, in their public form, mobilized civic and religious authorities against carnival. ... Carnival allowed the society involved to mediate into periodic ritual the culturally structured 'otherness' of its governing categories. We might call this process of periodic mediation *active reinforcement*. ... This contrasts strongly with the mechanism of hysteria which Freud called *reactive reinforcement* ... 'Contrary thoughts are always closely connected with each other and are often paired off in such a way that the *one thought is exaggeratedly conscious while its counterpart is repressed and unconscious'*.

(Stallybrass and White, 1986: 188, 189)

Psychoanalysis was one mode of active reinforcement that the *fin de siècle* developed. 'Periodic' in the regularity of the analysand's 'hour', psychoanalytic ritual utilised the potential space of the couch, as carnival utilised its site, to facilitate actively both the mediation of repressive categories and re-engagement with denied desire. To what extent does Gothic fiction also provide active reinforcement – in America as well as Europe?

The years when hysteria proliferated and Freud began his major work are also the time of the 'ghost story revival'. *Dr Jekyll and Mr Hyde*, 'The Phantom Rickshaw', 'The Yellow Wallpaper', *Dorian Gray*, *The Monster*, *The Turn of the Screw*, *Dracula*, plus the best short stories of Robert W. Chambers and M.R. James all appeared between 1885 and 1914. What Gothic and psychoanalysis share importantly is their utilisations of potential space. Gothic too is a site where human beings can forgo reactive reinforcement and actively re-engage with 'component' thoughts that have been repressed into the unconscious.

Moreover, Gothic, like psychoanalysis, has its strikingly carnivalesque features. These become clear in light of Bakhtin's claim that 'carnival celebrates temporary liberation from the prevailing truth of the established order' (in Stallybrass and White, 1986: 7). 'The Cask of Amontillado' is a carnival story which enacts the carnivalesque capabilities of all Gothic fiction, since Poe's story stages a temporary liberation even as it questions whether liberation is possible. Montresor uses the potential space of carnival for killing. His is, in effect, a counter-carnival where suppressed rage is vented, but repression is not escaped. Montresor utilises rather than abjures the binaries of good/bad, victim/victimiser which undergird social orthodoxy; his carnival is a reactive reinforcement disguised in motley. In turn, Poe's story is a true carnival, an active reinforcement. His readers experience the carnivalesque because we can escape Montresor's binaries and encounter the 'grotesque', as defined by Stallybrass and White – 'a boundary phenomenon of hybridization or inmixing, in which self and other become enmeshed in an inclusive, heterogeneous, dangerously unstable zone' (193).

This process of grotesque hybridisation is particularly prominent in *fin de siècle* Gothic. Dorian Gray exemplifies the 'grotesque body' which carnival celebrates and which 'transgressions of gender, territorial boundaries, sexual preference, family and group norms are transcoded into' (Stallybrass and White, 1986: 24). Grotesque bodies recur in *Dracula* where the Count grows physically younger every day he threatens Britain, in *The Monster* where a black man already effaced politically and socially in a racist culture is literally effaced by a fire that burns his face to a cinder, in 'The Yellow Wallpaper' where pregnancy so distorted the protagonist's self-image that she sees herself reflected in wallpaper patterns of 'bloated curves' that 'go waddling up and down in isolated columns of fatuity' (Gilman, 1892: 9). In these and other carnivalesque masterpieces of the *fin de siècle*, 'hybridization … produces new combinations and strange instabilities' (Stallybrass and White, 1986: 58). Gothic is reborn at the moment when psychoanalysis is born and carnival is dying, thus helping to assure that healing remains available to repression's many.

Subversion/Transformation

How does healing become subversive? My answer to the question posed in my subtitle is formulated in terms of 'transformation', rather than 'subversion', because the repression that damaged the Anglo-American middle class in the nineteenth century and that continues to dog us today was not imposed by some despot or oligarchy. It was taken on gradually, for reasons that seemed good or at least necessary at the time. Change therefore involved not a simple opposition and overthrow, as in a dictatorship, but a gradual alteration in desire and perception. This process is particularly difficult to chart in instances which produce no signal moment like the storming of the Bastille or the election of Nelson Mandela. There are no guarantees, with Gothic as with any other site of potential transformation. In so far as the plight of women and gays and blacks and religious minorities is certainly less arduous in Anglo-American society today than in, say, 1820, I have no great difficulty believing that Gothic has made a contribution, has helped effect changes in individual desires that produced a desire for change throughout the society. But there are no guarantees.

The March sisters in *Little Women* are reading sensation novels, but when the sisters close the covers of their books they go back to the sentimental life, just as their author wrote *Jo's Boys* long after the Gothic thrillers of *Behind a Mask*. Gothic fiction is a *potential* space precisely because actualisation depends upon each individual reader; and, especially given the private nature of reading, is anyone's guess. What does seem clear is that Gothic constitutes a site which readers return to generation after generation. Gothic has surely contributed more than its share of images to our permanent memory. Frankenstein, Jekyll and Hyde, Dracula above all, but the scarlet letter and the white whale too, images that proffer to each citizen in the terrifying privacy of readerly quiet the same healing question – why are you so afraid? The teeth of Heathcliff shining in death, the necrophilic bedroom of the Emily to whom Faulkner offered a rose, the rusty sawblade that Sethe passes across the throat of Beloved – why are we so afraid. I asked at the beginning of this essay how a popular text could be truly subversive. I end by asking, how could transformation occur any other way?

Works cited

Acton, William. 1857. *The Functions and Disorders of the Reproductive System*, London: n.p.

Chambers, Ross. 1991. *Room for Maneuver*, Chicago: University of Chicago Press.

Foucault, Michel. 1978. *The History of Sexuality*. Vol. 1. New York: Random House.

Gilman, Charlotte Perkins. 1872. 'The Yellow Wallpaper'. In *The Charlotte Perkins Gilman Reader*, ed. Ann J. Lane. New York: Patheon, 1980.

Poe, Edgar Allan. 1846. 'The Cask of Amontillado'. In *Edgar Allan Poe: Selected Prose and Poetry*, ed. W.H. Auden. New York: Holt, Rinehart, 1950.

Stallybrass, Peter and Allon White. 1986. *The Politics and Poetics of Transgression*. Ithaca: Cornell University Press.

Stevenson, Robert Louis. 1886. *The Strange Case of Dr Jekyll and Mr Hyde and Other Stories*. Harmondsworth: Penguin, 1979.

Stevenson, Robert Louis. 1911. *The Letters of Robert Louis Stevenson*, ed. Sidney Colvin. New York: Charles Scribner's.

Taussig, Michael. 1987. *Shamanism, Colonialism, and the Wildman*. Chicago: University of Chicago Press.

Winnicott, D.W. 1971. *Playing and Reality*. London: Tavistock.

Part II

Heartlands: the British nineteenth century

Chapter 4

Lost cities: London's apocalypse

Alexandra Warwick

> The Last Judgement begins, and its vision is seen by the imaginative eye or everyone according to the situation he holds.
>
> (William Blake)

Frank Kermode in *The Sense of an Ending*, that indispensable atlas for chroniclers of the Apocalypse, writes of what he calls the 'resilience' of apocalyptic thought. It is, he says:

> patient of change and of historiographical sophistications. It allows itself to be diffused, blended with other varieties of fiction-tragedy for example, myths of Empire and of Decadence and yet it can survive in very naive forms. Probably the most sophisticated of us is capable of naive reactions to the End.
>
> (Kermode, 1966: 9)

I am not sure at this point whether to lay claim to naiveté or sophistication, but what I do intend to do here is to examine the blending together of the apocalyptic with other myths of the late nineteenth century, Empire and Decadence among them, and also to look specifically at the function of Gothic in the dense mythical clusters of the *fin de siècle*.

The two strains, Gothic and apocalyptic, are not commonly linked together; indeed, it is rare to find mention of the Gothic in writing about the apocalypse, and work on the Gothic tends to take an association at least with elements of apocalyptic imagery somewhat for granted, without examination of its function. The question that arises is whether there is no more connection between them than the use of apocalyptic trappings to dress the Gothic set. Malcolm Bull, in his essay on the apocalyptic, includes a useful typology of apocalypse which locates theories ideologically on a continuum between the religious and the secular, and sociologically on the axis between high and low culture (Bull, 1995: 3). This yields four categories: high religious, high secular, popular religious and popular secular. Bull also suggests that the popular apocalyptic is not, as the other types are, concerned to effect personal spiritual transformation, but is deployed to shock, alarm or enrage (Bull, 1995: 5). It is my contention that Gothic can be identified by many of the same tropes as the popular secular strain of apocalyptic and further, that the particular cultural imprints of the late nineteenth century provide significant ways of making this identification. The myths of Empire, Decadence and apocalypse do indeed grow together and the language and structure of Gothic provide a frame for these exotic blooms.

Talking about the end has been the pastime of ages, though Norman Cohn suggests that only since the time of Zoroaster and the foundation of the first monotheistic system of belief has the specific notion of a new and perfect world to replace the present and imperfect one existed (Cohn, 1995: 21). As this was around 1500 BC, however, it seems fair to say that the end has already had a very long history. The end seems impossible to locate; clearly it cannot be found in the historical past, because that would mean that one was, impossibly, living after the end, but it has also proved difficult to locate in the future, subject to constant speculation and the periodic proposal of specific dates for its consummation. This kind of speculation has provided the possibility of thinking in detail about the Apocalypse, but paradoxically, as commentators from Augustine to Baudrillard have observed, has also produced the effect of its already having, in some sense, occurred. Augustine appears to be responsible for the origins of this effect; in his attempt to oppose popular millenarianism and to domesticate apocalyptic conjecture he contends that the end is immanent rather than imminent. The predictive apocalypse is blurred and its eschatology stretched over the whole of history; the end is always already present and not to come at some distant or not so distant date in the future. Baudrillard summarises it thus:

> the pole [of reckoning, dénouement and apocalypse] has come infinitely closer ... we have already passed it unawares and now find ourselves in the situation of having overextended our own finalities, of having short-circuited our own perspectives, and of already being in the hereafter, that is, without horizon and without hope.
>
> (Baudrillard, 1989: 34)

Fin-de-siècle indeed but, unfortunately for us it would seem, not *fin du globe*. Though Baudrillard is writing of the end of the twentieth century, his comment can equally be applied to describe some of the thinking that informs the writings of the late nineteenth century that I will be discussing here. Baudrillard's ideas of the already-having-happenedness of the end are close to those of Kermode. This is Kermode's application of his theory of apocalypse to tragedy: 'Beyond the apparent worst there is worse suffering, and when the end comes it is not only more appalling than anyone expected, but a mere image of that horror, not the thing itself' (Kermode, 1966: 82). For him the narrative effect that is the desire for a completed structure closed by an ending is both a product and a confirmation of the condition of existence. The reassurance of closure is at odds with the sense of always being *in medias res* in our own narratives, that we will never see our own end and thus be able to give pattern and shape to a personal history. Likewise, any account of the end of the world is a paradox; if the world has ended who is writing and who is reading? In fictions we constantly live beyond endings, giving rise to the double effect of ceasing and continuing to exist. The narrative of apocalypse is a sado-masochistic rehearsal in which readers and writers inflict destruction on themselves and others while gaining pleasure from surviving to witness the outcome. It allows an experience of death, but also produces a sense of living in-between, in a liminal space. Kermode identifies this as the sense of 'transition', derived from the very useful additional distinction he makes in his exploration of endings: the expansion of the short period of the reign of the Beast. This is found in *Revelation* and though it precedes the Day of Judgement it does not properly belong either to that or to the time before. He calls this period of transition characteristic and says: 'we are always somehow ready for the end, and for a beginning; we instantly identify our moment as transitional. So transition is the key term, and we recognise it or its onset by the unmistakable signs of decadence' (Kermode, 1995: 259). The cultural indicators of decadence obviously differ in any period, but the efflorescence in the 1880s and 1890s has been widely explored and the connections with the conventions of Gothic made explicit in the critical treatment of such well-known texts as Stevenson's *The Strange Case of Dr Jekyll and Mr Hyde* (1885), Wilde's *The Picture of Dorian Gray* (1891) and Stoker's *Dracula* (1897). The links have been made between apocalyptic and decadent on one side and decadent and Gothic on the other, and I want to try to show here that it is not simply a sequential shading of one into the other along a continuum, but that there are substantial ways in which the narrative and metaphorical patterns of apocalyptic and Gothic are similar if not identical.

One of the most important of the clusters of ideas that bring together these two forms is the city. The city is both lived experience and a powerful image, read and re-read constantly, used as a metaphor of ideal and of catastrophe, of promise and of horror. London was the focus of most of these imaginings and investigations; by the year 1900 it was the largest city on earth, with a population of almost six million people, and the centre of an empire that covered a fifth of the world's land surface and exercised authority over a quarter of its population. The celebration of Victoria's Diamond Jubilee in 1897 became a celebration of Britain and its empire, and London's place as the emblem of that empire was repeatedly stated, but many aspects of its social reality were already of great concern to the late Victorians. The only city that had ever equalled London in size and influence was Rome in the time of Hadrian (117–38). The narrative of Imperial Rome's decline and fall was a commonplace in historiography long before the nineteenth century; in 1788 Gibbon had located the reasons in the rise of Christianity and the intensification of internal conflicts, and Montesquieu, forty years earlier, had made the more familiar accusations of maladministration and overindulgence. The model of the apocalyptic end of the decadent empire assailed by destructive forces from within and without was a familiar one, and one that haunted the popular and political imagination of the Victorians. Matthew Arnold's short poem 'Revolutions', probably written in the early 1850s, surveys the history of dead empires, referring explicitly to Greece, Rome, France and England and suggesting that each of these attempts at a global civilisation is a stage on the way to perfection: 'One day, thou say'st there will at last appear/ The word, the order, which God meant should be' (17–18). The poem is a dense compression of the idea of the city, the empire and the word, proposing that the stones of the buildings are analogous to the elements of a divine word, and past and present empires are incorrect anagrams which fail to achieve the fusion of thing and name into a unified whole, the transcendental signifier that is the city of God, the new Jerusalem. Arnold clearly sees himself painfully in the time of Transition between ending and beginning, and he aspires to the point beyond the temporal scheme, eternity. Other writers made direct comparisons between Rome and England. Thomas Hodgkin, for example, produced an essay entitled 'The Fall of the Roman Empire and Its Lessons For Us' in which he remarks:

> There are many influences at work which may tend to enervate and to degrade us, to destroy our love of truth, to poison the fountains

of family life. But so long as we successfully resist these and keep the fibre of our national character undissolved, I believe the world will not witness the downfall of the British Empire.

(Hodgkin, 1898: 70)

He also makes the specific link between morality, a notion of nationality and the physical structures of empire.

Rome in the 1890s was notable chiefly for its ruins, and the similar vestiges of other lost empires were visible to the increasing numbers of tourists as well as to those with a more specialised interest. Archaeology was developing as a science, aided by new technologies and injected with new ideological concerns by the permeation of Darwinism into other disciplines. In archaeology concentration on the history of the human race focused on the histories of the great civilisations and the question of why such powerful empires had disappeared, fuelled by unspoken concerns about contemporary states. There were a number of significant discoveries in the period, such as Schliemann's unearthing of Troy, the finding of Knossos, Petrie's excavations in Egypt and the continued attempts to discover Babylon. These findings raised popular interest in picturesque ruins, and archaeology provided the subject matter for large numbers of cheap reproductions of grander works. The depiction of ruins in art was a well-established tradition by the late nineteenth century. Edmund Burke's treatise on the sublime, published in 1756, not only had a profound impact on the subsequent development of Gothic fiction but also on the representation of the landscape in painting, and large ruins, like those of Tintern Abbey, frequently featured as objects of aweful contemplation. Morton Paley suggests that the exhibition of John Hamilton Mortimer's drawing *Death on a Pale Horse* at the Royal Academy in 1775 inaugurated a new type of painting, the apocalyptic sublime, which existed only in England and took as its subject the terror of divine revelation (Paley, 1986: 1). These often took the form of depictions of Biblical stories of destruction and pictures such as John Martin's enormous triptych, *The Great Day of His Wrath, The Last Judgement* and *The Plains of Heaven* (1851–2) were extremely popular, exhibited widely throughout Britain and reproduced in a variety of media. The first of these has a vast city in the background and its toppling towers are directly linked in the pictorial space to the fate of the decadent masses in the foreground. With the depiction of ruins in fiction, non-fiction and painting as common currency, the leap of imagination required by the contemporary observer to see London in the same state of post-imperial dereliction was not great. The city is never absolutely new; the presence of older and decayed buildings casts a presaging shadow over those more recently constructed. James Thomson, in *The City of Dreadful Night,* wrote in 1874:

> The city is not ruinous, although
> Great ruins of an unremembered past,
> With others of a few short years ago
> More sad, are found within its precincts vast.

(Thomson, 1880: 1.36–9)

In Thomson's poem, although it does not name London, there is a series of ruins ancient and recent enclosed within the existing, and as he describes it, largely deserted city. The motif of enclosure is typically Gothic, 'an X within an X' as Eve Sedgwick calls it (Sedgwick, 1980: 20); we find it not only in the imprisoning edifices of castles and dungeons but in the narrative structures of Gothic fiction: in *Frankenstein* and *Melmoth the Wanderer,* for example, as well as in other texts like James Hogg's *Memoirs and Confessions of A Justified Sinner* and Stoker's *Dracula.* The desertion of the city is significant: the absence of human life emphasises the strangeness of the relationship between the city and inhabitants: it is their creation, yet it has an existence of its own, almost an organic life: it can survive without them. The image of the city as a body is recurrent: roads are arterial; it commonly has a 'heart', which raises difficult questions about the place of the human body within it; if it is a parasitical presence, then the imagined hostility of the city to its infestation has a foundation. H.G. Wells, in *The War of The Worlds* (1897), foregrounds these Gothic notions of infection and invasion of the body, though he blurs the bodies of Martians, Londoners and London. He sees London as a living body from which the life is sucked; the fortuitous succumbing of the Martians to a common virus restores the 'pulse of life' to 'the great Mother of Cities'. For Wells's narrator, surviving the invasion is like living after the end:

> I go to London and see the busy multitudes in Fleet Street and the Strand, and it comes across my mind that they are but the ghosts of the past, haunting the streets that I have seen silent and wretched, going to and fro, phantasms in a dead city, the mockery of life in a galvanised body.

(Wells, 1897: 192)

It is a city of the undead, uncanny; time has been undone and he exists between times, the last man in a city of ghosts, though he also senses that he may be the ghost and they the living.[1] There is another description of ruined London in Richard Jefferies's novel *After London*:

> the waters of the river, unable to find a channel, began to overflow up into the deserted streets, and especially to fill the underground passages and drains, of which the number and extent was beyond all the power of words to describe. These, by the force of the water, were burst up, and the houses fell in.
>
> For this marvellous city, of which such legends are related, was after all only of brick, and when the ivy grew over and trees and shrubs sprang up, and lastly the waters underneath burst in, this huge metropolis was soon overthrown.
>
> (Jefferies, 1885: 36)

It is interesting that in Jefferies's text flood is the major element of destruction; in many of the paintings of apocalypse the deluge is the agent of annihilation. There are obvious Biblical origins for this image, but it seems to be a hybrid of the sublime landscape and the apocalyptic sublime, with divine forces breaking through nature. There is also a specific *fin-de-siècle* anxiety at work here: the agents of London's destruction might be imagined to be fire and plague, also strongly Biblical but with very obvious precedents in seventeenth-century history. Water and its related imagery had a particular resonance for the Victorians; the building of sewers and fresh water pipes was an enormous project and the disruption caused was a conspicuous part of the urban environment. The water works were a source of great interest as well as raising fears about the safety of both the structures and their contents. Drawing on these anxieties, the metaphor of flood was a persuasive one, consistently employed to vivify warnings of being overrun, by revolutionary tides, by the rising waves of the working class and the creation of swamps of unhealthy life.[2]

Ruin, complete or partial, has actually been accomplished in the texts of Jefferies, Thomson and Wells, but the sense of the incipient destruction of the physical environment is a strong and characteristic Gothic device, from the castle of Otranto through to the house of Usher. The connection between the built environment and the identity of its occupants is common; Manfred is Otranto, Roderick and Madeleine are the house of Usher, swallowed by the rising lake, and in the same double sense of dynasty and edifice Harker speaks of Dracula: 'the pride of his house and name is his own pride, ... their glory is his glory, ... their fate is his fate. Whenever he spoke of his house he always said "we"' (Stoker, 1897: 28). The crumbling city is the representation of the decadence of empire and the morbid condition of its inhabitants. Wells sees the war with the Martians as a valuable counter to degeneration: 'this invasion ... has robbed us of that serene confidence in the future which is the most fruitful source of decadence' (Wells, 1897: 191), much as slightly later commentators saw the First World War as a necessary fire that would cleanse the nation.

   Decline in standards of sexual morality is consistently represented as a major indicator of decadence, and the corruption of the city, in contrast to the innocence of rural life, a contributor to this decline. In the late nineteenth century, London, through comparison with the doomed and sexually corrupt city of Babylon, is explicitly linked with one of the foundational Christian texts of apocalypse, the Book of Revelation. Perhaps the most well-known example of this kind of comparison is the journalist W.T. Stead's four part series in the *Pall Mall Gazette* in July 1885, 'The Maiden Tribute of Modern Babylon'. It is a lurid account of the sexual exploitation of young girls, constructed on a central metaphor that collapses the legend of the Minotaur in the labyrinth of Knossos with the story of the destruction of Babylon. Stead's report is a rich source for the exploration of the issues in this essay; he employs the structures and characters familiar from Gothic and sensation fiction, the villainous rakes and procuresses as well as the innocent female victims. He also utilises the architecture of Gothic: complex and unmappable streets and buildings and houses with underground rooms, thickly carpeted to silence the screams. He presents himself as an explorer of what he calls the 'strange inverted world' of the 'London Labyrinth' (Stead, 1885: 2), and in subsequent journalism and diary entries continues his 'night investigations' despite the prison sentence he received for his part in the purchase of an under-age girl when researching the 'Maiden Tribute' articles. The Babylon of the title of Stead's piece is the Babylon of Revelation; his reference is specifically to its sexual corruption, but also to the inescapable doom that it faces. Babylon is never going to be saved in Revelation; its history and future are simply a working out in temporal terms of the prophecy of destruction necessary to establish the kingdom of God in its place. Revelation is a curiously urban text, the thematic thread being the devastation of a series of cities and the final institution of the New Jerusalem. Historically the writing of Revelation was concerned with the struggle of empire, being written at about

90–5 AD, a nicely *fin-de-siècle* date. The 'great city' that is obliterated after visitation by various disasters seems obviously analogous with Rome, and the importance of presenting the Christian God in a city connected with the need to propose an alternative state and system. The nomadic character of early Christianity and the refusal to accede to the authority of Rome lead to the dream of a permanent city and state; the New Jerusalem is described in architectural terms: 'The city lieth foursquare, and the length is as large as the breadth, and he measured the city with reed, twelve thousand furlongs. And the length and the breadth and the height of it are equal' (Revelation 21: 16). It is knowable, regular and not labyrinthine, and it is splendidly jewelled, with a central river, and also gated, walled and defended. The use of the New Jerusalem as the expression of a utopian ideal is frequent, and many utopias are cities, Plato's Republic, More's Utopia, Augustine's City of God, Blake's Jerusalem, all represent the bright alternative to an observed contemporary state of corruption and degradation. These are cities of the heart, but also physically specific, illustrating the strength of the architectural metaphor.

In the late nineteenth century, London is the metonym for Empire; both are seen as expanding, but it is now more frequently a horrid fungal growth, pathological rather than benign. As London stands for empire, much of the writing by philanthropists like William Booth as well as by fantasists like Oscar Wilde figures the city in terms of east and west, and the west of London exists in the same philanthropic, exploratory but essentially voyeuristic and exploitative relation to the east as Britain to its Empire. The comparison of the problems of England, using London as a paradigm, with those of the Empire has been explored and indeed was a comparison made at the time. Booth's *In Darkest England* (1890) makes clear reference to Stanley's account of his expeditions *In Darkest Africa* (1890) and Conrad's *Heart of Darkness* (1902) makes a parallel between the Thames and the Congo, where Marlow's journey into barbarism is also a journey into the rotten heart of the Empire.

All of these texts focus on the place of the individual subject in relation to his larger environment and the experience of the individual inhabitant of the city is of crucial importance in the analysis of imperial urban Gothic. City planning was now designed to facilitate the movement of individuals in large numbers and simultaneously to discourage the formation of organised static groups in public spaces, at least partly because of the fears of civil insurrection such as actually occurred with the riots in Pall Mall in 1886 and the Bloody Sunday episode in Trafalgar Square in 1887. This meant that the individual, while still remaining part of a large moving mass, became detached from the crowd and a group identity as well as from an inhabited space that had become devalued by the increased speed of motion through it. This has been theorised extensively as the phenomenon of the Baudelairean *flâneur*: 'The individual sovereign of the order of things who ... is able to transform faces and things so that for him they have only that meaning which he attributes to them' (Tester, 1994: 6), and his occupation as 'the activity of the sovereign spectator going about the city in order to find the things which will occupy his gaze and thus complete his otherwise incomplete identity; satisfy his otherwise dissatisfied existence; replace the sense of bereavement with a sense of life' (Tester, 1994: 7). Although the same detachment of the individual from group and environment happens in London in the same period, London does not produce the *flâneur*, the man in easy mastery of his surroundings, but rather his negative double, the person in paranoid relation to his environment. It may be that this is the logical extension of the *flâneur*, the accomplishment of the short step from glorious individualism to isolation and alienation. The window shopping *flâneur* sees the products of empire displayed for his pleasure, the astonishing variety imaginatively extending the scope of his explorations to the boundaries of trade in China, Africa and India. For the paranoid wandering subject, however, the experience is one of terror: the outer environment has returned like a wave, threatening to engulf him, and instead of consuming he is consumed, in a neatly twisted version of cannibalism. It is the *unheimlich* manoeuvre, familiar from the Gothic, in which the position of the subject collapses from the illusion of coherent dominance into fragmentary dissolution. Part of this is due to the difference in architecture of London and Paris; London lacked a central government and although some clearing of slums and other spaces did happen in London it tended not to be on the same scale and planned in the same fashion as Paris. Paris offers views, allows ordered ways of seeing the city, awareness that there is plan and design; London crowds confirm the isolation of the single walker while simultaneously reminding him of his inescapable part in a pattern of which he cannot make sense. He is aware of loss and incompletion, and the patterns that he perceives are oppressive and threatening rather than liberating and empowering. Arthur Machen's writings contain many examples of this. Machen was a hack writer, a peripheral member of occult societies and a walker and observer of London streets. In his novel *The Hill of Dreams* the central character offers this perception of the city: 'All London was one grey temple of an awful rite, ring within ring of wizard stones circled about some central place, every circle was an initiation, every initiation eternal loss' (Machen, 1907: 176). He also repeats the images of post-imperial desolation and the sense of being the last person alive:

> it seemed to him as if he had strayed into a city that had suffered some inconceivable doom, that he alone wandered where myriads had once dwelt. It was a town great as Babylon, terrible as Rome, marvellous as Lost Atlantis, set in the middle of a white wilderness surrounded by waste places.
>
> (Machen, 1907: 176)

The structures of London do not offer uninterrupted vistas of visual pleasure, producing instead a kind of tunnel vision; Machen again provides an example: he and his fictional characters wander the streets, desperately hoping that they will be able to look along the long roads and see beyond the city. Their helplessness reminds us of Freud's wanderings in 'The Uncanny' in his illustration of the compulsion to repeat, as he tries to leave the street of brothels but is constantly returned to the same site of degraded fascination.

The clearing of spaces in London also emphasised the continued existence of the slums and complex alleys and courts that so occupied Dickens, and by the end of the century they become increasingly emblematic of the unknownness and unknowability of the city. The city cannot be comprehended by the individual; although it is a human artefact, it is beyond the grasp of the human subject and can only be partially known. The labyrinth of the streets that elude comprehension signifies the existence of secret information, mysteries and hidden truths, and hints at the possibility of revelation. Machen comments in his autobiographical text *The London Adventure*, 'London, it was true, was unknowable, an unplumbed depth ... we see nothing at all: though poets catch strange glimpses of reality, now and then, out of the corners of their eyes. I shall never forget the awe with which I first came upon the other Baker Street, the Baker Street which would enter no taxi-driver's mind' (Machen, 1924: 71). Revelation is the central experience of apocalypse; it is in fact the literal translation of the word. The action of revealing, of unveiling, is again characteristically Gothic. The experience of awe, that typical response to the sublime, is related to the revelation of the 'inverted world'. The inversion of the world is not a descent to the depths but a different reading of surface, a traversing project rather than an archaeological one. The labyrinth of Crete is not simply a replication of the city above it but an integral part of it, an enclosed space within, like Machen's vision of the concentric circles of stones. Just as Machen is vague about there actually being a centre to these rings, the labyrinth itself has no centre: each part of it is both centre and avenue; the structure is one of continuous surface. Sedgwick's work on the Gothic is again of relevance; she suggests that criticism has attempted to make sense of Gothic conventions by privileging the spatial metaphor of depth, whereas in her view the strongest energies inhere in the surface (Sedgwick, 1980: 12). There is a constant traversing of surfaces in the movement of the subject through the city; the Parisian *flâneur* encounters polished reflective surfaces of shop windows that confirm his identity, but the London walker experiences surfaces that reflect a problematic and confused subjectivity. They are both over-legible in their excess of signification and unreadable in that no satisfactory pattern can be imposed on them. The relation of the individual to London's urban space is one of paranoia; the fragmentary and tentative internal pattern created is projected outward onto the map of the city but the inscription of the pattern is unstable; it further fragments and then returns to menace the individual, resulting in the sadistic fantasies of destruction shown by the various narrators in the works of Wells, Thomson and Machen as they walk the deserted streets.

The Gothic world is similarly constructed. It is a world of surfaces: it has no form or shape of its own, it is unknowable in conventional terms, and is only made manifest in a kind of translation in which name and form are given through the conventional language of narrative. The Gothic environment and the city are worlds of utter subjectivity exploiting the subversion of the conventional assumption of the integrity of the self. The protagonists find themselves in a state of enthralment, first to the possibilities of the Gothic city and then to its horrors. Each approaches, or is brought to, in this case London, with a heightened apprehension and restless curiosity about what may lie within the apparently conventional reality. The vision of the Gothic world evokes both fear and desire in the subject. The stimulation of desire comes from the apparent possibilities of self-creation and gratification inherent in the other world: the examples are innumerable – Dracula, Dorian Gray, Machen's narrator – as well as the characters from sociological accounts like Booth's who believe the streets to be paved with gold. Yet the possibilities and the prospect of infinite desire infinitely satisfied prove illusory, and the object of desire becomes the object of disgust. As disgust and desire fuse, the fragmentation of the self that takes place leads to division and the doubling of identity. In *The Picture of Dorian Gray* Dorian anticipates hungrily the satisfactions of desire the city offers him, and maps all districts in his attempt to accomplish them, but the primal act of desire – transferring his soul to the portrait – has already rendered these satisfactions impossible. By the end of the narrative pleasures have become undifferentiated, the province of the other, the double, and not the self.

For the Gothic male protagonist, the will to know, to dominate his environment, deepens his enthralment, and all objects of desire become objects of fear. He engages in frantic activity seeking pleasure and power, but his actions in attempting to establish control lead to their opposite, complete loss of power. Any achievement is temporary, marking time before eventual destruction. In this sado-masochistic structure the Gothic protagonist is his own victimiser. Many of the texts that exhibit this structure, *The Castle of Otranto* and *Dracula* for example, can also be described as dynastic fictions, concerned with maintenance of identity and the ensuring of the continued existence of the family line through the passing on of this identity. It is always difficult and disallowed, the family line eventually defeated and another provided in its place.

The texts of Christian apocalypse, Revelation and Daniel, are also deeply concerned with the question of dynastic inheritance, Daniel particularly so: the whole book consists of the vision of a series of kingdoms set up, then fragmented and vanquished. The translation of the writing on the wall at Belshazzar's feast reads thus: 'God hath numbered thy kingdom and finished it … thy kingdom is divided and given to the Medes and the Persians' (Daniel 5: 26). The scene of this revelation forms the subject matter of possibly the greatest of the visual representations of the apocalyptic sublime, John Martin's *Belshazzar's Feast* (1826), in which the impossibly enormous palace is extended beyond the immediate scene into the receding towers and walls of the city. The end of the line of these insubstantial empires is the kingdom of God: 'And in the days of these kings shall the God of heaven set up a kingdom, which shall never be destroyed; and the kingdom shall not be left to other people, but it shall break in pieces and consume all these kingdoms, and it shall stand forever' (Daniel 2: 44). As with the Gothic patriarchs, the attempt to establish ruling lines and enduring architectural settings is futile, and can only end in destruction, or at best in the passing on of a distorted identity. Dracula's vampiric project is essentially an imperial one; he wishes to establish a new kingdom literally founded on shared blood. *The War of the Worlds* is a Darwinist apocalypse; the narrator wonders whether the Martians are a superior race to whom the future belongs, but we are reminded that they fall to a primitive viral organism: 'progress' is a hazardous movement. The preoccupation with blood as an index of race and anxiety about the debilitating effect on the empire of the weakening of the race can be found in a range of non-fictional as well as fictional texts, particularly those concerned directly with degeneration. In a pamphlet entitled *Degeneration Amongst Londoners* there is this comment: 'They are town dwellers, and thereby, a doomed race. Without infusions of new blood in a few generations they die out' (Cantlie, 1885: 45). This brief observation compresses many of the figures of the apocalyptic urban Gothic: the city, the death of the empire and the imperial race, the link between doomed structures and populations.

Inevitably, given the subject matter, any ending cannot be a true ending and there are many other issues that interrelate with these topics and merit further discussion. The question of gender is important; for example, Babylon is often described as a whore and the New Jerusalem as a bride; the monsters in the labyrinth are figures of exaggerated male sexuality and the perceived collapse of gender boundaries constantly articulated as a cause of imperial decadence. What can be seen from the few examples examined here is the complex relationship of apocalyptic thought and imagery to Gothic structures and conventions. Both these persistent figurations are recast in specifically *fin-de-siècle* terms and the tactics of shock, alarm and enraging identified as the effects of popular apocalyptic are deployed to produce a set of responses in the reader. These responses do not represent a personal spiritual transformation but a powerful admixture of voyeuristic moral outrage and the vertiginous disorientation of living beyond the end coupled with the satisfaction of having recuperated the end within narrative and within history.

Notes

1   *The War of the Worlds* is also an example of another distinct strain of London apocalypses, the invasion fantasy. For a comprehensive list of other examples see I.F. Clarke's study of 165 texts published between 1871 and 1900, *Voices Prophesying War 1763–1984*.

2   I am indebted to Rebecca Stott's as yet unpublished work on Victorians and water for these observations.

Works cited

Arnold, Matthew. 1965. 'Revolutions'. In *The Poems of Matthew Arnold*. Ed. Kenneth Allott. London: Longmans, 280–1.

Baudrillard, Jean. 1989. 'The Anorexic Ruins'. In D. Kamper and C. Wulf, eds. *Looking Back on the End of the World*. New York: Semiotext(e), 29–45.

Bull, Malcolm. 1995. 'On Making Ends Meet'. In *Apocalypse Theory and the End of the World*. Ed. Malcolm Bull. Oxford: Blackwell, 1–17.

Cantlie, James. 1885. *Degeneration Amongst Londoners*. London: Leadenhall Press.

Clarke, I.F. 1966. *Voices Prophesying War 1763–1984*. Oxford: Oxford University Press.

Cohn, Norman. 1995. 'How Time Acquired a Consummation'. In *Apocalypse Theory and the End of the World*. Ed. Malcolm Bull. Oxford: Blackwell, 21–37.

Hodgkin, Thomas. 1898. 'The Fall of the Roman Empire and Its Lessons For Us'. *Contemporary Review* 73, 51–70.

Jefferies, Richard. 1885. *After London*. Oxford: Oxford University Press, 1980.

Kermode, Frank. 1995. 'Waiting for the End'. In *Apocalypse Theory and the End of the World*. Ed. Malcolm Bull. Oxford: Blackwell, 250–63.

Kermode, Frank. 1966. *The Sense of an Ending*. Oxford: Oxford University Press.

Machen, Arthur. 1907. *The Hill of Dreams*. London: Richards Press, 1954.

Machen, Arthur. 1924. *The London Adventure, or The Art of Wandering*. London: Village Press.

Paley, Morton D. 1986. *The Apocalyptic Sublime*. London: Yale University Press.

Thomson, James. 1880. *The City of Dreadful Night*. Edinburgh: Canongate, 1993.

Sedgewick, Eve Kosofsky. 1980. *The Coherence of Gothic Conventions*. London: Methuen.

Stead, W.T. 1885. 'The Maiden Tribute of Modern Babylon.' *Pall Mall Gazette* 152 (6 July), 1–6.

Stoker, Bram. 1897. *Dracula*. Ed. A.N. Wilson. Oxford: Oxford University Press, 1983.

Tester, Keith, ed. 1994. *The Flâneur*. London: Routledge.

Wells, H.G. 1897. *The War of the Worlds*. London: Penguin, 1963.

Chapter 5

Hell is a city: symbolic systems and epistemological scepticism in *The City of Dreadful Night*

David Seed

Curtis Dahl's pioneering 1955 essay, 'The Victorian Wasteland', singles out James Thomson's poem *The City of Dreadful Night* for special comment since it 'expresses an unrelieved and hopeless pessimism deeper even than the sometimes posed gloominess of Swinburne' (Dahl, 1962: 39). Without ever explicitly suggesting an influence on T.S. Eliot, although this has now been established beyond doubt (see Crawford, 1985), Dahl finds that Thomson's pessimism is surprisingly modern in being so total. A label like 'pessimist', however, tends to hypostatise a general tone without examining the symbolic procedures of the work in question. Dahl does not mention a crucial fact about *The City*, for instance: it grew directly out of Thomson's atheism, which had in turn been shaped by his contacts in the 1860s with Charles Bradlaugh, the free-thinker and editor of the *National Reformer* where *The City* was first published in 1873.[1] Thomson demonstrates in this poem an awareness of the need to engage sceptically with the system of symbolism which he saw as underpinning Christianity and which was coming under increasing pressure from contemporary developments in evolutionary thought. *The City*, then, is far more complex than an expression of hopelessness. This would reduce it to a Victorian tone-lyric writ large. Nor does it exploit a single view of the city. The analogy with Hell is one among many. In his management of shifting perspectives Thomson draws on an association traditional to Gothic literature between visual obscurity and difficulties of understanding. His night-time settings and his evocation of a murky atmosphere reflect a quality in the text itself whose 'dark words' emerge from the received collapse of a commonly shared system of signification. Thomson's very scepticism results in an obscurity that is quite deliberate and examined even as it is created; and this scepticism is articulated in ways very different from one of the classic Victorian documents of religious doubt – Tennyson's *In Memoriam.*

A comparison between the openings of *In Memoriam* and *The City* will clearly show the different rhetorical strategies pursued by each writer to negotiate spiritual doubt and overt scepticism respectively.[2] Tennyson crucially addresses the 'strong Son of God' right from the first line, asserting the existence of the deity independent of any means of proof. Indeed an opposition between faith and knowledge is quickly established so strong that any lapse of faith or sign of doubt becomes a criticism of humanity itself – 'we are fools and slight'. The choice of pronoun suggests that Tennyson is extending his own personal grief to speak on behalf of mankind in general. As he told his son, '"I" is not always the author speaking of himself, but the voice of the human race speaking thro' him' (Tennyson, 1905: 255). Death self-evidently is the central problem addressed in the poem and Tennyson's insistence on the creative power of the deity gives him a means simultaneously of situating mortality within a larger scheme of things. The stars can thus be read as the signs of God's creativity and Tennyson makes a prediction (and plea?) to be lifted out of the traditional metaphor of mortality: 'thou wilt not leave us in the dust'. Similarly the contrast between faith and doubt is expressed in an equally traditional contrast between light and dark ('a beam in darkness').

Thomson, on the other hand, situates utterance within mortality – 'in the dust I write' – even evoking a posture (prostration) which could signify either physical exhaustion or spiritual awe. In fact, the second possibility is scarcely glimpsed before Thomson produces his boldest inversion by presenting faith as an agency of darkness and death. The first Gothic image of *The City* ironically expresses the revival of faith as a morbid act of exhumation, an anachronistic appeal to the 'spectres of black night'. Tennyson attempts to validate the grandeur and permanence of the deity by diminishing human constructs, therefore mocking what he calls 'our little systems'. Behind these systems and exempt from their mutability stands the deity. If it were not for the latter, to Tennyson all-important, proviso, Thomson would echo those sentiments and more or less does so in his 1876 essay 'On the Worth of Metaphysical Systems', but here he consistently views creeds as human constructs not ways of systematising transcendental truth.[3] On the contrary, the clearest role Thomson adopts at the beginning of *The City* is that of truth-teller and he mounts an assault on all means of deception. The figure of unclothing (used in Arnold's 'Dover Beach' as a metaphorical contrast between enclosure by a 'bright girdle' and naked exposure to express the attenuation of faith and resultant vulnerability of the self) thus renders a necessary process of revealing truth 'stripped naked of all vesture that beguiles'. It is typical of Thomson's care over his vocabulary that he should use a term ('vesture') close to the ecclesiastical 'vestment', a resemblance which implicates the church in deception. Whereas Tennyson in the 'Prologue' establishes a meditative sequence of thoughts through spiritual address, Thomson problematises the very nature of his own utterance, placing a line and a half within quotation marks as if it represents the speech of another. Tennyson denigrates his own lines as if they are confused: 'Forgive these wild and wandering cries', but the very regularity of the iambic stressing belies the uncertainty he is claiming. Thomson's atheism denies him the possibility of a transcendental addresses so he immediately begins to question his own purposes as soon as the poem opens. Indeed his main difficulty at this stage is to identify an implied reader, another enormous difference from Tennyson. The latter packs the prologue to *In Memoriam* with general statements ('our wills are ours', 'we have but faith', etc.) where the pronomials imply that it is still possible to speak for a community of believers. Thomson cannot make this assumption and foregrounds his ruminations on a possible readership, rehearsing and dismissing potential groups ('the hopeful young', 'pious spirits'), ending finally with a hidden community of sceptics. Thomson then casts himself as an enabling voice for the 'mute and lonely'. The writing of *The City* is viewed in advance as an exercise in risk because Thomson is consciously reordering traditional signs. Where Tennyson's overlapping anxieties concern access to the deity and the decorum of expressing grief, Thomson foregrounds the broader problem of the potential comprehensibility of his own poem.

Thomson's difficulties of identifying a readership were compounded by his awareness of the depersonalising effects of city life.[4] In his 1857 poem 'The Doom of a City', a sage, an obvious surrogate for the poet himself, identifies one of Thomson's general premises later built into *The City*: 'What – Solitude in midst of a great City, / In midst of crowded myriads brimmed with Life! – ' (xix). From at least Wordsworth onwards, nineteenth-century writers on the city had located a central irony of urban life: the physical proximity with countless others actually increased the individual's isolation. Book VII of *The Prelude* depicts Wordsworth's recoil from the London crowds as a series of defensive rationalisations: the scenes of the streets are 'spectacles', 'entertainments'. But the climax of St Bartholomew's Fair overwhelms the poet with the sheer medley of sense-impressions that he can no longer organize, even rudimentarily as spectacle. And so the result is 'blank confusion'.[5]

Thomson's most important prose fantasy, 'A Lady of Sorrow', similarly describes a recoil from the crowded city, but this time at night. The speaker is led by the eponymous lady around a city where, like Wordsworth, his senses are bombarded by more sights and sounds than he can organize:

> At first she used to lead me, and still she often leads me, hour after hour of dusk and night through the interminable streets of this great and terrible city. The ever-streaming multitudes of men and women and children, mysterious fellow-creatures – and even this knowledge is sometimes darkened and dubious – overtake and pass me, meet and pass me; the inexhaustible processions of vehicles rattle and roar in the midst; lamp beyond lamp and far clusters of lamps burn yellow above the paler cross shimmer from brilliant shops, or funereally measure the long vistas of still streets, or portentously surround the black gulfs of squares and graveyards silent; lofty churches uplift themselves, blank, soulless, sepulchral, the pyramids of this mournful desert, each conserving the Mummy of a Great King in its heart; the sky overhead lowers vague and obscure; the moon and stars when visible shine with alien coldness, or are as wan early spectres, not radiant rejoicing spheres whose home is in the heavens beyond the firmament. The continuous thunders, swelling, subsiding, resurgent, the innumerable processions, confound and overwhelm my spirit, until as of old I cannot believe myself walking awake in a substantial city amongst real persons.
>
> (Thomson, 1881: 18)

Thomson here rehearses many of the effects he was to develop in *The City of Dreadful Night*: the bewildering endless sequence of passers-by, unknown to the narrator except as members of a common species; perspectives along interminable streets marked out by lamps; the emptiness of churches and the 'alien coldness' of the stars; and finally the fluctuations in the general noise of the city. All these factors result in the perceptual data streaming before the observer with increasing phantasmagoric rapidity. Thomson acknowledges a debt to de Quincey in a pseudo-editorial foreword, and the influence of the earlier writer can be seen in the surreal transformations which take place within the narrator's vision, further destabilising the sights before him.[6]

The streets of the city described here and in Thomson's most famous poem then grant him no access to understanding. They become the recurring site of perceptual confusion and the narrators within both works join the other citizens in wandering to and fro in bewilderment. But at least the narrator of 'A Lady of Sorrow' has a companion, albeit one who is attenuating into a Shadow. In stark contrast with Dante's *Inferno* where Virgil's role as expositor is crucial, Victorian poems of religious doubt either depict the *search* for a guide or contain a figure transformed into an embodiment of threat (the 'gray and gap-tooth'd man as lean as death' (60) in Tennyson's 'Vision of Sin') and trickery (the 'hoary cripple' (2) at the opening of Browning's 'Childe Roland').[7] A different possibility of guidance is suggested in Kipling's 1888 description of Calcutta which borrows Thomson's title *The City of Dreadful Night* and which uses a quotation from the poem as an epigraph. As Kipling is taken round Calcutta at night he records his astonishment at the sights which confront him: 'the eye has lost its sense of proportion' (Kipling, 1901: 203).[8] The result is never too confusing because Kipling is protected at every point by being in the company of members of the Calcutta police force. So while there is a certain frisson from the reader vicariously seeing areas of Indian life normally barred to Europeans, our imaginative security is never brought under very heavy pressure because the narrator is protected and the descriptive genre is familiarised through repeated comparisons with Dickens's sketches where the latter's forays into darkest London were similarly done with police protection.

Whether the city in Thomson's poem is read metaphorically as an emblematic landscape of spiritual absence or metonymically as a social location, guiding figures are conspicuous by their absence. It is as if no one knows the city. This suggestion is introduced as early as section (ii), the first narrative segment of *The City*, when the narrator follows a frail old man who 'seemed to walk with an intent' (ii). Pursuit reflects the narrator's urgent desire to gain access to a purpose – any purpose – but the results are anticlimactic. The old man leads him to a graveyard, a prosperous villa and a poor house, encoding them symbolically as the places where the cardinal virtues died. The story inverts spiritual quest as a 'drear pilgrimage' (ii) which the old man will repeat endlessly. When confronted with his own despair the latter ascribes a purely mechanical movement to life through the figure of a watch after the hands and dial have been removed: 'the works proceed until run down' (ii). This analogy constitutes a literal defacement of the example used by William Paley at the beginning of his *Evidences* (1794) to prove the existence of God. Suppose we find a watch; 'this mechanism being observed ... the inference, we think, is inevitable, that the watch must have had a maker.' Following the argument from design, Paley proposes that the watch can be taken as an analogue of the 'works of nature' which collectively imply the 'workmanship of an all-wise creature' (Paley, 1837: 1, 4).[9] Thomson's personification of despair, needless to say, blocks such consoling inferences and the narrator learns a bleakly negative lesson of 'perpetual recurrence'.

The encounter is typical of those in *The City* in its denial of consolation and reinforcement of alienation. Thomson's narrator characteristically overhears or catches glimpses of other figures who are so wrapped up in their own feelings that they resent his intrusion. In 'A Lady of Sorrow' Thomson generalises a hostile reaction to strangers as the inevitable result of solicitations by beggars and prostitutes: 'if one whom you know not ventures to address you, your first feeling is of distrust and defiance: this is your instinctive judgement of each other' (Thomson, 1881: 40). It is tempting to read Thomson's narrator as an urban *flâneur*, a figure discussed by Walter Benjamin with reference to Baudelaire and to Poe's story 'The Man of the Crowd'. For Benjamin the latter demonstrates Poe's fear of the crowd: 'there was something menacing in the spectacle they presented' (Benjamin, 1973: 128).[10] Poe's narrator sits securely inside a window observing the different social types who emerge at different phases of the London day. Then he notices a man who challenges his categories and pursues him around the streets for an entire night only to conclude that he personifies the spirit of the crowd itself.[11] Poe anticipates Thomson in narrating a kind of pursuit and also in depicting a more anxious and uneasy guise of the *flâneur* who is normally a dilettantish stroller. In either case the figure's attitude to the city is crucial since, as Marie Maclean has argued, 'the *flâneur* ... is constantly reading the text of the streets and, in the case of the Baudelairean narrator, constructing his own narrative from the signs he finds there' (Maclean, 1988: 56).[12] Thomson's narrator is never as leisurely as Baudelaire's and his anxious scrutiny of the urban scene typically discloses, as it does for Blake in 'London', 'marks of weakness, marks of woe' (4). Other humans within the city become potential sources of knowledge which can be verbalised but also glimpsed through the signs of suffering inscribed in their features. Towards the end of *The City* the narrator wanders into a northern suburb where the country lanes in fact offer no release from town. As he walks he encounters a human derelict based partly on Blake's Nebuchadnezzar who turns a 'haggard filthy face with bloodshot eyes'

(xviii) on him.[13] Once again the result is immediate hostility. The creature wants to cling on to his 'clue' of life which he reifies as a cherished possession and he threatens the narrator with assault from a 'poisoned blade' or a phial of acid. The precious clue turns out to be a metaphor of connectedness, a 'golden thread which reunites my present with my past' (xviii). This thread takes him back to the innocence of childhood where he becomes a 'nursling soft and pure' (xviii). The narrator, however, is unimpressed by this fantasy of regression. William David Schaefer sees the episode as marking a turning-point since 'Thomson denies the possibility of escape into a world of innocence' and 'shuts the door on what he came to think of as the "diseased" Blake' (Thomson, 1967: 214).[14] The city is figured repeatedly by Thomson as a maze and the old man clearly sees his own blood-spots as marking out a meaningful trail, but this is rejected by the narrator in favour of a linear concept of time: 'the thing which has been, never is again' (xviii).

The inhabitants of Thomson's city 'murmur to themselves' (i) or respond to address by 'gasping' or 'hissing'. The narrator is therefore tantalised by the proximity of voices which only rarely engage in dialogue. At one point a wild-looking man declaims to an empty square 'as if large multitudes were gathered round' (iv), at another the narrator intrudes on a private funeral. In both cases place sets up expectations which are undermined: of a public meeting-place or of bustle from a brightly lit 'mansion' (x). Sections vi and viii of *The City* are set on a river-walk almost certainly based on the new Embankment for the Thames built through the 1860s. This place for leisurely promenades offers Thomson the possibility of overhearing speech which is immediately assimilated into his reverie:

> I heard strange voices join in stranger talk,
> Although I had not heard approaching feet;
> These bodiless voices in my waking dream
> Flowed dark words blending with the sombre stream.
>
> (vi)

We have already seen how the city challenges the observer's assumptions of a stable reality. Here the alienness of the heard voices is stressed but, because the speakers remain unseen, their words are all the more easily appropriated into the narrator's field of consciousness where river and utterance blur together. In the second instance of overheard conversations a couple is actually seen, but never particularised. It is enough for the narrator to note that they repeat his own meditative posture in gazing at the 'stream profound' (viii). Thomson in effect disperses the narrating function among the different examples of suffering humanity which his narrator encounters in his travels around the city.

Thomson's city is defined as an expanse and a labyrinth. It cannot be seen all at once and therefore can never be properly known. Even local scenes exploit chiaroscuro effects arcing from the limits to street lighting:

> Although lamps burn along the silent streets;
> Even when moonlight silvers empty squares
> The dark holds countless lanes and close retreats.
>
> (iii)

The dark also holds the possibility of horizontal as well as lateral extension. Thomson's terminology of 'gulfs' and 'abysses', clearly derivative from Dante and the Gothic tradition generally, indicate depths with all their connotations of concealment: 'the lanes are black as *subterranean* lairs' (iii: emphasis added).[15] The city also contains ruins, but its past is forgotten; and, even more importantly, Thomson renders the external as an expression of states of mind. Thus the narrator enters a mansion to find a man grieving over the corpse of a loved one, spatialising his feelings within the 'mansion of my heart' (x). Thomson's city in short is a composite, extending its expressive range by including resemblances to Victorian London, Dante's Inferno, and a city of the dead. It is an obvious signal to the reader that the place lacks geographical specificity for it to be called 'this Venice of the Black Sea' (iv). Isobel Armstrong has identified this quality of inclusiveness: 'Thomson's endless city holds within itself the landscapes of all and any latitudes, the monumental buildings of all and any cultures ... The city does not transcend space and time: it is always being built indifferently, destroyed and rebuilt out of the same material elements' (Armstrong, 1993: 466).

In fact, Thomson uses three main analogies in his poem between the city as necropolis, Hell, and Limbo. The first articulates the 'certitude of Death' (i), constantly foregrounds mortality, and links *The City* with the graveyard school of reflective poetry from the eighteenth century. Thomson's landscape is packed with the signs of death, whether in a 'God's-acre' (an archaic term for a graveyard) or a 'necropolis', a term which was used increasingly from the 1820s onwards to designate the newly landscaped cemeteries of London. Thomson had drawn on the latter's etymology to mean a 'city of the dead' in 'The Doom of a City' where the protagonist enters a modern metropolis literally turned to

stone. It is as if time has suddenly stopped so that the city and its population have been 'arrested in full tumult of its strife'.[16] This literal
transformation is rendered metaphorically in *The City* where the suffering of its inhabitants has frozen their features – 'worn faces that look
deaf and blind / like tragic masks of stone' (i). Thomson's use of stone
as a traditional metaphor of the atrophy of feeling blurs the distinction
momentarily between the living and the monuments to the dead. Just
for a moment people are turning into inanimate matter, an effect
repeated when Thomson makes his only reference in the poem to
transportation. As he walks the streets a laden wagon thunders by and
the observer speculates on its contents: 'what merchandise? whence,
whither, and for whom?' (ix). These questions partly echo Emerson's
metaphysical query in *Nature* (1836): 'What is matter? Whence is it?
and Whereto?' (Emerson, 1960: 49).[17] Thomson answers his own questions by reducing human beings to cargo, reifying the hopes and 'abor-
tions' into the contents of a 'Fate-appointed hearse' (ix). And so once
again the distinction between the animate and inanimate collapses.

Indeed it seems at times that every feature of Thomson's city relates
to death. The only time the 'mighty river' of the city is described it is
encoded psychologically as the 'River of Suicides' (xix). Partly Thomson
was exploiting the notoriety which Waterloo Bridge had gained by the
1850s as the favourite location for suicides. His 1865 poem 'Polycrates
on Waterloo Bridge' burlesques suicide by substituting a meerschaum
pipe for a human body which will join the garbage in the river. Dickens,
by contrast, made no bones about stressing the bridge's association
with death in 'Night Walks', a sketch collected in *The Uncommercial
Traveller* (1860):

> the bridge was dreary ... the river had an awful look, the buildings
> on the banks were muffled in black shrouds, and the reflected lights
> seemed to originate deep in the water, as if the spectres of suicides
> were holding them to show where they went down. The wild moon
> and clouds were as restless as an evil conscience in a tumbled bed,
> and the very shadow of the immensity of London seemed to lie
> oppressively on the river.
>
> (Dickens, 1964: 129)

The analogies organize the entire scene around the funereal, suicide,
crime and a general atmosphere of heaviness.

In comparison with Dickens's language, Thomson's is positively aus-
tere. Drawing on mythical associations with Lethe, he depicts the river

simply as a source of oblivion, unlike Dickens who locates the place of suicides within a wider social context.[18] While the latter implies that these deaths represent the night-side of the prosperous metropolis, Thomson refuses pathos to the anonymous instances he cites ('one plunges from a bridge's parapet' [xix], etc.), representing death instead as a release. Dickens moves in his sketch from Waterloo Bridge to sombre reflections on the deserted theatres of the South Bank; Thomson similarly uses the notion of suicide to attack social behaviour as theatre: 'When this poor tragic-farce has palled us long, / Why actors and spectators do we stay?' (xix).[19] Death here becomes a means of release from the tedium of inauthentic action, paradoxically a fatal way of penetrating layers of illusion.

The second main analogy Thomson uses is with the city as Hell, and here of course he draws on Dante, quoting him in an epigraph and through allusions within the poem. Thomson's city can be read as a landscape of despair since the words over the portal of Dante's Inferno are quoted in the opening section of the poem. But a complication occurs when exactly the same words are quoted by a man who has returned to the city *from* Hell (vi). The analogy shifts to Limbo where the city becomes read as a place of exile distinct from either spiritual extreme. Here we need to bear in mind the circumstances of the poem's composition. Schaefer has argued that Thomson's original conception was to produce a Dantesque allegory (as evidenced in sections ii, xviii, and xx, the first to be written). Then he developed a further series of sections, all drafted in 1870, which were 'fantastic, supernatural, lightly allegorical' (Schaefer, 1962: 613). Finally, in 1873, he added a series of more narrative sections which would alternate with the latter. What Schaefer does not explain is the paradox of how a poet who has lost his faith, indeed developed an outright scepticism towards the symbolic system of Christianity, could even contemplate imitating an allegory based on medieval Catholicism, in other words, based on the very system Thomson had rejected. The answer seems to be that the Hell analogy was never a stable one since both sections where it is made explicit (i and vi) were drafted in the same year, 1870. The comparison is never as clear-cut as it is in, for instance, Hume Nisbet's story 'The Phantom Model' where an artist is painting a representation of Dante's Beatrice. His journey down river to find the perfect model is figured as a voyage down the Acheron to the inferno of Wapping where human figures move like 'dark shadows'. Here the Dantesque analogy articulates the polarisation between the East and West Ends of London, signalling a social distance so extreme that the inhabitants of each district scarcely seem to belong to the same species.[20]

The analogy between the city and Hell slides into a further comparison, this time borrowed from *The Ancient Mariner*, with Death-in-Life. Reinhard Kuhn finds in this figure the very embodiment of nineteenth-century ennui, especially its expression of endless duration (Kuhn, 1976: 276). Thomson clearly incorporates the Coleridgean intertext by using two sections (iii and v) containing designations of the city as Death-in-Life to frame his own version of the mariner's narrative, this time locating events on land. A wild-featured man (with 'glances burning with unnatural light') declaims his story of traversing a featureless desert and being beset by apocalyptic creatures until he encounters a 'woman with a red lamp' who triggers a fracture of his self into two guises. In a travesty of spiritual guidance she makes off with his 'corpse-like' self leaving his 'vile' self behind.[21] The predictable body/soul division never materialises and the local narrator joins the other inhabitants of the city as falling victim to a common state of subjection to a necessity they can only glimpse. The supposed privileges of citizenship reverse into a liability and the inhabitants' permanent site of homelessness is expressed figuratively as an attenuation of their persons into 'phantoms'.

No single analogy can make total sense of the city, so it can only be apprehended through a series of synecdoches, and this is one reason why Thomson situates sections in different parts of the city: a square, the streets, a river-walk, the suburbs, and so on. The city, in effect, spatialises Thomson's subject and allows him to use different locations, each one with its own tonality and social expectations. Like *Maud*, *The City* circles round its subject, alternating reflective sections with passages of narrative and descriptions which are constantly modifying each other. Given Thomson's attention to different areas of the city, we might expect a sequence focusing on the prime landmark of a cathedral to be the most prominent.

These cathedral sections pose the question whether religion can still draw humanity together. Thus the narrator follows a line of people passing into a cathedral specifically to answer this question. As usual the situation takes on a nightmarish dimension from the 'warder' who questions each newcomer 'with deep eyes burning through a black hood' (xii). From this point on Thomson temporarily fragments the narrating voice to cover a number of instances of those thronging into the cathedral, each case exemplifying the ironic refrain, 'I wake from daydreams to this real night'. The trope of waking, here used to express confronting an unwelcome reality, establishes a series of previous actions where the spiritual is reduced to the same level of fantasy as drinking and whoring. The very function of the cathedral is negated in advance by the dismissal of 'preaching to an audience fired with faith / the Lamb who died to save our souls from death' (xii). Indeed, the whole project of writing a Miltonic epic becomes ridiculed. Once a speaker appears the anti-Miltonic ironies get stronger and stronger since he turns out to be none other than Satan displaced into an alien context. But even the context is negated. The cathedral proves to be a shell, a mere place for people to come together, with 'no swelling organ-strain, / no chant, no voice or murmuring of prayer' (xiv). Religion then is referred to as a liturgical absence, clearing the ground for the preacher and throwing maximum weight on to his words.

Thomson temporarily produces a pastiche of Milton's epic similes to convey the stature of the speaker and repeats one of Satan's primary signs – 'two eyes which burned as never eyes burned yet'. Thomson's 'preacher' conflates Milton's Satan and Samson speaking from a position of spiritual loss and promising the congregation the results of having examined the universe. The climax comes as a further reversal, this time of the Christmas message:

> And now at last authentic word I bring,
> Witnessed by every dead and living thing;
> Good tidings of great joy for you, for all:
> There is no God; no Fiend with names divine
> Made us and tortures us; if we must pine,
> It is to satiate no Being's gall.
>
> (xiv)

Thomson has cleverly lured the reader into a position similar to the listeners in the cathedral. The verbal echoes of Milton seem to promise a satanic figure although the speaker is never named, and the latter's adopted role as truth-teller actually involves negating his own resemblances. The remainder of his message elaborates on his main denial, this time reducing the connotational language to a minimum so that the speaker can expound a totally secularised evolutionary world-view where humanity is as subject to change and potential obsolescence as any other species. Death is now described materialistically as a recycling of matter 'Whose elements dissolve and merge afresh / In earth, air, water, plants, and other men' (xiv). 'Men' is the last unprivileged term in a series and a necessitarian version of life is propounded as characterised by laws of time and by eternal conflict.[22] Like Hardy and Tennyson, Thomson's speaker dwarfs humanity by situating it within 'infinite aeons' (xiv) which precede mankind's origins.

Thomson's cathedral speaker is clearly a surrogate for the poet himself. His words possess a rare authority in *The City* and, as if that was not enough, they were echoed in an article which Thomson published only months after his poem had appeared. Commenting on an attack which had been mounted on the physicist John Tyndall by Bishop Alford, after ridiculing the latter's hostility to evolutionary secularism, Thomson concludes:

> What myriads say in their hearts (not to speak of the millions who say it in their lives), There is no God; but are afraid even to whisper the fact except to their nearest friends! Fools, indeed, as cowards always are; for if all the unbelievers freely proclaimed themselves, if all the scribes and pharisees, who now miserably cant, spoke out, it would be found that already 'There is no God' is the true creed of the mass of the intelligence and energy of this very Christian country.
>
> (Thomson, 1967: 105)

The crowning irony in *The City* is that this anti-creed should be put forward within the context of an imitation of a Christian sermon.

If the speaker acts as a surrogate for Thomson, then the whole cathedral episode can be read as a metaphor of the delivery and reception of *The City* where the congregation represent potential readers. Out of the reflective silence following the 'sermon' there bursts forth a shrill voice of agreement which confirms the speaker's general proposition with a story of the frustration of life's chances. The response challenges the very possibility of meaningful utterance:

> Speak not of comfort where no comfort is,
>   Speak not at all: can words make foul things fair?
> Our life's a cheat, our death a black abyss:
>   Hush and be mute envisaging despair.
>
> (xvi)

This response recognises the deliberate austerity in the speaker's message and then slides into an attack on words, ironically quoting from the first witches' song in *Macbeth* where a ritual formulation *does* reverse such opposed qualities.

Since the cathedral sections of *The City* introduce the secularism which lies at the poem's heart it is only fitting that they should be followed by a brief consideration of man's place in Nature, and particularly of the symbolic potential in the moon and stars. We have seen how Thomson uses quotation and allusion to evoke Christian mythology or ceremonies of Christian devotion, only to invert or negate them. For Isobel Armstrong this procedure gives a duplicity to Thomson's language since his poem 'uses the language of hell and of Christian despair to enter fully into that condition, and at the same time withdraws from it to expose it as a mystified mythology which collapses under an antagonistic materialist mythology' (Armstrong, 1993: 463). This is finely put because Thomson typically purports to be operating within the conventional symbolic system of Christianity before he attacks it. And it should by now be obvious that the stylistic manifestation of his atheism is a series of attacks or inversions of such conventional symbolism. A passage from his 1865 essay 'Open Secret Societies' will exemplify the rhetorical procedures Thomson's scepticism involves. Here he parodies the churches as the organisers of spiritual sanitation: 'These Churches have been elaborated and organised by man as patent reservoirs and cisterns (with a parson-tap for nearly every street) of the Waters of Life; and behold, these waters scarcely flow into them at all, but turn away and make for themselves truly secret and mysterious channels' (Thomson, 1881: 201). A metaphor is here transformed into a startlingly literal (and, for the 1860s, topical) metonym, diminishing the churches to civic bodies where the liquid of life becomes a commodity to be dispensed so sparingly that its circulation is scarcely perceptible. In a similarly parodic spirit Thomson elsewhere reduces the deity to a leading commercial figure in his 1865 allegory 'The Story of a Famous Old Firm' (in Schaefer, 1967: 42–54).

These effects are of course dependent on language – here the transposition of terminology – and a general characteristic of *The City* is its unusual self-consciousness of expression, a characteristic which would contrast with Thomson's contemporaries. The opening of Arnold's 'A Summer Night' (1852) for instance, sketches out a nocturnal scene of urban solitude:

> In the deserted, moon-blanch'd street,
> How lonely rings the echo of my feet!
> Those windows, which I gaze at, frown,

> Silent and white, unopening down,
> Repellent as the world
>
> (1–5)

Drawing on the trope of the body as the dwelling of the soul, Arnold can use the buildings as particularly charged images of hostility. Since the street repels the observer these lines cue in the excited moment of visual relief when a gap between roofs brings the moon into sight and 'doth a whole tract of heaven disclose!' (10). Having established the moon in contrast to the gloom and silence of human habitation, Arnold then attributes a voice to the moonlight as a substitute for either human or supernatural silence. Although he expresses this speech tentatively ('*seems* to say' [26, emphasis added]), nevertheless the plausibility of a voice coming from above, and therefore of the supernatural, depends on Arnold's willingness to leave the connotations of the term 'heaven' unmodified and unexamined.

Thomson will have none of this. Immediately after the cathedral episodes he attacks the pathetic fallacy:

> How the moon triumphs through the endless nights!
> How the stars throb and glitter as they wheel
> Their thick processions of supernal lights
> Around the blue vault obdurate as steel !
> And men regard with passionate awe and yearning
> The mighty marching and the golden burning,
> And think the heavens respond to what they feel.
>
> (xvii)

Moon and stars are half-personified through such terms as 'triumph' and 'throbs', and their symbolic role as spiritual signs is hinted at in 'supernal'. But the latter might mean no more than 'higher' and Thomson attributes an unusual hardness ('obdurate' in the Latin sense) to the vault of heaven which blocks off that area of connotation and introduces the humanisation of the moon and stars as self-delusion.[23] The moon can, therefore, not supply a spiritual voice as happens in some of Arnold's poems. Here the pacing of vocabulary and the careful control of connotation are two aspects among others of a general lexical mobility in Thomson's poem. He also repeatedly uses puns (for example, 'end' meaning 'purpose' and 'demise'), half-echoes, and etymology to shift the reader between different areas of meaning, the metonymic and the metaphorical, and so on. One of the most traditional tropes in spiritual symbolism, for instance, is the metaphorical connection between breath and spirit. It is this figure which Thomson deconstructs in section xv of *The City* where he collapses together prayer and all other human utterances as two physical phenomena: sound vibrations and the expellation of breath. The latter is expressed through Saxon and Latin terms as weighing down the communal air ('it') of the city: human feelings and thought 'are breathed into it with our respiration; / It is with our life fraught and overwrought' (xv). Feelings and thought become concretised as the 'freight' (cognate of 'fraught') of the air and all these terms converge on the city's 'atmosphere' (again 'breath' etymologically, this time from Greek). By the end of this section through a series of linkages between feeling, utterance and breath Thomson can suggest that the prevalence of city diseases is directly caused by the common presence of so many inhabitants. Whether the 'infections' are physical or emotional, human proximity becomes well-nigh fatal.

It should be clear by now that Thomson articulates his scepticism by deconstructing Christian metaphors and symbols. He was concerned to avoid what Charles Bradlaugh described in 1873 (the year Thomson was completing *The City*) as a dualistic view of the world. Speaking as a 'Naturist' Bradlaugh declared: 'we only know the phenomenal and the conditioned', whereas a believer also knew the transcendental realm of the deity (Bradlaugh, 1873: 41). Thomson's constant reduction of metaphor to metonymy should therefore be seen within the context of a secularisation of his thought and this process is summed up in a coda to the cathedral sequence just discussed. Thomson's 1876 essay 'On the Worth of Metaphysical Systems' renders the system of Christianity in the metaphor of a cathedral and that building is described in section xx of *The City* as a 'wave-worn rock', apparently drawing on the traditional figurative opposition between the sea of doubt and the rock as embodiment of faith. In front of the cathedral stand two stone images: an angel and a sphinx. The observer falls asleep twice and each time awakes to find that the angel has fallen, fracturing into a 'trunkless head'. The image of militant Christianity by this time has quite literally become a synecdoche and Thomson here narrates, through the figure of the fall, the emptying of meaning from a spiritual emblem. The result is a cryptic fragment: 'I pondered long that cold majestic face / Whose vision seemed of infinite void space' (xx). The sphinx as the very embodiment of enigma makes an appropriate object to juxtapose to the fallen angel; Thomson had elsewhere drawn on the former to express the inscrutability of life's processes: 'fate the Sphinx in the desert of life'.[24] The implication of such sequences is that Thomson's atheism does not manifest itself as a settled intellectual position.

Rather it is a process which he sums up in his 1882 poem 'Proem' where once again he recounts the discarding of the archive of Christian or mythic narratives and symbology: 'Our world is all stript naked of their dreams' (15). But as the poem progresses this nakedness becomes less a matter of liberation and more a matter of regret over humanity's loss of consolatory fictions. This pathos of loss and absence informs many sections of *The City* also. Since the symbolic system which Thomson is destabilising is always larger than any of his individual utterances he is compelled into recurrent exercises in deconstruction which enact the impulses within his scepticism but which always retain the melancholy traces of the very system under attack.

In order to conclude his poem Thomson at one and the same time retains the fiction of a city by describing a statue presiding over it, and reminds the reader of the fictionality of the poem by describing Dürer's drawing of Melancholia. Once again we find Thomson conflating the activities of narration and scrutiny as he tries to explain the power of this figure. Stressing size and materiality, he recognises the inadequacy of verbal representation ('words cannot picture her' [xxi]) and finds yet another cryptic embodiment of hidden meaning. This time, though, the point is that there is no point. Thomson denies interpretative depth to this figure: 'there is no light beyond the curtain' (xxi). Blocking off the transcendental reference of the phrase 'beyond the veil' (which occurs in *In Memoriam*), he reads the statue as all surface. Accordingly it becomes the appropriate embodiment of 'vanity and nothingness' (xxi) and the fitting culmination to a poem whose rhetoric has been consistently negative. Thomson's insistence on the statue's physical actuality rounds off a poem which has austerely refused any note of relief from its materialistic gloom. The first part of my title comes from Shelley's famous statement in 'Peter Bell the Third':

> Hell is a city much like London –
> A populous and a smoky city;
> There are all sorts of people undone.
> (3. 1–3)

Shelley makes explicit his secularisation of Hell in the dedication of the poem where he declares : 'you will perceive that it is not necessary to consider Hell and the devil as supernatural machinery. The whole scene of my epic is in "this world which is."'[25] Thomson too preserves aspects of an epic tonality in *The City*, like Shelley relocating his Gothic imagery in contemporary situations of lost transcendental belief and the anonymity of the Victorian metropolis.

Notes

1 The best account of Bradlaugh's impact on Thomson is given in Schaefer, 1965. Schaefer pinpoints Thomson's shift to atheism in an 1864 poem, 'Desolate' (subsequently retitled as 'Night').

2 All quotations from *In Memoriam* are taken from the Prologue. Quotations from *The City* are identified by section; unidentified quotations are taken from the Prologue. Other poems quoted are identified by line number.

3 After surveying a number of systems figured metaphorically as buildings Thomson reflects: 'And now that we have seen in history so many such systems arise and disappear, all with the same assurance of plan, all with the same instability of structure, it is natural that we should ask the question I have put, What is their worth?' (Thomson, 1881: 299).

4 By the 1840s this had become a commonplace of Victorian writing on the city; see Hulin and Coustillas, 1979: 18.

5 Thomson also describes the carnivalesque aspects of a London fair in 'The Fair of St Sylvester' (1875), collected in *Essays and Phantasies*.

6 Thomson acknowledges his debt to de Quincey in the foreword to 'A Lady of Sorrow', which derives from the latter's 'Levana and our Lady of Sorrow' (1845), collected in *Suspiria de Profundis*. De Quincey was planning a four-part work, the last part of which was to centre on the Mater Tenebrarum (i.e. 'mother of Shadows'). Thomson himself published a poem with that title in 1859.

7 Thomson disliked Tennyson's poem and in 1859 himself published 'A Real Vision of Sin', a kind of poetical corrective. On the other hand, he admired Browning's poem, describing it as follows: 'It is a series of pictures very powerful, weird and Rembrandt-like, elevated above grotesqueness by the stern heroic fortitude of the Childe' (Thomson, 1967: 212).

8 Kipling also uses the same epigraph from Thomson's poem for 'Under the Deodars' in *Wee Willie Winkie*, 1895.

9 I am grateful to my colleague Bernard Beattie for bringing this work to my attention.

10 Benjamin also finds the lighting crucial to Poe's tale: 'In the course of his story, Poe lets it grow dark. He lingers over the city by gaslight. The appearance of the street as an *intérieur* in which the phantasmagoria of the *flâneur* is concentrated is hard to separate from the gaslight' (Benjamin, 1973: 50).

11 In the course of an essay on Blake, Thomson describes Poe as a 'fine artist' (Thomson, 1967: 218).

12 The tradition of the *flâneur* as leisured observer in English prose only obliquely touches on Thomson and more typically stretches from Addison and Lamb up to Symons at the turn of the century.

13 See Harper, 1952.

14 The derelict's confidence about having found a connecting thread is ironically contradicted by his final movement: 'he turned to grope' (xviii).

15 Connected with this effect is Dickens's evocation of 'two cities in one, an overworld superimposed on an underworld' (Punter, 1980: 220). Of course Dickens's doubleness has much more to do with the social knowability of the metropolis than Thomson's.

16 The dream figure at the end of de Quincey's 'English Mail Coach' also takes the protagonist to a necropolis – a 'city of sepulchres'. Thomson's city in his

earlier poem becomes the subject of spiritual judgement and condemnation, finally being swamped by the sea. Its fate anticipates Richard Jefferies's futuristic fantasy, *After London* (1885), where the city has been drowned in an enormous black pool of its own effluent.

17 Thomson admired Emerson's writings. Emerson's own formulation is itself a part-echo from Carlyle's *Sartor Resartus*: 'Sure enough, I am; and lately was not: but Whence? How? Whereto?' (39).

18 Most famously in the opening chapter of *Our Mutual Friend* which describes characters earning a livelihood by salvaging corpses from the Thames.

19 A similar perceived estrangement from life is expressed in Arnold's 'The Buried Life': 'I knew they lived and moved / Trick'd in disguises, alien to the rest / Of men, and alien to themselves' (20–2).

20 'The Phantom Model' was published in Nisbet's *The Haunted Station* (1894). Exactly the same polarisation of urban areas occurs in Wilde's *The Picture of Dorian Gray* (1891).

21 The resemblances with 'The Ancient Mariner' and this narrative lie in the hallucinatory extremity of the torments evoked, the sheer suddenness of their appearance, and the narrator's loss of direction and bearing. The lady with the lamp represents a reversal of a symbol of heroic femininity found, for instance, in Longfellow's poem 'Santa Filomena' and popularised in the person of Florence Nightingale.

22 For commentary on the impact of evolutionary thought on Thomson, see Forsyth, 1962.

23 In so doing Thomson excludes a whole area of poetical expression where the moon and stars might be used as a symbolic focus for consoling reflections on human life, as occurs, for example, in Wordsworth's 'A Night-Piece' or Longfellow's 'Light of the Stars'.

24 In 'A Lady of Sorrow' Thomson describes 'Fate the Sphynx in the desert of Life, whose enigma is destruction to all who cannot interpret, and a doom more horrible before destruction to him who does interpret' (Thomson, 1881: 16–17). Michael R. Steele finds a source for this episode in Winwood Read's *The Martyrdom of Man*.

25 Thomson admired the irreverent energy of Shelley's poem, describing it as 'that long wild laugh of a young Greek god at the vision of a highly respectable English Sunday school teacher, toiling up Parnassus with a heavy bundle of sermons and hymn-books and moral old clothes on his back, resolved to convert and civilise those poor shameless heathen Muses' (Thomson, 1967: 188–9).

Works cited

Armstrong, Isobel. 1993. *Victorian Poetry. Poetry, Poetics and Politics*. London: Routledge.

Arnold, Matthew. 1961. *Poetry and Criticism of Matthew Arnold*. Ed. A. Dwight Culler. Boston: Houghton Mifflin.

Benjamin, Walter. 1973. *Charles Baudelaire: A Lyric Poet in the Era of High Capitalism*. Trans. Harry Zohn. London: NLB.

Blake, William. 1989. *Blake: The Complete Poems*. Ed. W.H. Stevenson. 2nd edn. London: Longman.

Bradlaugh, Charles. 1873. *Christianity in Relation to Freethought, Scepticism, and Faith: Three Discourses by the Bishop of Peterborough with Special Replies by Mr Charles Bradlaugh*. London: Austin.

Carlyle, Thomas. 1914. *Sartor Resartus; On Heroes, Hero-worship and the Heroic in History*. London: Everyman.

Crawford, Robert. 1985. 'James Thomson and T.S. Eliot'. *Victorian Poetry* 23, 23–40.

Dahl, Curtis. 1962. 'The Victorian Wasteland'. In *Victorian Literature: Modern Essays in Criticism*. Ed. Austin Wright. New York: Oxford University Press, 32–40.

Dickens, Charles. 1964. *The Uncommercial Traveller, and Reprinted Pieces, etc.* London: Oxford University Press.

Emerson, Ralph Waldo. 1960. *Selections from Ralph Waldo Emerson*. Ed. Stephen E. Whicher. Boston: Houghton Mifflin.

Forsyth, R.A. 1962. 'Evolutionism and the Pessimism of James Thomson (B.V.)'. *Essays in Criticism* 12, 148–66.

Harper, George M. 1952. 'Blake's *Nebuchadnezzar* in *The City of Dreadful Night*'. *Studies in Philology* 50, 68–80.

Hulin, Jean-Paul, and Pierre Coustillas, eds. 1979. *Victorian Writers and the City*. Lille: University of Lille Press.

Kipling, Rudyard. 1901. *From Sea to Sea*. Vol. 1. London: Macmillan.

Kuhn, Reinhard. 1976. *The Demon of Noontide: Ennui in Western Literature*. Princeton: Princeton University Press.

Maclean, Marie. 1988. *Narrative as Performance. The Baudelairean Experiment*. London: Routledge.

Paley, William. 1837. *Natural Theology, or Evidences of the Existence and the Attributes of the Deity, Collected from the Appearance of Nature*. Edinburgh: Chambers.

Punter, David. 1980. *The Literature of Terror: A History of Gothic Fictions from 1765 to the Present Day*. London: Longman.

Schaefer, William David. 1962. 'The Two Cities of Dreadful Night'. *PMLA* 77, 609–16.

Schaefer, William David. 1965. *James Thomson (B.V.): Beyond 'The City'*. Berkeley: University of California Press.

Shelley, Percy B. 1977. *Shelley's Poetry and Prose*. Ed. Donald H. Reiman and Sharon B. Powers. London: Norton.

Steele, Michael R. 1974. 'James Thomson's Angel and Sphinx: A Possible Source'. *Victorian Poetry* 12, 373–6.

Tennyson, Alfred. 1987. *The Poems of Tennyson*. Ed. Christopher Ricks. 2nd edn. London: Longman.

Tennyson, Hallam. 1905. *Alfred Lord Tennyson. A Memoir*. London: Macmillan.

Thomson, James. 1881. *Essays and Phantasies*. London: Reeves and Turner.

Thomson, James. 1919. *The City of Dreadful Night and Other Poems*. London: Dobell.

Thomson, James. 1967. *The Speedy Extinction of Evil and Misery: Selected Prose of James Thomson (B.V.)*. Ed. William David Schaeffer. Berkeley: University of California Press.

Chapter 6

'A pestilence which walketh in darkness':[1] diagnosing the Victorian vampire

Robert Mighall

This essay attempts to place on a more secure historical footing a suggestion made by Ernest Jones – that the nocturnal and sanguinary exploits of the vampire can 'only point to a natural and common process, namely nocturnal emissions accompanied with dreams of a more or less erotic nature. In the unconscious mind blood is commonly an equivalent for semen' (Jones, 1931: 119). C.F. Bentley applies Jones's idea to *Dracula*, suggesting that Jonathan Harker being visited by the three female vampires has 'the unreal quality of a masturbatory fantasy or erotic dream' (Bentley, 1972: 28). Similarly, Christopher Craft states that in *Dracula* 'blood substitutes for semen', and points out that the 'symbolic interchangeability of blood and semen in vampirism was identified as early as 1931 by Ernest Jones' (Craft, 1989: 230). The problem with such comments, however, is that they suppress the historical dimension. They suggest that this perceived relationship is somehow essential, that one activity – vampirism – 'symbolises' autoeroticism, and that this equation finds its source in the 'unconscious'. It is the role of the post-Freudian critic to bring this to light and explain the real significance of this 'fantasy'.

The following will attempt to historicise the relationship between autoeroticism and vampirism in the Victorian period. It will proceed by considering the differences between the vampire of folklore and the type found in nineteenth-century fiction. These differences are important, but are often overlooked. Vampire mythology is neither universal nor coherent. Before nineteenth-century fiction took up the vampire, his or her traits were neither universal nor standardised (for example, not all vampires from folk traditions drink blood).[2] After Stoker, vampire lore has come to resemble the language of science or medicine, with standardised laws, symptoms and aetiologies. As I will now demonstrate, it is testimony to the pseudo-scientific and medical influences on Stoker's novel that Count Dracula has fixed the iconography and attributes of the vampire.

I

In 1855 Dickens's *Household Words* carried a short piece entitled 'Vampyres', describing the terrors of vampiric visitation:

> For every night comes the terrible Shape to your bed-side...and sucks your life-blood in your sleep... Day after day you grow paler and more languid; your face becomes livid, your eyes leaden, your cheeks hollow. Your friends [advise] you to seek medical aid...but you are too well aware that it is all in vain. You therefore keep your fearful secret to yourself; and pine, and droop, and languish, til you die... You are then yourself forced to become a vampyre, and to create fresh victims; who, as they die, add to the phantom stock.
>
> (Ollier, 1855: 39)

This outline will be familiar to most people, even if their knowledge of vampirism is based entirely on Bram Stoker's *Dracula* (1897). As this popular account implies, a mysterious debilitating illness is a clear indication of vampiric activity. In 1855, however, this pathological emphasis was of a relatively recent vintage. It was not quite an aspect of Polidori's *The Vampyre* (1819) in which the vampire's victims die instantly, but it did form a part of James Malcolm Rymer's *Varney the Vampyre* (1847), where it is explained that a victim could languish 'from year to year', slowly 'wast[ing] away' (Rymer, 1847: 157). Whilst this pathological emphasis became central to vampire fiction, it was largely absent from the folklore as recorded by eighteenth-century scholars.[3] Here the vampire's victim dies immediately, or at the most lasts two or three days. In folklore medical diagnosis was rarely an issue. The villagers instantly recognized that a vampire was at large, and set about discovering which of the victim's neighbours had returned from the grave and attacked him, while the cause of death was as likely to be strangulation as loss of blood.

A possible imaginative model for this new narrative structure can perhaps be found in another mysterious illness which preoccupied

Rymer's and Stoker's contemporaries. The following passage appears in Samuel Tissot's *Onanism*:

> The health of a young prince was gradually declining and the reason could not be ascertained. His surgeon suspected the cause, waited, and detected him in the act...the evil progressed, he lost strength daily, and was saved only by guarding him night and day for more than eight months.
>
> (Tissot, 1758: 47)[4]

This passage includes the key elements of the typical Victorian vampire tale. It involves a person of high birth, who is attacked by a mysterious debilitating illness. A knowing physician is called in, who suspects the real cause and sets about catching the fiend/victim in the act. Finally, the masturbator, like the vampire, is prevented by round-the-clock surveillance. As will now be explained, this narrative structure is just one of many points of comparison between these two discourses. The following will identify other 'vampiric' traits in clinical and quack literature on the perils of self-abuse;[5] it will then offer an explanation for these correspondences and finally assess their influence on Victorian vampire fiction.

The closest parallels between vampirism and masturbation can be identified on the rhetorical level, and principally in the way the latter was personified. As W.A. Hammond wrote in *A Treatise on Spermatorrhoea*, 'the lurking foe creeps insidiously to his murderous work. ...It besets youth like some infernal demon, ever on the watch to kill body and soul' (Hammond, 1862: 5).[6] This 'monster evil of civilization', this 'silent assassin', should, according to one writer, be termed ' "diabolical". For the Enemy himself could scarcely have devised [a practice] more destructive of body and soul' (Henery, 1861: 43, 79, 34).[7] A diabolical, creeping foe which kills body and soul; such medico-moral rhetoric might easily be describing another dark figure who stalked the pages of nineteenth-century literature.

As the terms 'self-pollution' and 'self-abuse' suggest, the patient is both the agent of destruction and its helpless victim. Similarly, the vampire is both a monster and the victim of an earlier attack. This is brought out clearly in the handling of Lucy's illness in *Dracula*. By day she is a helpless languid invalid; at night she invites Dracula to feed on her by deliberately pulling the garlic away from her throat. Eventually she metamorphoses into the 'callous devil', the 'foul Thing which had taken Lucy's shape without her soul', whom The Crew of Light are forced to destroy (Stoker, 1897: 271, 274). At her death she is restored to her role as the victim whose destruction they must now avenge. The patient suffering from self-abuse was invariably described as its (his or her own) 'victim'. Thus one authority describes the spectacle of a female onanist, looking 'like a skeleton', and encountered on what threatened to be her death bed: 'Even in her semi-conscious state, the polluted hand, *governed by the foul habit,* mechanically sought the source of lustful and sinful gratification' (Henery, 1861: 48, emphasis added). The onanist, like Lucy in her transitional state, is only 'semi-conscious' (and therefore only partly guilty), being 'governed' by a habit that is both personified and given independent agency. This duality is clearly seen in Samuel La'Mert's remarks when he asks,

> Whither may he fly from the plague that is within him, the evil that haunts him alike in darkness and in light? ... No sooner has this uncleanness got the ascendancy over the passions, but forthwith it pursues its slave everywhere, and retains possession of him at all times and places.
>
> (La'Mert, 1852: 48–51)

Here masturbation is the agent, and the patient its helpless victim, a victim who is 'governed', 'haunted', 'pursued' and 'possessed' by some extraneous evil.

However, the onanist was often a victim in a more obvious sense, having been initiated into this practice by another. Tissot records an epidemic of vampiric proportions: 'Some years since, it was discovered in the city, that a company of libertines, fourteen or fifteen years old, used to assemble to practise this vice, and that a whole school is still polluted by it' (Tissot, 1758: 48). It would appear that the onanist, like his fictional counterpart, feels a compulsion to 'infect' others, and so the vice spreads. A fine example of onanistic 'infection' is found in Curtis's *Manhood* from 1840. He quotes a letter from a patient's father, who heard of his son's illness and visited his boarding school:

> Alas! my dear sir, what a shock I received. I beheld a skeleton, a living skeleton! ... My honest misguided boy was moved at the sight of my affliction, and the *dreadful* secret was unfolded to me. ... I need not be very explicit; the Hon. Augustus ——, had introduced a vice! irresistible alas! the secret practice of which, was slowly undermining the vitality of every youth in the seminary.
>
> (Curtis, 1840: 92)

A fiendish aristocrat thus infects the youth of the respectable classes. The novelistic convention of substituting a dash for the name of the offender shrouds him with further mystery.

All writers on this subject, whether quacks or physicians, agreed that masturbators had 'a peculiar stamp to their characters' (Lallemand, 1851: 354). They constituted a recognisable pathological type, presenting distinctive symptoms and behavioural codes for those who could read the signs. As the authors of *The Silent Friend* observe: 'When once the destructive practice is established, the barrier of intellectual control falls [and he becomes] a misanthrope, a nadir-point of discontent!' (Perry, 1847: 52). Like Polidori's Lord Ruthven, Rymer's Varney or Stoker's Count Dracula, the onanist 'becomes an outcast on earth... [and] bids adieu to the circle of mankind' (Brodie, 1845: 15–16). The general advice offered to parents by Cooke is to 'have an eye...upon those who prefer darkness and solitude': sensible advice, whatever the suspected cause (Cooke, 1871: 114).[8]

II

Both Laura in Le Fanu's 'Carmilla' and Stoker's Lucy Westenra experience vampirism as a 'bad dream'. As Lucy tells Dr Seward: 'All this weakness comes to me in sleep; until I dread the very thought' (Stoker, 1897: 164). Bad dreams were also common symptoms of those suffering from masturbational illnesses and seminal disorders. According to *The Silent Friend*, the masturbator's sleep is 'interrupted by the most frightful dreams. Indeed, the individual becomes terrified to go to bed, lest sudden death should be his fate' (Perry, 1847: 65–6). This is perhaps the logical consequence of the personification of masturbation and seminal emissions, and the suggestion that they have an independent (malevolent) agency. It also points to intriguing correspondences between this discourse and an earlier tradition which ascribed nocturnal emissions to the activities of incubi and succubi. This subject preoccupied a number of medieval and early modern demonologists, and is explained here by Ludovico Sinastrasi, author of *De Demonialitate*:

> When women are desirous of becoming pregnant by the Demon... the Demon is transformed into a Succubus, and during the act of coition with some man receives therefrom human semen; or else he procures pollution from a man during his sleep, and then he

preserves the spilt semen at its natural heat ... This, when he has connexion with the woman, he introduces into her womb, whence follows impregnation.

(in Summers, 1930: 13)[9]

Such demonological works (one early thirteenth-century source suggested that 'demons collect all wasted human seed, and from it fashion for themselves human bodies' [Caesarius, 1929: 139]) provide a rhetorical and imaginative precedent for the writings on masturbation and seminal weakness. The latter's prevalent use of (demonic) personification perhaps survives as an echo from this earlier discursive domain. Tissot's treatise, published less than a century after the learned belief in witchcraft receded (see Thomas, 1991), includes a passage which underlines the conceptual connection between the supernatural and the physiological in this discourse. As the physician records:

Some years since, I saw a young man who was affected with nocturnal emissions almost every night; and who already had some attacks of nightmare [*cochemar*] ... the two diseases returned every night: the phantom of the nightmare was a female, which caused at the same time the emission. Enfeebled by these two causes ... he was rapidly advancing into consumption.

(Tissot, 1758: 94)

The scientific term for the popular 'Nightmare' was 'Incubus', because it, like the demon of that name, would 'sit' on the sufferer, causing a sensation of suffocation or strangulation. Attributed to respiratory or digestive causes, in its purely physiological form, which was firmly established by the time Tissot wrote, the incubus disorder was almost without erotic associations.[10] But whilst the erotic had been purged from learned comment on the incubus, the incubus had not entirely been exorcised from discourses on the erotic. Thus although Tissot separates these two 'diseases' nosologically, he none the less equates them imaginatively and functionally. They are not *actually* the same, and the 'phantom' is imaginary; but they produce the same effects, and can be characterized in a similar way to the experience described by demonologists. The demonological belief lurks behind such representations, suggesting that one quack's remark that it has often taken all his skill to 'snatch from the verge of the grave' the victim of seminal weakness, and 'remove the incubus from his soul', was only partly metaphorical (Hammond, 1862: 11).

This last observation provides an explicit (albeit metaphorical) confirmation of the supernatural prehistory of clinical discourse on masturbation, but also points to an important development which suggests that vampirism would have been a more appropriate metaphor here. For although the vampire and the incubus were often associated or confused,[11] there was the fundamental difference that the activities of the former (in either demonology or physiology) were rarely fatal, whereas in folklore vampirism invariably was. As quacks were keen to stress the potentially fatal consequences of this practice, and thus urge the swift necessity of their expensive intervention, they would profit by updating their metaphors to conform to the tastes of sensational literature, and 'feed off' the more appropriate imagery found therein. Many did. And this exchange, as will now be suggested, was reciprocal.

III

The following introduces S.G. Howe's chapter on self-abuse: 'There is [a] vice, a monster so hideous in mien, so disgusting in feature, altogether so beastly and loathsome, that in very shame and cowardice, it hides its head by day, and vampyre-like, sucks the very life-blood from its victims by night' (Howe, 1848: 83–4).[12] *The Silent Friend* similarly refers to masturbation as 'a vampyre feeding on the life-blood of its victims' (Perry, 1847: 54). Masturbation was like vampirism because both practices supposedly depleted the body of vital fluids, a process believed to be fatal. The term 'life-blood' is a metaphor for semen. However, to a large extent, this usage is only partly metaphorical. Underwriting such statements is the widespread belief that, 'the loss of one ounce [of semen] enfeebles more than forty ounces of blood' (Tissot, 1758: v). This statement derives from Tissot, but it is found in countless quack treatises on this habit, at least until the mid nineteenth century.[13] Therefore Ernest Jones's observation that 'In the unconscious mind blood is often an equivalent for semen' (Jones, 1931: 119) is somewhat redundant, while the 'modernity' of this insight is rather put into perspective. For as Samuel La'Mert points out: 'Loss of blood, if repeated … is a sure and readily acknowledged index of corresponding failure of the vital powers: but the deadly drain upon the nervous system from the loss of [semen, that] *most curiously elaborate secretion from the blood* is more rapidly destructive' (La'Mert, 1852: 17–18). This material analogy between blood loss and seminal emission encourages this metaphorical equation between vampirism and

masturbation. It also helps to explain many of the rhetorical correspondences between the respective discourses responsible for representing them.

When vampirism was transported from the mountains and forests of
folklore into the drawing-rooms and boudoirs of a (semi-)realist fictional context it was made to conform to the explanations and expectations of its new social milieu. And thus in the Victorian period
vampirism became a disease. The logic which informs this model is the
'common sense' reasoning that if vampires drink blood and the victims
only have a limited quantity of blood, then *eventually* the victim will
die after a slow wasting illness. Such a 'sanguinary economy' is central
to the dramatic interest of Bram Stoker's *Dracula*, and is clearly seen
operating in the scenes involving blood transfusions. Lucy revives with
the infusion of Arthur's blood, only to relapse after Dracula's next
nocturnal visitation: 'All our work is undone; we must begin again'
(Stoker, 1897: 167). Dracula drains it, the men restore it. He waxes as
she wanes.

A similar physiological 'economy' informs the literature on masturbation and seminal weakness. As Lallemand, an expert on 'Spermatorrhoea', observed: 'When the patients have passed a few days in
succession, without suffering from pollutions, they manifest rapid
increase of strength and activity: a single discharge again reducing
them to their debilitated condition' (Lallemand, 1851: 341). The complaint which he describes was the result of earlier excesses, which were
now involuntary, resulting in both nocturnal and diurnal emissions.
The latter, passed in the urine, at stool, or (nice occult touch) through
a 'misty impalpable moisture' escaping through the pores (Henery,
1861: 16), was imperceptible to the ordinary observer. The 'occult'
nature of this cause meant that inexperienced or incredulous physicians were baffled by their patients' disorders, and, like Dr Seward,
chose 'to ignore the existence of the most dangerous foe to life [and]
act as if no such foe existed' (Henery, 1861: 20). At least Seward has an
advantage over his real-life counterpart in achieving what one authority claimed was impossible: 'could we but lift the veil of the grave, how
should we startle at the long train of the victims of sensualism!'
(La'Mert, 1852: 44).

A problem appears to present itself at this point, however. If masturbation is a 'vampyre-vice' because it drains semen the way a vampire
sucks blood, then this could hardly inform the most famous Victorian
vampire tales such as 'Carmilla' and *Dracula* where the principal victims are female. However, at least in the early writings on onanism,

when the formula was being established, there was a belief that females did 'ejaculate', and that this was essential to reproduction and therefore just as 'vital' to the female's animal economy.[14] This idea was soon relegated to 'folk' wisdom and replaced by a more sophisticated version. A model of 'nervous economy' existed alongside the logic which equated semen with blood, and eventually superseded it when the latter was discredited around the mid-century. The nervous model principally served to explain why masturbation was also harmful to infants and females who had no 'seed' to lose. When the seminal model became the preserve of quacks, the nervous model was triumphant and served for both sexes. However, the latter was really only a more sophisticated or 'metaphysical' version of the former, and retains the notion of a physiological 'economy' essential to both vampire tales and quack treatises. Instead of losing seed, the masturbator lost 'nervous' energy, the supply of which was also finite. And therefore excessive nervous losses had the same effect as seminal drain. As Lallemand asserted: 'I am convinced that the effects produced by seminal discharges may be brought on by *any other debilitating cause*, whose action on the *economy* is rapid and important' (Lallemand, 1851: 367). This, supposedly, would include blood loss from vampiric attack; an experience which, as will now be explained, produced identical symptoms to self-abuse.

The passage from *Household Words* previously quoted implies that extreme pallor is an attribute of the vampire/victim. Similarly, Polidori's Lord Ruthven is conspicuous for his 'dead grey eye', and the 'deadly hue of his face' (Polidori, 1819: 7). Rymer's Sir Francis Varney is described as being 'perfectly white – perfectly bloodless', and whose face 'wore a singular cadaverous-looking aspect', with, 'a curious pinkish-looking circle round his eyes' (Rymer, 1847: 3, 180). And finally, Count Dracula, who served to fix the popular iconography of the pale, gaunt vampire, is described as producing 'a general effect of extraordinary pallor', while Lucy is described by Dr Seward as 'more horribly white and wan-looking than ever' (Stoker, 1897: 28, 167). In short, fictional vampires are rarely healthy-looking, with florid faces and portly physiques. But the ones from folklore were. In fact, the appearance of the typical folkloric vampire is the complete antithesis of the type found in Victorian fiction. As Paul Barber points out, the vampire of folklore 'is never pale, as one would expect of a corpse: his face commonly is described as florid, or of a healthy color, or dark'. Moreover, these vampires have 'a tendency to be plump or swollen ... quite unlike the vampires of fiction' (Barber, 1988: 41, 42).

'Hideous and frightful' is the aspect of the typical onanist, 'a faded...
wandering corpse' (Henery, 1861: 75–6) who by almost universal
assent presents the following symptoms: 'the face [is] pale, bloated,
and cadaverous, [while] the body is generally...emaciated, with coldness in the extremities' (Perry, 1847: 65). Another writer asserts that:
'when a general state of languor and lassitude [is] joined to a pallid
face, emaciation of the frame, foetor of breath, and the appearance of a
bluish circle around the eyes, [these are] grounds for suspecting that a
patient is addicting himself to some secret practices.' As one of his
cases lamented: 'my face has become as it were cadaverous – so pale, so
livid' (Curtis, 1840: 42, 40). Combined, therefore, the paleness, emaciation, lassitude, sunken eyes, bad breath, nightmares and nocturnal
preferences suggest that the medico-moral discourse on masturbation
somehow contributed to Victorian fiction's refashioning of the vampire. (Figure 6.1 depicts a distinctly vampiric representative of the masturbatory type, provided by Brodie's *The Secret Companion*, 1845: 19.)
I would suggest, therefore, that Victorian authors adapted vampirism
to the model of morbidity found in the literature on self-abuse.
Fictional vampirism does not so much 'symbolise' masturbation;
rather, it approximated the way it was represented at the time. This
may be largely a consequence of the 'physiological economy' model
common to both discourses; however, as will now be suggested, it may
have been more deliberate.

IV

The final section of this essay will suggest that given these close parallels between vampire fiction and a literature that was equally homogeneous and 'generic', some practitioners in the former mode may have
been aware of this proximity and exploited it in their fiction. The question asked of a young man by Doctor Phillips, called to investigate a
case of vampirism in Florence Marryat's *The Blood of the Vampire* (1897),
might be addressed to so many victims of vampirism or similar 'vices':
' "Hullo! young man, and what have *you* been doing to yourself?"
exclaimed the doctor. He was certainly looking ill. His face was chalky
white, and his eyes seemed to have lost their brightness and colour'
(Marryat, 1897: 112). Any reader who had a knowledge of the pathological literature on self-abuse (and this literature was vast and conspicuous; most of the publications featured in this essay were advertised on
the front pages of daily newspapers) might be wondering the same
thing. The conventional physician, often serving as foil to the occult

Figure 6.1 First published in *The Secret Companion, a Medical work on Onanism or Self Pollution* (London: Brodie & Co., 1845).

expert, became an important part of the fictional formula, and principally served to establish the modernity of the context into which the supernatural threat intrudes. The following discussion will turn Doctor Phillips's question around and ask the doctors in these tales what *they* thought their patients had been doing to themselves before the 'true' diagnosis is accepted.

The most famous foil to the occult doctor is of course Stoker's Dr Seward, who is confronted by a mystery illness that defies all conventional logic. As his real-life counterpart Dr Henery reasons: 'If a man is bleeding to death, or subjected to a severe course of blood-letting, he sees the process going on.' Not so the victim of seminal weakness or other vampire vices: 'The juices and essences of his life may be passing away from him ... in imperceptible emissions' (Henery, 1861: 15–16). Seward faces a similar dilemma. He believes that Lucy died 'of nervous prostration following on great loss or waste of blood', but as Van Helsing sensibly asks: 'And how the blood lost or waste?' (Stoker, 1897: 246). As Seward informs Holmwood in the early stages of Lucy's illness: 'there is not any functional disturbance or any malady that I know of. At the same time, I am by no means satisfied with her appearance' (145). Her appearance is, of course, 'ghastly pale' (150).

Shortly after this, Seward makes the intriguing confession that he 'did not have full opportunity of examination such as I should wish; our very friendship makes a little difficulty which not even medical science or custom can bridge over' (146). What Seward thought too delicate to ask Lucy will never be known, but perhaps he should have taken Dr Howe's advice to those confronted with similar symptoms. As Howe remarks: 'many a fond parent looks with wondering anxiety upon the puny frame, the feeble purpose, the fitful humors of a dear child [unaware that] the victim hugs the disgusting serpent closely to his bosom, and conceals it carefully in his vestment.' Howe's advice is to 'throw aside all reserve; to charge the offence directly home; to show up its disgusting nature and hideous consequences in glowing colors' (Howe, 1848: 86). Such a scene takes place much later, but of course, the malady turns out to be only vampirism after all.

Sheridan Le Fanu's 'Carmilla' (1871) perhaps offers the most 'knowing' use of such a dual-pathological structure, almost inviting the reader to imaginatively conflate these two 'disorders'. Le Fanu's tale is narrated by a young girl, who, shortly after the arrival of a mysterious young woman, suffers bad dreams, and starts to exhibit the by now familiar symptoms: 'My sufferings had, during the last week, told upon my appearance. I had grown pale, my eyes were dilated and darkened underneath, and the languor which I had long felt began to display itself in my countenance' (Le Fanu, 1871: 106). If Dr Dawson encountered Laura he would know exactly what to think. With the onanist, 'changes in the general appearance and countenance gradually but steadily unfold themselves. ... the patient emaciates [and then ...] the pale sharpened features, the haggard look, but *too clearly denounce* the hidden mischief' (Dawson, 1845: 16). If this was so 'clear' to real physicians, then why not the fictional ones? Or perhaps it was. Laura is not the only one to suffer these symptoms, she finds them 'so exactly described' (Le Fanu, 1871: 125) in the interpolated narrative of General Spielsdorf, who tells of his own daughter's death by a mysterious illness that had baffled the physician. The 'occult' doctor is called in, who argues with his more materialist counterpart about his, as yet unspecified, hypothesis. He tells the father that the patient was near death, but that 'one more assault might extinguish the last spark of vitality' (129). But what kind of assault is not immediately specified. Instead, the doctor writes the name of the disorder on a piece of paper, hands this to the patient's father and makes a discreet exit. The General responds to this note: 'At another time, or in another case, it might have excited my ridicule. But into what quackeries will not people rush for a last chance...?' (129–30). As is spelt out shortly, the complaint is actually vampirism; but until this is established a masturbatory disorder stands as a more likely candidate. However, not only is there a 'double' pathology at work here, exploiting the reader's expectations, Le Fanu's tale actually highlights the way fiction departs from folklore along the lines established in this essay. Both the 'pathological decline' and the appearance of the fictional vampire are scrutinized; an emphasis that implicitly encourages the reader to frame an alternative diagnosis to 'vampirism'. It is Laura who encourages this awareness. Directly after the passage which describes her symptoms she reasons: 'It could not be that terrible complaint which the peasants call the oupire, for I had now been suffering for three weeks, and they were seldom ill for much more than three days, when death put an end to their miseries' (106). Laura evidently knows her folklore. This categorical denial throws doubt on the supernatural hypothesis even before it is offered, thus compelling the reader to consider an alternative disorder which matches her symptoms. When a doctor attends her, he, like the authority on onanism, advises 'not to let Miss Laura be alone for one moment' (112): advice that could equally be to prevent solitary vices as ward off vampires. Laura's response to it, believing that she is *not* suffering from vampirism, suggests that she is thinking along more conventional lines: 'I fancied, perhaps luckily for my nerves, that the arrangement was prescribed...[to prevent me] doing any of the fifty foolish things to which young people are supposed to be prone' (113). If not fifty, then perhaps one in particular.[15]

Not only does Laura invite the reader to doubt pre-emptively the 'vampiric' diagnosis of her case on the basis of its marked departure from folkloric precedents, she also provides an explicit rejection of the literary construction of the vampiric type according to western models of morbidity. For, as she asserts: 'the deadly pallor attributed to that sort of *revenants*, is a mere melodramatic fiction. They present, in the grave, and when they show themselves in human society, the appearance of healthy life' (135). As both pathological decline and the unhealthy pallor of the vampire are *the* key fictional departures from folklore, and as both find direct parallels in the symptomatology of self-abuse, then it is difficult not to suspect a knowing manipulation of these expectations on Le Fanu's part.

I am not suggesting that vampirism 'really is' masturbation in this or any other tale from the period; rather, that Le Fanu was aware of these parallels and slyly pointed to them in his tale. By looking at the contemporary representations of masturbation, an alternative to the 'symbolic' approach to the correspondences between this practice and fictional vampirism is possible. What I propose are material correspondences, rather than symbolic 'equivalents', conscious modellings rather than unconscious 'substitutions'.

I will conclude by quoting from Franz Hartmann's article on real-life (psychic) 'Vampires' from the esoteric journal *Borderland*. According to him the vampire's typical victim 'may be very intellectual and refined, but they are always sensually inclined people, and *usually given to secret vices*. To a sensitive person the shake of their hand feels clammy and cadaverous' (Hartmann, 1896: 354).[16] It is difficult to know which discourse has inspired which here: whether these attributes derive from the masturbator as vampire or the vampire as masturbator. The exchange appears to have reached equilibrium. Interestingly, Stoker's novel, which fixed the image of the pale, cadaverous vampire, was published the following year.

Notes

1 Howe, 1848: 84.
2 On the differences between the vampire of folklore and the type found in nineteenth-century fiction, see Barber's excellent *Vampires, Burial and Death: Folklore and Reality*.
3 For selections from these testimonies, see Barber, 1988, *passim*, and Frayling, 1991, 87–103.
4 Tissot's book was the 'seminal' work in the development of the medical discourse on the perils of self-abuse. It was published originally in Latin in 1758, in French in the 1760s, and in most European languages by the 1770s.

It went through numerous reprints, last appearing as late as 1905. This work established the formula for most clinical and quack treatises on the subject for the next 150 years. On the history of the pathological literature on self-abuse, seminal weakness and masturbatory insanity, see Spitz, 1952; Hare, 1962; Macdonald, 1967; Gilbert, 1980; Jordanova, 1987; and Wagner, 1983.

5   On the differences and similarities between quacks and respectable physicians on the effects of masturbation, see Porter and Hall, 1995: 145; and Mason, 1994: 187–90, 211–16.

6   Spermatorrhoea was a disorder attendant on masturbation or sensual excesses, resulting in both nocturnal and diurnal emissions; see Mason, 1994: 295–8.

7   The 'demonic' imagery was largely the preserve of the quacks who sought to terrify the gullible into purchasing their nostrums, and derived largely from the biblical lexicon inaugurated by the anonymous pamphlet known as the *Onania: or, The Heinous Sin of Self-Pollution, and Its Frightful Consequences, in Both Sexes consider'd, &c...* (London, 1720).

8   Although the vampire's extreme photophobia largely originated with Murnau's film *Nosferatu* (1922), there are precedents for this in the literature. Dracula's powers are severely restricted 'at the coming of the day', while Lord Ruthven, Varney and Carmilla display distinct preferences for the moonlit hours. This is another trait exhibited by the vampire's onanistic cousin, who is 'painfully affected by any bright light...some even are unable to bear any light more brilliant than twilight...they are obliged to avoid mid-day', Lallemand, 1851: 348.

9   *De Demonialitate*, written in the late seventeenth century, was first published in 1875. On the activities of incubi and succubi see Robbins, 1959, sections on 'Incubus'; 'Succubus'; 'Sexual Relations with Devils'; 'Nightmare'. I am greatly indebted to Dr Gareth Roberts for his advice on matters demonological and in assisting research for this essay.

10 For the 'Incubus' as physiological disorder, see Bond, 1753; Waller, 1816. The nightmare was primarily a physical experience which was *accompanied* by bad dreams. It did not take its more figurative sense until the twentieth century.

11 On the confusions between the vampire and the 'mora' or 'mare' (nightmare), see Perkowski, 1989.

12 Later published as *On the Causes of Idiocy*, Edinburgh, 1848. Howe was certainly not a quack, but a highly influential philanthropist and asylum inspector.

13 On the analogy between blood and semen in medical and quack literature, and on masturbation generally, see Mason, 1994: 205–15.

14 On this see Laquer, 1992; Mason, 1994: 204.

15 Significantly, as is later revealed, the reason her complaint differed from those attacked by the folkloric 'oupire' was that it was erotic in its characteristics 'resembling the passion of love' (135).

16 Interestingly, the focus of the piece is really incubi or 'demon lovers', and Stead, the journal's editor, remarks that the 'physical mischief' caused by such 'intercourse' would be similar to that occasioned 'on the material plane', i.e., masturbational disorders (353).

Works cited

Barber, Paul. 1988. *Vampires, Burial and Death: Folklore and Reality*. New Haven: Yale University Press.

Bentley, C.F. 1972. 'The Monster in the Bedroom: Sexual Symbolism in Bram Stoker's *Dracula*'. *Literature and Psychology* 22, 27–34.

Bond, John. 1753. *An Essay on the Incubus, or Nightmare*. London: Wilson and Durham.

Brodie, R.J. & Co. 1845. *The Secret Companion, a Medical Work on Onanism or Self-Pollution*. London: Brodie.

Caesarius of Heisterbach. 1929. *The Dialogue of Miracles*. 2 vols. Trans. H. Von E. Scott and C.C. Swinton Bland. London: Routledge, Vol 1.

[Cooke, F.] A Physician. 1871. *Satan in Society*. Chicago: Vent.

Craft, Christopher. 1989. '"Kiss Me With Those Red Lips": Gender and Inversion in Bram Stoker's *Dracula*'. In Elaine Showalter, ed. *Speaking of Gender*. London: Routledge, 216–42.

Curtis, J.L. 1840. *Manhood; the Causes of its Premature Decline with Direction for its Perfect Restoration*. London.

Dawson, Dr. 1845. *An Essay on Marriage*. London: Hughes.

Frayling, Christopher. 1991. *Vampyres, Lord Byron to Count Dracula*. London: Faber.

Gilbert, Arthur N. 1980. 'Masturbation and Insanity: Henry Maudsley and the Ideology of Sexual Repression'. *Albion* 12, 269–82.

Hall, Lesley. 1995. *The Facts of Life: The Creation of Sexual Knowledge in Britain, 1650–1950*. New Haven: Yale University Press.

Hammond, W.A. 1862. *A Treatise on Spermatorrhoea*. London: Hooper.

Hare, E.H. 1962. 'Masturbatory Insanity: The History of an Idea'. *Journal of Mental Science* 108, 1–25.

Henery, A.F. 1861. *Manly Vigour: The Art of Preserving, Improving and Recovering It*. London: n.p.

Howe, Samuel Grindley. 1848. 'Self-Abuse'. Supplement to the *Report Made to the Legislature of Massachusetts, Upon Idiocy*. Boston: Collidge and Wiley.

Jones, Ernest. 1931. *On the Nightmare*. London: Hogarth Press.

Jordanova, Ludmilla. 1987. 'The Popularization of Medicine: Tissot on Onanism'. *Textual Practice* 2, 68–79.

Lallemand, Claude. 1851. *On the Causes, Symptoms, and Treatment of Spermatorrhoea*. English Translation. London: John Churchill.

La'Mert, Samuel, M.D. 1852. *Self-Preservation: A Medical Treatise on the Secret Infirmities and Disorders of the Generative Organs, resulting from solitary habits, youthful excess, or infection*. 47th edn. London: La'Mert.

Laquer, Thomas. 1992. *Making Sex: Body and Gender from the Greeks to Freud*. Cambridge, MA: Harvard University Press.

Le Fanu, J. Sheridan. 1872. 'Carmilla'. In Alan Ryan, ed. *The Penguin Book of Vampire Stories*. London: Penguin, 1987, 71–137.

Macdonald, R.H. 1967. 'The Frightful Consequences of Onanism: Notes on the History of a Delusion'. *Journal of the History of Ideas* 28, 423–31.

Marryat, Florence. 1897. *The Blood of the Vampire*. London: Hutchinson.

Mason, Michael. 1994. *The Making of Victorian Sexuality*. Oxford: Oxford University Press.

Ollier, Edmund. 1855. 'Vampyres'. *Household Words* 11, 39–43.

Perkowski, Jan L. 1989. *The Darkling: A Treatise on Slavic Vampirism.* Columbus: Slavica.

Perry, R. and L. 1847. *The Silent Friend: A Medical Work (With Observations on Onanism and its Baneful Results).* 3rd edn. London: Perry.

Polidori, John. 1819. 'The Vampyre'. In Alan Ryan, ed. *The Penguin Book of Vampire Stories.* London: Penguin, 1987, 7–24.

Robbins, Rossell Hope. 1959. *The Encyclopedia of Witchcraft and Demonology.* Middlesex: Hamlyn.

Rymer, James Malcolm. 1847. *Varney the Vampyre; or, The Feast of Blood.* London: E. Lloyd.

Spitz, René A. 1952. 'Authority and Masturbation: Some Remarks on a Bibliographical Investigation'. *Psychoanalytic Quarterly* 21, 490–527.

Stoker, Bram. 1897. *Dracula.* Ed. Maurice Hindle. London: Penguin, 1993.

Summers, Montague. Trans. 1930. *Demonolatry*, by Nicholas Remy. London: John Rodker.

Thomas, Keith. 1991. *Religion and the Decline of Magic.* London: Penguin.

Tissot, S.A. 1832. *A Treatise on the Diseases Produced by Onanism.* Trans. by 'A Physician'. New York: Collins and Hanny.

Wagner, Peter. 1983. 'The Veil of Science and Morality: Some Pornographic Aspects of the *Onania*'. *British Journal for Eighteenth-Century Studies* 6, 179–84.

Waller, John. 1816. *A Treatise on the Incubus, or Night-Mare, Disturbed Sleep, &c.* London: Cox.

Part III
America: states of instability

Chapter 7

American Gothic landscapes: the New World to Vietnam

Jeannette Idiart and Jennifer Schulz

The proliferation of proposed Amendments to the United States Constitution in recent years, particularly since the Republican Party regained control of both houses of Congress in 1994, brought tensions over the interpretation of this national narrative to the forefront of partisan politics. Informing debates over terms limits, welfare reform, and a balanced budget is the question of how much government the Constitution authorises. In the case of welfare reform, the debate circulates around the extent to which the government should intervene in the lives of individuals to ensure their equal access to the rights and protections of democracy. These questions regarding equality have demanded constant revision and reinterpretation of the document since its ratification. While the parties' competing attempts to revise the Constitution to reflect the framers' original intent have dominated the popular media, American Gothic literature reflects the 'haunted consciousness' of the nation: the awareness that at the heart of its governing text are contradictions that threaten to unveil American democracy as a fiction. These texts bring to the surface the repressed knowledge that the founding value of the Constitution, equality, is predicated on the exclusion of selected populations on the basis of race, gender and property. They reveal that embedded within the national narrative is the ideological construction of the inferior 'other' whose exclusion effects national solidarity. Charles Brockden Brown's *Edgar Huntly* (1799), Herman Melville's *Benito Cereno* (1855) and Francis Ford Coppola's *Apocalypse Now* (1979) all point to the fact that the Constitution is founded upon conflicting ideologies. They represent a clash of interpretations, historical moments of national division when these conflicts cannot be subsumed within a national narrative.

Charles Brockden Brown published his novel *Edgar Huntly* in 1799, more than a decade after the ratification of the Constitution and during the bitter presidential elections of 1800. The novel, one of the earliest in the American canon, was written in a political and social atmosphere saturated with the chilling rhetoric of national dissolution, civil war, and foreign and internecine invasion. Such hysterical rhetoric, first voiced during the Constitutional Congress of 1783, returned to haunt the public debate over the still-nebulous forms of government a decade later.

Indeed, the dissolution of the new republic became a very real possibility during the Whiskey Rebellion of 1794. Western settlers, frustrated by what they perceived as 'taxation without representation' by a distant and unresponsive government located in the eastern city of Philadelphia, threatened to secede. In his analysis of the Whiskey Rebellion, Stephen Ambrose writes, 'The rhetoric of the Whiskey Rebels was all but identical to the rhetoric of Sam and John Adams, Thomas Jefferson, and Patrick Henry. The logic of the rebellion was the logic of the Revolution – just as the ocean that separated England from America dictated that they should be two nations, so did the mountains separate the East from the West and dictate two nations' (Ambrose, 1997: 39). The Whiskey Rebellion brought to the surface the conflicting values of revolution and government that underpin the Constitution. This conflict threatened the document's ability to govern an expanding and therefore unstable geopolitical landscape.

Debates, generated by these conflicts and fears, became particularly vituperative during the late 1790s and the presidential campaigns of 1800 when there was rioting in the streets of the major cities of the new republic. Republicans and Federalists – the two major political factions which had formed at the time of the Constitutional Congress – bitterly contended over the interpretation and implementation of the Constitution. In short, the Federalists favoured a broad reading of the Constitution which allowed for a strong national government and championed this version of the document as the only adequate check on depraved human nature and, in the words of Edmund Randolph, delegate to the Constitutional ratification convention of Virginia, the 'unspeakable calamities which discord, faction, turbulence, war and blood have produced in other countries' (in Smith, 1980: 103). Yet the Federalists still voiced distinct fears about the efficacy of the Constitution. They wondered aloud whether a document could restrain what they perceived to be the anarchic impulses of the masses or the potential for disorder that an expanding frontier engendered, a threat that they regarded with special horror after reports of the bloody excesses of the French Revolution made their way across the Atlantic. In response to these threats, the Federalists implemented the Alien and Sedition Acts of 1798. This legislation restricted immigration and naturalisation and authorised the government to seize and deport aliens from countries in conflict with the United States. It also imposed fines and prison sentences for speaking or printing malicious or seditious opinions against the government, challenging the newly passed First Amendment to the Constitution that guaranteed freedom of speech (Smith, 1980: 266–7).

The Republicans, led by Thomas Jefferson, feared that Federalist schemes to fashion a sovereign national government from the Constitution and narrowly define the freedoms granted in the document would all too effectively quash the project of democratisation. For Jefferson, the project of democratisation was continuous with expansion of the frontier, with peopling the entire continent with a viable, private property owning, culturally homogeneous republican citizenry. The cultivation of the land and the cultivation of American subjects, Jefferson believed, were mutually constitutive processes. Native Americans, in Jefferson's vision, would also be subject to this process; as the wilderness turned into farmland, they would be transformed into yeoman farmers idealised in republican ideology. A centralised, all-powerful government would impede the organic process of citizen-making that westward expansion allowed.

Nevertheless, at the heart of both this Republican notion of citizen-making and the Federalist terror of anarchy of the masses was deep ambivalence over the possibility of codifying democracy and creating a coherent narrative of national consensus in the face of a changing landscape and populace. Charles Brockden Brown's *Edgar Huntly*, an epistolary novel self-consciously preoccupied with the instability of written documents, takes up such anxieties about the Constitution. The novel not only questions the ability of narrative to effect a coherent understanding but also warns of its power to awaken irrational impulses in its readers. In fact, the central character fears that a stolen cache of letters arguing for religious scepticism will find its way into circulation and 'communicate the poison when the antidote could not be administered' (Brown, 1799: 126). Edgar Huntly is terrified that the persuasive letters, without the counter-agent of opposing or alternative narratives, will exert a terrible power over the readers of them. In a strange reversal of the rationalist goals of the Constitution's framers and of Edgar Huntly's written attempts to make sense of the novel's strange events, these letters become a source of infection.

The novel opens with the eponymous hero writing a letter to his sweetheart, a letter that relates the drama surrounding her brother's death. Edgar prefaces his letter with the warning that 'the incidents and motives which it is designed to exhibit will be imperfectly revived and obscurely pourtrayed' (6). He is not sure that when he 'exhibits' the incidents and motives for Waldegrave's murder he will find an explanation for it. Indeed, one of the horrors Edgar recounts in his letter to Mary is that narratives, and in particular written documents, rather than create coherence, may instead foment madness. Indeed, Edgar's attempts to reconstruct narratively the past of a man he suspects of murder prove fruitless and, in fact, devastating. His failure echoes Federalist fears that narrative, and in particular the Constitution, cannot legislate the individual actions of a heterogeneous population.

Clithero, the man Edgar suspects of murder, is an Irish emigrant, a 'stranger, whose adventures and character, previously to his coming hither, were unknown' (14). Clithero's obscure origins automatically make him an object of suspicion and presumed guilt especially in a climate of intolerance and fear manifested in the Alien and Sedition Acts of 1798 which specifically targeted Irish immigrants. Clithero misinterprets Edgar's attempts to establish his guilt or innocence and instead reads them as attempts to re-establish his Old World identity as a murderer. Clithero cannot remake himself in the New World because he subscribes to the logic, shared, at least initially, by Edgar, that his past determines his identity. Once Edgar employs his rationalist methods of detection and finds him innocent of the murder, he resolves to save Clithero from his irrational and superstitious self-judgement. However, instead of acting as an agent of rationality and assimilation, Edgar, in pursuit of Clithero, loses himself and all vestiges of civilisation in the wilderness. These scenes lay bare the Federalist fear that the wilderness cannot be tamed, and in fact infects those who inhabit it with savagery. In this novel, the wilderness is a very real and physical threat (Edgar falls in a cave, is nearly eaten by a jaguar and almost drowns in a river) but it also functions as a metaphor for the 'otherness' – the unassimilability – of Native Americans and immigrants. Where the former reflect the wilderness in which they live, the latter, in effect, carry a wilderness within, manifesting in superstition, disease and anarchy.

Clithero, in his blatant madness, is too disruptive to be assimilated into both Edgar's rationalist narrative and into republican society and at the end of the novel drowns on his way to fulfil what he perceives to be his murderous fate. However, we are left with the more insidious problem in the character of Edgar Huntly. For Edgar's murderous rampage against the band of Native Americans he encounters in the wilderness – which he rationalises as necessity – eludes reason and justice. In fact, the more Edgar justifies his bloody and clumsy killing spree, the more clearly he emerges as Clithero's double. He begins to read his situation as predestined when he realises that the Native Americans that died at his hands were those who murdered his own family. Edgar resigns himself to the forces of fate when he asks 'Was I born to a malignant destiny, never tired of persecuting?' (178). By the end of the novel, Edgar has relinquished reason as a method for understanding and being understood and instead relies on the sympathy of his reader, in this case, his mentor Sarsefield. He tries to recoup his actions as those motivated by a 'misguided, indeed, but powerful benevolence' (281). Yet Sarsefield's final 'farewell' signals his disassociation from, rather than his sympathy with or understanding of, Edgar. The breeding, education and familiarity that they shared and that once created a sympathetic identification between Edgar and his mentor become unstable, made manifest in the moment in which Sarsefield misrecognises Edgar as a Native American 'other' and opens fire on him. This moment suggests that the changing social, cultural and physical landscape destabilises the conditions for understanding one another, rendering everyone 'other': unreadable, unpredictable and ungovernable.

Throughout the nineteenth century, writers continued to underscore the problems of trying to construct a national narrative in the face of this expanding landscape and diversifying populace, especially as the nation was poised to dissolve into Civil War. The influx of disruptive 'others', the result of expansion and the colonisation of 'foreign' populations into the United States, the slave trade and immigration, continued to challenge the narration of a coherent national identity. The Wilmot Proviso of 1850, which sought to ban slavery from newly acquired western territories, was essentially an attempt to inscribe upon the West the future (political, social, cultural and economic) identity of America: one that was free-labouring and white. The debate surrounding this legislation (which ultimately failed) instead highlighted the contradiction at the heart of the Constitution, specifically the ways that a full citizen and full person is in part constructed in contradistinction to the black slave who is granted only three-fifths personhood. This definition is both reflective and productive of an ideology wherein freedom is dependent on slavery, wherein the national narrative of democracy necessitates an 'other' who functions to level the differences between disparate populations of European immigrants. Historically, black Africans were forcibly imported as slaves to replace the system of indentured servitude. The dramatic cultural and physical differences of these slaves were employed in the ideological construction of essential difference and racial hierarchy. Such fictions provided fertile ground for nineteenth-century writers, who made visible the injustices inherent in American democracy that haunted the consciousness of the nation. In his 1850 novella *Benito Cereno*, Herman Melville dramatises the instability of these racial definitions and the dangerous misreadings they engendered.

Melville's tale of a slave mutiny set aboard a Spanish slaver in the middle of the Atlantic stages the drama of national dissolution within the framework of the international slave trade. Delano, the American captain who stumbles upon the ship in revolt, misreads the conspiracy by translating it through American racial ideology. Delano alternates between reading slaves on the Amistad through a Constitutional lens, which renders them not quite human, and a sentimental lens, which casts them in a cosy paternalistic light. In fact, the two readings come out of the same ideological justification for slavery: that it is the white man's Christian responsibility and burden to civilise the African savages. In either case, Delano cannot credit them with seizing control of the ship and staging an elaborate charade of a well-ordered slave ship under a powerful and scheming Spanish captain.

Delano casts the Spanish captain, Benito Cereno, as the true danger to Delano's own ship and person. However, the perceived threat of foreign invasion blinds Delano to the internal revolt on the slave ship – Delano constantly misreads the situation by overdetermining Benito Cereno's 'foreignness'. Delano locates this foreignness in the Spanish captain's ambiguous relationship to his slaves. Benito Cereno inconsistently maintains the boundaries between master and slave: on the one hand, he appears to give his slaves too many liberties (letting them strike white sailors with impunity), and on the other hand, he seems to crave the spectacle of his authority over them (he demands extravagant displays of obeisance from a former African king). This inconsistency threatens the racial hierarchy, making Delano's identification with Benito Cereno unstable. After all, the Middle Passage allowed European and American captains to establish their racial identification and international trade partnership over the bodies of the black slaves. Through his behaviour toward his slaves, Benito Cereno seems at least to betray this relationship, at worst to have designs on Delano's ship. When, in response to this threat, Delano contemplates 'relieving' the 'unfit' Benito Cereno of his command, Delano describes his actions as motivated by 'benevolence': 'There was a difference between the idea of

Don Benito's darkly preordaining Captain Delano's fate and Captain Delano's lightly arranging Don Benito's' (Melville, 1855: 60). The difference is figured in racial terms: dark versus light, and in Old World/New World dichotomies. Where Spanish imperialism is aligned with preordination and fate, evocative of Clithero's superstitious irrationalism, American expansionism becomes an exercise in rational beneficence. Delano thus assuages his anxieties of Benito Cereno's racial loyalties under the rubric of essential difference: 'How unlike are we made' (51). In Delano's eyes, Benito Cereno is not only 'foreign', he has become less than white.

However, after the slaves' conspiracy is unmasked and Delano's readings of the slaves are proven woefully inadequate, Delano works to reestablish his identification with Benito Cereno and the racial hierarchies upon which that identification depends. Specifically he works to replace his narrative of paternalism with that of white international solidarity against black aggression. Delano focuses on the final outcome of his defeat of the slaves which, to him, is emblematised in 'yon bright sun [that] has forgotten it all, and the blue sea and the blue sky… [that] have turned over new leaves' (103). To the naïvely optimistic Delano, the hierarchy of white over black and the harmonious relationship between Spaniard and American is safely naturalised once again.

If not for the 'shadow' that hangs over Benito Cereno, which he sums up in one word, 'The Negro': neither the gentle trade winds, nor the now-unrestrained alliance between him and Delano, nor the trial and execution of the slaves can erase the events of the revolt. The conspiracy, evidence of the intellect of the black man and against Social Darwinist ideology, cannot be naturalised, nor can it be recontained within the proliferation of legal documentation that attempts to narrativise the events. In the last paragraphs of the novel, the severed head of the leader of the conspiracy meets 'unabashed[ly] the gaze of the whites' and its ominous silence resonates beyond the clamouring legal depositions (104). Babo's head, silently facing down his white persecutors, evokes the slave uprisings in Haiti and Nat Turner's rebellion, and foreshadows the eruption of the Civil War just ten years after Melville's novel is published.

Babo's unabashed gaze forces the reader to examine the inequities embedded in the Constitution, which instead of ensuring the stable rule of white property owners, incited internal division. In the twentieth century the spectre of that disembodied head continues to haunt the consciousness of the nation. In the middle of the century, in the face of the Civil Rights movement, Cold War foreign policy deflected public attention onto a so-called 'Third World' that threatened collusion with the Soviet empire. The alien 'other' that required 'containment' was no longer a domestic population but were populations in the newly emergent Communist states in Latin American, Africa and Asia against whom the American people (black and white) could join forces. The ideology of America's civilising missions to 'make the world safe for democracy' fell apart, however, in Vietnam during the 1960s and 1970s. The loss of the war, while challenging the ideology, spurred the anxious proliferation of narratives that attempted to explain that loss, to conceal it and to mitigate it. So disillusioned was the American public by the United States's complicity in the senseless loss of life that documentation of this war continues to multiply and circulate in the 1990s. Recently former Defence Secretary Robert McNamara catalogued the mistakes he and the United States government made during the Vietnam War and laid out lessons for the future in his repentant memoir *In Retrospect*. *In Retrospect* is less a indictment than a plea to the American people to recognise the 'honest mistakes' the government made during the eleven-year siege of Vietnam.

His insistence on positing 'honest mistakes' suggests his conviction that there was a coherent game-plan to which the US government and the soldiers should have adhered. Further, he suggests that the 'honest mistake' was in not realising that the Vietnamese were not playing by the same rules. He locates this disjunction in the ways the Vietnamese and US governments interpreted actions and images during the conflict. In the summer of 1997, two years after the publication of *In Retrospect*, McNamara initiated a conference in Vietnam with American and Vietnamese historians, government officials, retired military officers and diplomats. The ostensible purpose of the conference was to collect documentary evidence that would help to locate and evaluate the 'honest mistakes' that both sides made in the war. McNamara wanted nothing less than to rewrite the history of the Vietnam War in accordance with his assumption that there was a logic to the war, that a coherent narrative exists – it just needed to be found. As David Shipler, in a recent *New York Times* article notes, 'The way McNamara examined his failure in Vietnam was to intellectualize it, diagnose it, pinpoint the variables that might have been revised' (Shipler, 1997: 32). This almost scientific approach is evocative of Edgar Huntly's belief that a rational historical narrative could function as a palliative for an incomprehensible past. McNamara hoped to arrive at his diagnosis by, as Shipler puts it, 'flushing information out of every hiding place' (34). Information, especially documentary evidence that the

Vietnamese have zealously guarded over the years, was the raw material with which he hoped to rewrite history. When the Vietnamese, instead of turning over the documents, offered their analysis, McNamara read their actions as uncooperative. They were not playing their part in the drama of meaning making, of which McNamara envisaged himself to be the author. Their part, clearly, was to provide the statistics, military orders and battle plans that McNamara could then mould into a history palatable to his American audience.

McNamara was also working against the less palatable representations of the Vietnam war that have proliferated in American culture since the war. The media, Hollywood, the government and individual testimonies have contributed to the profusion of contradictory and chaotic images of the war. These images, in their very denial of cause and effect logic, have actually precluded the 'logical' narrativisation of the war that McNamara seeks. As Susan Jeffords puts it in her analysis of Vietnam representation in contemporary American culture, these texts 'must be read, not as increasingly refined attempts to arrive at an explanation of the war, but as increasingly deferred logics that produce a (con)fusion from which explanation cannot occur' (Jeffords, 1989: 22).

One of the texts Jeffords includes in her analysis, Francis Ford Coppola's 1979 film *Apocalypse Now*, while participating in the project of imperialism, also dramatises and criticises the government's project of deferring logic. As Amy Kaplan has noted, while filming *Apocalypse Now* in the Philippines, Coppola relied on the US's military and economic dominance over its former colony, appropriating the landscape and the Philippine army as props and sets. Kaplan notes that 'The documentary on the making of the film... which stands awkwardly between an exposé and a publicity reel, refuses recognition of the film's complicity with the imperial context that enables its production' (Kaplan, 1993: 18). Yet, Coppola's incisive representation of covert and extra-legal government assignments reveals the elaborate machinations of the government that denied its own imperialist actions.

Early in the film a hungover Willard, on the verge of nervous breakdown, walks into his covert lunch meeting with CIA and Special Forces officials to receive his next assignment. 'Have you ever seen any of these men?' the commander asks him. Willard responds in the negative. This exchange, performed in front of and in reference to men for whom he initially registers recognition and who have probably sent him on his previous missions, tests and proves Willard's ability to misread the wholly legible, or deny recognition of the wholly recognisable. He likewise denies any knowledge of the last covert operation which he supposedly executed for the CIA. Despite, or perhaps because of, his visibly fragile physical and psychological state, Willard's programmed responses prove him fit for a mission that he cannot refuse. Indeed, how can Willard refuse an assignment that, like his last mission, 'does not exist, nor will it ever exist'? How can Willard act independently of a government that contradicts or erases all its own actions?

In fact, these government erasures underscore the more far-reaching blurring of distinctions between fact and fiction, between sane and insane, between friend and enemy, between soldier and murderer that this mission and that this war depended upon in order to preclude logical narration and dissent. Jeffords contrasts blurring with deconstruction in that 'rather than challenging the sufficiency of categories themselves ... blurring maintains oppositions by (con)fusing them' (Jeffords, 1989: 22). Willard's assignment is, in effect, to assassinate a hired assassin who has been charged with murder. There is a kind of arbitrariness to the government orders that resists cause-and-effect logic and thus any attempts at rational legislation of actions; as Willard puts it, 'charging a man with murder [in Vietnam] was like handing out speeding tickets at the Indy 500.' It is never clear where the line between murder and 'termination with extreme prejudice' is actually drawn. And Willard could just as easily be the next target for termination. Willard literally embodies the blurring that Jeffords describes; when his superior's messengers knock on his hotel room door, they could just as easily be there to arrest him as to give him his next assignment.

Like Willard, Kurtz, his target for termination, embodies the blurring in a way that threatens to backfire on the military. His 'unsound methods', as the military defines them – assuming a god-like reign over 'the natives', murdering at whim – are less acts of dissent than a kind of exaggerated fulfilment of his mission and rank, in fact, a perfected imperialism. After he planned and executed his first mission, the press reconstructed what the army deemed a crime into a heroic action and circulated Kurtz throughout the United States as a model of patriotism. So when Willard reads Kurtz's dossier as he travels up the Nyong River to carry out his mission, he is once again forced to misread the wholly legible. For the documents within the dossier provide what seems to be a bullet-proof narrative of the perfect soldier, endorsed at every step of the way by the US military, posterboy for the American public. Yet, Willard, in order to fulfil his mission, must read Kurtz's accomplishments as symptoms of madness. Kurtz's actions must either be subsumed within the fictions of order, coherence and patriotism collected in the dossier, or he must be erased completely. As Willard travels further up the river into Cambodia, and outside the 'legal' geographic boundaries of the war, the dossier, like the landscape, ceases to signify. Kurtz's exemplary resumé can mean anything and nothing out of context: depending upon the mission and the place where it is played out, Kurtz can be either a hero or criminal. The dossier functions as more than just another source of dissonance for the disoriented Willard; the dossier demonstrates the ways in which documents, images, artefacts and statistics produced by the war and employed by the government created the semblance of logic and meaning, actually deferring the narration of the war and thus perpetuating the illogical and random violence in Vietnam.

One of the major themes of the 1997 conference in Vietnam was the misreading of 'images' on both sides and how those misreadings shaped policy and action. The US government, for example, misread the political geography of Vietnam as a microcosm of Cold War politics and therefore drew a national boundary between the Communist North and the 'Democratic' South. The Vietnamese read their political geography through a nationalist lens and located the threat in foreign domination rather than in internal political division. The US misread the nationalism that drove Ho Chi Minh's movement; the Vietnamese underestimated the anti-Communist fear that drove US foreign (and domestic) policy (Shipler, 1997: 34). As the government officials in the film ask Willard to misinterpret Kurtz's dossier, so too did the US government ask the public to misread the images produced by and productive of the War.

In *In Retrospect*, McNamara sadly admits that he measured the progress of the war by enemy 'body counts' and asked the public to do the same. Prior to the 1997 conference McNamara conceded that 'body counts' were a false measure of success or failure in the face of both the Vietnamese indifference to their staggering casualties and the American public's demand for withdrawal in response to the unacceptably high number of American casualties. McNamara rationalised, 'There were some people to whom life was not the same as to us.' General William Westmoreland, commander of US forces in Vietnam, seconded McNamara's assessment of the Vietnamese indifference to death, when he fiercely maintained, 'We did not lose a single battle against those people...they defeated us psychologically' (in Shipler, 1997: 33). Although Westmoreland and McNamara have radically different views of the outcome of the war, they agree that the US withdrew because Americans value life more highly than do the Vietnamese. Their readings of the war ultimately depend on racist ideology which renders the Vietnamese less than human. This ideological undercurrent ran through McNamara's assessments of the 1997 conference in Hanoi. He called the conference on the pretext that 'Human beings have to examine their failures' (in Shipler, 1997: 30). When the Vietnamese did not cooperate with this standard of humanity by enumerating their own failures, McNamara simply took their resistance to his plan as evidence of their inhuman 'otherness'. Where he was frustrated in his attempts to construct a new, acceptable historical narrative, McNamara defaulted to essentialist explanations. These explanations come to stand in for history: in reference to his belief that the Vietnamese did not care about their dead, he cautions, 'we better understand that and write it down' (in Shipler, 1997: 50).

Prior to the 1997 conference, McNamara lamented that US foreign policy makers do not understand their opponents, 'We don't understand the Bosnians, we don't understand the Chinese and we don't really understand the Iranians' (in Shipler, 1997: 32). After the 1997 conference McNamara came to the conclusion that what we need to 'understand' is that the Vietnamese, the Chinese, the Bosnians and the Iranians cannot be understood. Their essential difference renders them unknowable and precludes rational negotiations with the United States. His insistence on 'writing it down' suggests that a 'lesson' can be drawn from this understanding. McNamara's project points to a willingness, on the part of some of those who directly resisted narrativisation of the war, to find a lesson, a portable narrative to apply to future foreign policy. So effective are these 'lessons' that they have been instituted again and again as domestic policy. From the Alien and Sedition Acts of 1798 to the anti-immigration legislation throughout the twentieth century (most recently, Proposition 209 in California), alien unknowable 'others' have been marked as internal threats to national stability.

The process of constructing a national narrative in the United States has been marked by a constant return of the repressed contradictions at the heart of its founding text. Our very political process is haunted by the conditions of its inception, by the irrational and repressed prejudices that underpin it. American Gothic literature offers counternarratives to the official stories. The American Gothic is not simply an aesthetic or psychoanalytic category but an unofficial political history and a methodology for hearing the voices of dissent that interrupt narratives of national consensus.

Works cited

Ambrose, Stephen. 1997. *Undaunted Courage: Meriwether Lewis, Thomas Jefferson, and the Opening of the American West*. New York: Simon and Schuster.

Brown, Charles Brockden. 1799. *Edgar Huntly: Or, Memoirs of a Sleep-walker*. New York: Penguin, 1988.

Coppola, Francis Ford. 1979. *Apocalypse Now*. Zoetrope.

Jeffords, Susan. 1989. *The Remasculinization of American Culture: Gender and the Vietnam War*. Bloomington: Indiana University Press.

Kaplan, Amy. 1993. '"Left Alone With America": The Absence of Empire in the Study of American Culture'. In *Cultures of United States Imperialism*. Ed. Amy Kaplan and Donald Pease. Durham, NC: Duke University Press.

McNamara, Robert, with Brian VanDeMark. 1995. *In Retrospect: The Tragedy and Lessons of Vietnam*. New York: Random House.

Melville, Herman. 1855. *Benito Cereno*. New York: Dover, 1990.

Shipler, David. 1997. 'Robert McNamara Meets the Enemy'. *New York Times Magazine*, 10 August .

Smith, Page. 1980. *The Shaping of America: A People's History of the Young Republic*. Vol. 3. New York: McGraw-Hill.

Chapter 8

Gothic numbers in the new republic: *The Federalist* No. 10 and its spectral factions

Helen F. Thompson

Representing faction: Gothic parts

In the 1835 translation of the first volume of *Democracy in America*, Alexis de Tocqueville states:

> Fetters and headsmen were the coarse instruments that tyranny formerly employed; but the civilization of our age has perfected despotism itself, though it seemed to have nothing to learn. Monarchs had, so to speak, materialized oppression; the democratic republics of the present day have rendered it as entirely an affair of the mind as the will which it is intended to coerce. Under the sway of one man the body was attacked in order to subdue the soul... Such is not the course adopted by tyranny in democratic republics; there the body is left free, and the soul is enslaved.
>
> (de Tocqueville, 1835: 274)

In its dramatic inversion of body and soul, de Tocqueville's assessment of republican tyranny justifies the inclusion of *The Federalist* paper No. 10 in the present volume. Republican tyranny, in de Tocqueville's account, works upon the matter of the soul, rendering the 'coarse instruments' of absolutism irrelevant to the uncanny scenario of free bodies and enslaved minds. The instrument that would displace the monarch – the newly non 'materialized' bogeyman of de Tocqueville's republic – is, of course, the majority. In this essay, I will pursue this immaterial majority as it is imagined in an earlier text, one that necessarily promotes it: James Madison's *Federalist* No. 10, written in 1787 to endorse the ratification of the American Constitution despite the gap between an expanding population and a small representative body.

Madison, in defusing his readers' concerns about the development of factions in the new union, envisages a subtilised form of representation that anticipates the rhetorical co-ordinates of de Tocqueville's account. It is, in particular, the mathematics of factionality – the equivocal relation of faction to the terms 'majority' and 'minority' – that makes Madison's text a suggestive precedent to the event of ratification that would, for de Tocqueville, drive the ghostliness of the new union deep into the American political unconscious.[1]

I will read *The Federalist* No. 10 as the infrastructural or quantitative imagining of republican majority. Because this majority is for Madison, as for de Tocqueville, not 'materialized', the mathematics it projects are obviously improper: their more evocative counterpart will be a spectral part of the union's body, which incarnates as phantasmatic predilection Madison's fantastic math. The pivotal idiosyncrasy of that maths occurs in Madison's definition of faction:

> By a faction I understand a number of citizens, whether amounting to a majority or minority of the whole, who are united and actuated by some common impulse of passion, or of interest, adverse to the rights of other citizens, or to the permanent and aggregate interests of the community.
>
> (Madison, 1787: 886)

Even though a faction is composed of a 'number of citizens', that number is qualified not by its relation to a larger whole but by its 'interest'. A faction, in other words, is *either* a 'majority or minority of the whole', its distinctness from the body of the entire community conceivable only as adverse 'passion'. Madison invokes a deviating number of citizens, indifferently proportional to the union as a whole. The peculiarity of this definition inheres in its insistence that the relation of one 'number of citizens' to a group of 'other citizens' can be thematised (as deviant) without being quantified: that Madison's invocation of standardising rights denies any relation to a consensus imagined in numbers.

Madison would be the first to concede that factionality – or, more specifically, a union's 'propensity to this dangerous vice' (886) – cannot simply be wished away. This is because factionality is the marker of both a deviant interest and an aptitude that republican government wants to protect:

> As long as the connection subsists between [man's] reason and his self-love, his opinions and his passions will have a reciprocal

influence on each other; and the former will be objects to which the latter will attach themselves. The diversity in the faculties of men from which the rights of property originate, is not less an insuperable obstacle to a uniformity of interests. The protection of these faculties is the first object of Government. From the protection of different and unequal faculties of acquiring property, the possession of different degrees and kinds of property immediately results: and from the influence of these on the sentiments and views of the respective proprietors, ensues a division of the society into different interests and parties. (887)

I have, in fact, cited the *two* causes of faction provided by Madison: first, the distorting effects of self-love upon an ideally dispassionate reason; and, second, the 'diversity in the faculties of men' from which the 'first object of Government' proceeds. Faction would, then, impose upon the abstract ground of republican consensus (reason, and a uniformity of interests) two apparently symmetrical expressions of the real: self-love and property. Feelings of self-love 'attach themselves', with almost fleshly insistence, to rational political opinion; property would map upon the mutualising force of the social contract the palpable distractions of class. Yet Madison adds a final twist to the protracted cause-and-effect logic that defines the latter category. He cites 'the possession of different degrees and kinds of property', faction's most obviously material incentive, in the capacity of an 'influence', one bringing about, finally, the divergent 'sentiments and views of the respective proprietors'. It may seem pedantic to insist that, perhaps only by some tic of grammatical order, the imagined trajectory of class faction ends in the domain not of material difference but of differing 'sentiments': this is, however, the last moment in Madison's text where he will, even in passing, solicit the Lockean imagining of differently-sized parcels of land (or money).[2] As such, Madison's final turn to sentiment brings us to the unquantifiable factions cited above. Indeed, not only does this final cause of faction cease to imagine difference as real, it leaves unthematised the even *more* real parts of the future union not in possession of the 'faculties' that serve to delimit the range of potentially countable citizens, parts like, for example, women, who are neither quantifiable nor prone to the subjectivising effects of self-interest. I will return to this other real – a real even more real than the property that asserts itself as sentiment – below.

    Like a deviating interest, property is unquantifiable. Thus it comes, perhaps, as less of a surprise to find Madison's example of factionality in action weighted against the apparent mandate of the majority: 'measures are too often decided, not according to the rules of justice, and the rights of the minor party; but by the superior force of an interested and over-bearing majority' (886). It is easy to imagine, keeping Madison's discussion of the faculties of acquisition in mind, who might comprise this 'minor party' (the few with, perhaps, the most to lose); but such speculation is not the immediate (Gothic) interest of this passage. In his designation of an 'interested and over-bearing majority', Madison seems to anticipate the terms of de Tocqueville's tyranny, positing, in the face of a ubiquitous tendency towards self-love and interest, the minority as the faction that alone remains untainted. This is an important possibility of Madison's text, because it engages with a particularly ghostly aspect of the political imaginary informing his argument: the notion of virtual representation. I will turn to this notion because it so explicitly arises from Madison's emphatic attempts to de-quantify the meaning of faction, and because, in dismissing virtual representation later in his text, Madison will formulate the central compromise of *The Federalist* No. 10.

Virtual representation is well defined by Edmund Burke in his letter to Sir Hercules Langrishe:

> Virtual representation is that in which there is a communion of interests and a sympathy in feelings and desires between those who act in the name of any description of people and the people in whose name they act, though the trustees are not actually chosen by them. This is virtual representation. Such a representation I think to be in many cases even better than the actual … it corrects irregularities of literal representation, when the shifting current of human affairs or the acting of public interests in different ways carry it obliquely from its first line of direction.
>
> (Burke, 1894: 293)[3]

The benefit of virtual representation as asserted by Burke – its undeviating fidelity to the 'first line of direction', the public good – is a function of its *lack* of proximity to the people in whose name the representative acts. By restricting the franchise, severing the connection of those who act and those in whose name they act, virtual representation would assure that the interests of the unenfranchised majority are served by a disinterested minority. This is a notion of government whose reception in the American colonies is charted by Bernard Bailyn, who states that,

144 Helen F. Thompson

far from being in a position to embrace it, the colonists had

> drifted backward, as it were, toward the medieval forms of attorney-
> ship in representation ... The colonial towns and counties, like their
> medieval counterparts, were largely autonomous, and they stood to
> lose more than they were likely to gain from a loose acquiescence in
> the action of central government.
>
> (Bailyn, 1967: 64)

Indeed, American colonists like James Otis were capable of invoking
political representation as precisely the 'literal' or 'actual' function left
unqualified by Burke: 'every man, woman, boy, girl, child, infant, cow,
horse, hog, dog, and cat who *now* live, or ever *did* live, or ever *shall* live
in this province are fully, freely, and sufficiently represented in this
present glorious and august Provincial Congress' (in Bailyn, 1967: 172).

In his exhaustive inclusion of every imaginable 'man, woman, boy,
girl, child, infant, cow, horse, hog, dog, and cat' in the representative
operations of the Provincial Congress, Otis would, rhetorically at
least, iterate the proximity of representation to its referents. To a dematerialised, imaginary consensus like that later invoked by de
Tocqueville, this vision opposes the inextricability of congress and the
bodies it stands for. Otis counters Burkean 'sympathy' with an index
whose taxonomic materiality would necessarily include the body of the
representative himself. Yet Otis's rhetoric, penned in 1765, is as fantastic
as Burke's: if Burke would posit a virtual 'communion' that does away
with the need to enlarge the franchise, Otis's vision of women, children
and animals clearly also dissolves that franchise's real limits, projecting
instead the comically microscopic realisation of what Bailyn has called
'the active and continuous consent of the governed' (Bailyn, 1967: 172).

In 1787, Madison must defuse the Antifederalist attack upon centralised government – an attack most frequently couched in opposition
to the elitist or even aristocratic pretences of virtual representation –
without recourse to language like that of either Burke or Otis.[4] The
Burkean vision was, as Bailyn suggests, an ideological and a real irri-
tant provoking the colonists' rejection of their would-be representatives in England; the rhetoric employed by Otis, however, comes too
close to popular government, precisely that source of faction whose
instability and unruliness Madison would counter in the new Union.
Madison clearly addresses these alternatives, first flatly rejecting virtual
representation's central fiction: 'It is in vain to say, that enlightened
statesmen will be able to adjust these clashing interests, and render

them all subservient to the public good. Enlightened statesmen will not always be at the helm' (Madison, 1787: 888). Popular government is even less recoupable: 'a pure Democracy, by which I mean, a Society, consisting of a small number of citizens, who assemble and administer the Government in person, can admit of no cure for the mischiefs of faction...there is nothing to check the inducements to sacrifice the weaker party, or an obnoxious individual' (888-9). Madison will, inevitably, imagine a compromise, whereby representation is neither purely virtual nor purely actual:

> It must be confessed, that in this, as in most other cases, there is a mean, on both sides of which inconveniences will be found to lie. By enlarging too much the number of electors, you render the representative too little acquainted with all their local circumstances and lesser interests; as by reducing it too much, you render him unduly attached to these, and too little fit to comprehend and pursue great and national objects. The Federal Constitution forms a happy combination in this respect.
>
> (Madison, 1787, 888-90)

Madison's 'mean' is, fundamentally, a mediation of Burke's mystified sympathy and Otis's cats, dogs, cows, hogs and women. The Madisonian statesman would exactly mediate between a diffuse and an imminent electorate, a constituency that is not-him (he has no corrupting interests) and one that is (he is on Otis's list); he would accommodate the local (cats and dogs) without diverging from the national (the union's first line of direction). The interest of Madison's mean to the present essay inheres in its negotiation of, at bottom, the virtual and the actual – and, again, in its unquantifiable mathematics. A 'mean' should make numerical sense, but this one cannot: Madison's 'happy combination' cannot be (really) in-between the large and the small because, as we have seen, the terms that would designate those proportions of the union claim their significance only as deviant passion. Madison's mean has no real meaning; I return, then, to the language of faction in *The Federalist* No. 10, to evoke the irresolution of actual and virtual that generates such an unmeaning mean.

The most suggestive description of faction in *The Federalist* No. 10 occurs, again, as Madison attempts to reconcile popular and virtual attributes of government:

> If a faction consists of less than a majority, relief is supplied by the republican principle, which enables the majority to defeat its sinister

views by regular vote: it may clog the administration, it may con-
vulse the society; but it will be unable to execute and mask its
violence under the forms of the Constitution. When a majority is
included in a faction, the form of popular government on the other
hand enables it to sacrifice to its ruling passion or interest, both the
public good and the rights of other citizens. To secure the public good,
and private rights, against the danger of such a faction, and at the
same time to preserve the spirit and the form of popular government,
is then the great object to which our enquiries are directed. (888)

Perhaps the most pressing observation to be made about this set of
equations is that minority factions have no (imaginable claim to)
rights. A minority faction can only be 'sinister', an equivalence which
allows it to be flushed from the administrative workings of popular
government's best-case scenario. Let us play out the logic of this passage. When Madison's maths is straightforward, and a faction is equivalent to a minority, he is able to invoke the 'republican principle' as a
source of relief from its constipative effects and the nameless 'violence'
that threatens to accompany them. While here mathematics confirm
that the 'sinister' be safely forestalled by the 'regular', in the case of a
majority faction Madison can only imagine the gratification of sinister
passion at the expense of the slighter body of the public good, a viola-
tion sanctioned by the literal equivalencies of popular government.
Presumably, the spectre of such a 'sacrifice' amply illustrates the monstrosity of popular government – at least to those friends of a well-
constructed Union who do not want to find themselves struggling
against the heavy body of popular opinion. As I suggest above, Madison
drains majority and minority of their numerical sense, leaving the
sinister and the regular as their only index of relevance to the public
good; indeed, even the barest embodiment, the additive tallies that
register the interests of popular government, provides that public good
with no prophylactic against the majority's passion. For the public
good to remain untouched by factionality, Madison's arithmetic cannot register the interest of the majority as anything other than a
passion whose depravities are off the scale of the natural numbers (as
they are called), whose sinister desires cannot be added up.

   The implicit violence of this passage varies greatly from the later,
more abstractly paranoid, tyranny of the majority as imagined by de
Tocqueville.[5] At the same time, however, Madison's scenario is also semi-
spectral, in so far as the majority are never fully embodied in his text:
it might then materialise as most of the body of the union, quantifiable,

if not in number, then in obvious bulk. Such a body might, theoretically at least, be able to wrest the meaning of the central, mystified term in Madison's text – the public good – from the weaker grasp of the minority (indeed, from the grasp of Madison himself). Madison's metaphorics of contagion – of convulsive violence and mortal disease – occupy a peculiarly unstable relation to the views he repeatedly qualifies as sinister and 'secret' (890), throwing into relief, despite himself, the problematic substance of a majority faction. If a majority faction can never be (most of) a body, it might, instead, be more happily imaginable as a sinister and secretive body part, one that can be excised from the union. Let us take as a possibility the organ obliquely solicited in Madison's transition from majority to minority in the above passage, 'on the other hand'. This might fortuitously indicate the appendage in which even the grossest proportion of popular passion can be localised and removed from the new union. (Sinister is, of course, 'left' in Latin; the OED adds 'situated on the left side of the body; lying on or towards the left hand; astray from the right path'.) As a presumably useless (even illiterate) hand, a hand whose irrational embodiment opposes it to the right (writing) one, and thus possibly even a self-loving hand, this body part can be imaginatively amputated from the union to ensure the unimpeded progress of the public good. At the same time, however, the left hand inevitably figures the almost-indistinguishability of sinister demands from right ones. It offers both the spectral possibility of an uncorrupted union and portends the vulnerability of Madison's public good to some other, inalienable grasp.

Madison's text cannot unequivocally imagine the excision of faction from the union. If sinister desires added up to body parts, a majority faction would survive the operation: the minority's definition of the public good would, instead, find itself vestigial to government's larger, deviant remainder. Thus sinister faction might, instead, be figured as a suspect appendage, representing a predilection and not a finite number of bodies. The amputation of one sinister organ is the corrective to a Gothic mathematics that can never quite count all of its members.

Madison closes his text with the far more concrete representation of a body's sinister part:

> The influence of factious leaders may kindle a flame within their particular States, but will be unable to spread a general conflagration through the other States: a religious sect, may degenerate into a political faction in a part of the Confederacy; but the variety of sects dispersed over the entire face of it, must secure the national Councils

against any danger from that source: a rage for paper money, for an abolition of debts, for an equal division of property, or for any other improper or wicked project, will be less apt to pervade the whole body of the Union, than a particular member of it; in the same proportion as such a malady is more likely to taint a particular county or district, than an entire State.

In the extent and proper structure of the Union, therefore, we behold a Republican remedy for the diseases most incident to Republican Government. (890)

The most striking aspect of this summation is its movement between an imagining of faction as virtualising 'conflagration', a 'taint' that 'pervades' the matter of the union, and an imagining of faction as local and localisable, a discrete 'part' or 'member' remote from the interests of the national council. This is the adjudication of the virtual and the actual prescribed in Madison's math. Faction would be withstood by the disinterested statesman who best knows what is right for the nation; at the same time, it materialises in a 'variety of' small bodies 'dispersed over the entire face of' the union, whose conflicting demands efface each other, leaving the blankness of a public good that no body (except Madison) really knows or wants. The states and localities whose 'wicked and improper projects' – including the 'equal division of property', which would, ironically, neutralise faction as Madison has defined it – would cancel each other out are, then, something like a host of hands working at cross purposes. In their deviating and improper interests, the states are the left hand(s) of Madison's union. They add up to nothing: nothing, that is, but the final spectre of the public good. Madison's concluding 'therefore' would finesse this spectral logic. The future union's 'extent', the matter of Madison's 'Republican remedy', is an extent whose parts cannot be summed, whose states, far from making up the public good, loosen each other's hold upon it. It remains for de Tocqueville, over forty years later, to resolve these states into a phantom majority, the extent of whose passions can only be calculated in the spread of Gothic numbers.

Theorising union: Gothic wholes

I have suggested above that *The Federalist* No. 10, in its attempts to mediate between actual and virtual forms of representation, constitutes an infrastructural imagining of American consensus. Forty-eight years later, de Tocqueville gives a vividly reified depiction of that consensus.

In this second section of my essay, I will suggest that two other, contemporary, accounts of America's self-ratification are predicated upon an agency that is as reified, and as ghostly, as that imagined by de Tocqueville. In their stress upon the abstracted assent constituting the new nation, these accounts neglect Madison's imagined recombination of actual and virtual. Such neglect would turn modern political subjects into spectres, rather than the less easily qualified beings suggested in Madison's text. In the ambivalence of its attempt to reconcile local passion with national extent, *The Federalist* No. 10 opens a wide (and equally ambivalent) field of possibilities for our present-day imaginings of national *and* – at the same time – local subjecthood.

In *Democracy in America*, de Tocqueville offers the following definition of the terms majority and minority: 'A majority taken collectively is only an individual, whose opinions, and frequently whose interests, are opposed to those of another individual, who is styled a minority' (de Tocqueville, 1945: 269). Strikingly, he effaces these terms' quantitative meanings to posit each of them as a single, unified agent: even more strongly than in Madison's evocation of uncountable numbers of citizens, de Tocqueville levels the real difference between majority and minority, positing instead differences of opinion held by two 'individuals'. This would, on the one hand, seem to reflect de Tocqueville's assessment of modern, un-'materialized', sociality; on the other, however, he suppresses precisely what might seem to make the tyranny of the majority different from that of a king, the diffuse, random particulateness that resists focalisation in a single body. Here, for an account of mathematics that speaks of a roughly contemporaneous cultural moment, we might turn to Michel Serres's discussion of the transition from geometry to thermodynamics, from visible, transcribable lines of force to the fields of heat and cold driving the engines of industrialisation.[6] Michel Foucault, speaking more directly about political force, is equally insistent that modern power is non-geometric: the 'new physics of power', which postdates the monarch, requires, he states, 'mechanisms that analyse distributions, gaps, series, combinations... a physics of a relational and multiple power' (Foucault, 1979: 208).[7] De Tocqueville's insistence upon the majority and minority as 'only' individuals would seem to belie these later historicising accounts: they amplify de Tocqueville's obvious simplification of political causality, his suppression of the stochastic variables that might constitute modern political agency in favour of counters that can (still) be mapped in opposition to each other. Anchored to a geometric point, de Tocqueville's majority would be in one place at the same time that it is everywhere and nowhere. The ghost haunting his text is that of both the monarch and the 'individual' who cannot really take the monarch's place.

De Tocqueville's definition of the majority is unified precisely in the face of the disintegration of kingly force that would render such unity obsolete. Even more significantly, de Tocqueville's imagining of the majority is far more coherent than Madison's. Madison's text registers the difficulty of accommodating a majority faction within a minority vision of public good – a difficulty that, despite itself, surfaces in his argument as one of stubbornly physical consensus; de Tocqueville, in no longer referencing the figurative equivalence of a majority and a large number of people, avoids this tension between the virtual and the actual. In its abstracted but still geometric integrity, de Tocqueville's majority claims a kind of virtual unity, leaving far behind Madison's laboured reconciliation of cats, dogs, women and disinterested (we might even say disembodied) statesmen.

I will now briefly turn to two contemporary assessments of the union: one, Jacques Derrida's reflections upon the signing of the American Declaration of Independence; the other, Michael Warner's related discussion of the ratification of the Constitution.[8] These accounts are of interest here because they thematise precisely the novel paradox of de Tocqueville's dematerialised but geometric majority: virtual unity. Indeed, both are concerned with what could be called the textual mechanics of virtual unity, the phantasmatic inclusivity of a set of documents opposed, in theory, to nobody. If Madison's, and later de Tocqueville's, visions of the power of the majority derive their sinister interest from the weakness of the minority (or, for Madison, of the public good), Derrida and Warner envisage a consensus that would already include everybody, whose sinisterness resides not in superior force but, instead, in rhetorical or textual effect. Recalling Madison's unquantifiable majorities and minorities, we could say that Derrida and Warner explore the textual event of unquantifiable union: they each deal in a mathematics whose smallest unit is the indissoluble assent of a whole nation.

Derrida expresses his interest in the Declaration in the terms of speech-act theory, which distinguishes between constative statements (like those making up a scientific text, 'whose essential value must be dissociable from its author and thus proves its objectivity') and performative ones (like a vow of marriage or the founding of an institution, which presumes an 'individual or collective subject' whose intentions are actualised in speech) (Derrida, 1984: 16–17). The difference between constative (authorless) and performative (authored)

statements collapses, for Derrida, in the event of the Declaration's signing: are the 'good people' referenced in their representatives' signatures
really already free – 'and only affirm that emancipation in the
Declaration' – or, rather, do they 'liberate themselves in the instant and
by the signature of this Declaration?' (20). The crucial undecidability
between constative and performative statements – which has been
stressed by J.L. Austin in terms of the finally performative nature of
what would be objective truth (and, for that matter, objective freedom)[9] – is here exposed in the 'good people' who would both describe
and declare themselves free. These good people are, of course, *themselves* the ultimate referent constituted from the play of redundancy
and novelty. As Derrida states, 'But this people does not exist. ... The
signature invents the signer. The latter can only authorize itself to sign
when it has reached the last letter, so to speak, of its signature, by a
sort of fabulous retroactivity' (22). The Declaration's signatures, then,
constitute a fabulous performative because only at their ends do they
reference truth (as freedom).

This twinned act of erasure and inscription 'dissolves the lines of
colonial paternity or maternity' at the same moment that it founds
'the signature of each American citizen' (24). Derrida deconstructs
its independence by exposing its necessary audience: 'One can understand this Declaration as a vibrant act of faith, as an indispensable
hypocrisy ... so that this declaration has a meaning *and* an effect, it
must have a final hearing. God is the name, the best, for this last hearing and this ultimate signature' (27). Most interesting here, in the context of the faculties of acquiring property that Madison's *Federalist*
paper defends, are the possibilities of either good or bad faith opened
by Derrida's designation of 'indispensable hypocrisy'. Yet these cannot,
without diverting Derrida from phenomena of grammar to those of
demography, crack the seamless mutuality of this 'vibrant act': indeed,
that vibrant act of faith, that indispensable hypocrisy, retroactively
effects unity itself, in so far as 'each American citizen' would, even
now, find his or her own signature inevitably contributing to the constitutive incoherence of self-reference and self-legitimation.

Michael Warner's discussion of the Constitution builds upon Derrida's
reading: here, however, Warner is concerned not with the event of the
signature, but the medium of print, which diverges crucially from that
of writing in the abstractness and the mechanical reproducibility of
its inclusive claims. Warner states: 'whereas the climactic moment for
the Declaration of Independence was the signing, for the Constitution
the climactic moment was the maneuver that deprived signing of any

personal meaning... The Constitution's printedness allows it to emanate from no one in particular, and thus from the people' (Warner, 1990: 107–8). Thus, if Derrida's citizen affirms his or her Americanness in signing his or her name, Warner's does so in reading the printed pronoun 'we'. The passage in which Warner describes this effect proceeds:

> In the preamble the reading citizen interpellates himself – even herself – into the juridical order precisely at its foundation... Not only does it [the consumption of the preamble in print] enact the consent of every citizen – male and female, old and young, black and white, rich and poor – it also reads that consent as the transcendent grounds of subjection... There is no legitimate representational space outside the constitutive we. (111–12)

'Male and female, old and young, black and white, rich and poor' is reminiscent of, if not even *more* deliberately inclusive than, Otis's cats, dogs, cows, hogs, children and women. Yet the rhetorical directions of the two passages are utterly at odds. Otis would, in listing all these distinct bodies, suggest that the Provincial Congress occupies the same level of resolution as the quotidian particulars of the governed. Warner, however, lists all these types of citizen to assert the abstracting capacities of the Constitutional 'we'. In Otis's account, the congressman is coextensive with the bodies that he represents; in Warner's, he is as unlocalisable as 'every citizen' who integrates him or herself into 'the juridical order' through the consumption of print. Indeed, the illegitimate 'representational space outside the constitutive we' designated by Warner is precisely the space occupied by the (mostly illiterate) bodies Otis cites: this space outside the transcendent ground of the 'we' is, necessarily, occupied by those whose local detail resists interpellation into the newly abstracted criteria of subjection.[10]

Derrida is interested in the anti-metaphysical event of the signature, the fissure in the self-presence of the name that, in acting ineluctably as a performative and as a constative, would by itself found a nation. Warner, while concerned with the same conundrum of self-legitimation, of law that must legislate its own authority, would open this instability of the name into the quintessentially abstracted capacities of the printed 'we' – which, in being reproduced and read over and over, makes the ambiguity of performative and constative, of self-interpellation and self-representation, the subjectivising a priori of 'every citizen'. The main point that I will make here thus concerns the fantastically virtual operation of print – which acts more intangibly and more seamlessly, it goes almost without saying, than Burke's imagining of the perfectly disinterested statesman. After Burke, after even the featureless body of statesman drops from the equivocation of the people and the public good, in the passage from the signature to pronominal print, the barest taint of the personal drops from the mediating substance of the name. This is precisely Warner's point in stressing the endlessly inclusive and recuperative capacity of the 'we'. It offers no resistance (and, indeed, no opportunity) to the reader who is also a citizen. It would subsume (some of) Otis's subject bodies, Burke's statesman, and the people into its virtualising operation – its residue is not the spectacular body of the king but, recalling Madison, the 'local'. The states, supplemental to the ubiquity of the national 'we', are this nation's remainder. If we can assume the largest property-owners (whom we can also assume to be Burke's ideal statesmen) to be the real referent of the Madisonian public good, then in Warner's account there is no body left in whom we might imaginatively focalise the real interests of the nation. This is the fantastic endpoint of de Tocqueville's paranoia. The phantasmatic majority, that individual who is everywhere and nowhere, is now a fantastically unified we. To repeat Warner, there would be no space left outside of de Tocqueville's majority: we can only imagine ourselves inside it.

My main point here, then, is that the only imaginable difference from Warner's constitutive we must be found in embodiment itself. His account of the inclusive powers of print must necessarily posit its difference in irreducible, indissoluble, embodied particularity – what he designates in his text as the personal and the local.[11] I have spent this much time recapitulating Warner's discussion because of this ending. In returning to Madison's *Federalist* No. 10, I will suggest another trajectory, one that cannot so clearly imagine (or fail to imagine) what its other is. This is Madison's mediation of actual and virtual representation, which is suspended between embodied particulars and featureless abstraction. As I have suggested above, Madison's text projects phantasmatic body parts, and a phantasmatic 'mean', as ways of reconciling national extent with the public good. As a way, also, of thematising a subject body that diverges both from Burke's intangible constituency and Otis's cats and dogs, the Madisonian mean would offer a partially abstracted citizen, who from the irresolution of actual and virtual would claim both particularity and representative abstraction.

If part of the pressure upon this essay is the application of the term 'Gothic', then here I will offer a final possibility of its use.

De Tocqueville's majority, and Warner's 'we', are obviously ghostly, setting up the perilous equivocation of virtual consensus and the nation's bulk; but the distinction upon which such an opposition rests, that of virtual and embodied, abstract and personal, is, I would suggest, distinctly unGothic in so far as it (re)produces the theoretical equivalence of embodiment and difference. The operation of the 'we' as evoked by Warner over-abstracts the (Foucauldian? republican American?) citizen, leaving as that transparent subject's remainder either nothing (but cats and dogs – 'we' readers are all included) or, inversely, everything ('our' bodies have always been left out).[12] Thus while Warner provides obvious leverage for a tally of the bodies that the Constitution fails or refuses to represent in the very act of representation, he cannot thematise those bodies as anything other than other, either radically external or imminently subject to the endlessly expansive operations of the subjectivising we. In an application of Foucault that would drain discipline of any shred of corporeal meaning,[13] we find the undisciplined subject (the illiterate subject who cannot interpellate him/herself into the 'we') ironically both *more* (as a manual labourer, propertyless woman or slave) and *less* subject to the consolidating order of the new nation. This incoherence – how subject is the embodied subject? how subject is the reading subject? – signals, I would suggest, an overly sharp distinction between the Constitution's reader and the rest of the nation's (indeed, the rest of his, or her) body. Might not the Constitution's reader 'interpellate himself – even herself' into the abstracting category of national citizenship in a partial way, through a recombination of actual and virtual whose unpredictable outcome is signalled in Madison's text by his unreal mean?

Madison's mean, what can be invoked as its monstrous and irresolved recombination of virtual and actual, offers another way of imagining the spookiness of national subjectivity: it would contain local difference as a phantasmatically real part of itself. Instead of situating embodiment on its nether side, the Madisonian mean confuses the (theoretical) distinctness of virtual and actual, collapsing them in an uneven mediation whose Gothic interest inheres in its inability to assert fully its dissimulating powers. Unlike a ghost story based in the displacement of materialised by virtual force, then, Madison's mean projects a story with no clear ending, whose irreducible but proximate terms dictate its continued suspense. The subject of this story is a composite of local and national, actual and virtual, whose subjection to the new union can be thematised in its endlessly unstable reconciliations of those two imperatives.

One more part: the case of gender

This will be a brief, necessarily inconclusive, case study. I have suggested that in *The Federalist* No. 10 we might imagine the statesman's body as it equivocates between actual and virtual representation. His interested or sinister particularity might be thematised as his left hand. I will invoke a roughly contemporary feminist text – Mary Wollstonecraft's 1792 *Vindication of the Rights of Woman* – to reference another equivocation of actual and virtual that generates a spectral body part. If Wollstonecraft's rhetoric would situate feminine subjecthood in a relation obviously opposed to the disinterested statesman – women are 'slaves to their bodies' (Wollstonecraft, 1792: 44) – she just as obviously excludes herself from that final reduction, projecting instead a feminine body that will make a meaningful contribution to 'social virtue' and 'public spirit' (140). This contribution cannot be a purely embodied one – tellingly, Wollstonecraft compares women and kings, those final representatives of materialised force, to dismiss Louis XIV's roster of ('ludicrous' and 'frivolous') corporeal accomplishments in favour of interiorised assets like 'knowledge' and 'judgment' (56–60). Yet, at the same time, the substance of a woman's civic duty can never be absolutely opposed to the king's, in so far as Wollstonecraft affirms that women's contribution to the public good cannot distract them from the bodily exigency of reproduction: 'whatever tends to incapacitate the maternal character, takes woman out of her sphere' (177). Thus Wollstonecraft defends women's maternal function even while complaining, in her mention of kings and elsewhere, that feminine social or rational capacity has historically been subsumed in feminine embodiment.[14] This paradox leads us to the spectral part of her text.

The part of the female body that Wollstonecraft finds most problematic is the breast. Its collapse of frivolous (to Wollstonecraft) and properly reproductive femininity occurs precisely, she states, after childbirth – when, 'during the first effervescence of voluptuous fondness [husbands] refuse to let their wives suckle their children. They are only to dress and live to please them' (73). The multiple advantages that she attaches to the maternal breast – as a 'way of cementing the matrimonial tie', preserving the mother's health and preventing 'a houseful of babes' (142, 190–1) – would sublimate erotic or decorative anatomy in reproductive duty. This effects a mediation of civic function and feminine embodiment that is neither wholly textual nor wholly materialised. The breast is thus the local (gendered) organ of

Wollstonecraft's national body, sublimated into the abstractness of the public good at the same time that it supplies the matter nourishing the nation. It resonates with Madison's 'mean' in so far as the irresolution constituting both mark their mutual appeals to the local and to the national. Wollstonecraft's imagined embodiment of rational gender, instead of signalling its foreignness to the Madisonian statesman, articulates another way in which the spectral parts of this unevenly national subject might continue to assert themselves.[15]

I have claimed that the spectral factions of *The Federalist* No. 10 offer one vision of the newly American subject: this subject can be evoked as Gothic not in its absolute transparency but, rather, in its inability to resolve the actual and virtual parts of itself. Its relation to the subjectivising force of the union is both forestalled and negotiated in the relation of embodiment to abstraction; in its anteriority to the textualising event of ratification, this subject would thematise the difference of local and national without rendering either of those terms external to itself. Its interest to the present critical moment, then, lies in the way that it thematises this binary without reifying it. In a critical present in which the polarisation of abstraction and embodiment threatens an overly reductive hermeneutic – whereby dematerialised force would contain everything but the most radically exteriorised difference – Madison's text suggests a subtilised imagining of assent that is nonetheless terminally stalled, implicated in the alterity of virtual and actual but never quite able to mobilise it coherently. Thus the subject evoked by *The Federalist* No. 10 displaces the event of textualised assent with the more resonant event of irreducible compromise. This compromise is a fruitful resting-place for contemporary imaginings of a national citizen who is virtual *and* actual, occupying the unstable ground of subjection as the ever-negotiable terrain of Madison's fantastic mean.

Notes

1   De Tocqueville warns: 'Absolute monarchies had dishonored despotism; let us beware lest democratic republics should reinstate it and render it less odious and degrading in the eyes of the many by making it still more onerous to the few ... The majority lives in the perpetual utterance of self-applause, and there are certain truths which the Americans can learn only from strangers' (275). Certainly, de Tocqueville imagines himself to be one of the 'strangers' informing America of this newly persuasive form of despotism.

2   See John Locke, *Two Treatises of Government*, especially the Second Treatise, where Locke discusses appropriation (of land by labour), and the conversion of property into money, as the funding premise of modern sociality,

compressed in the rapid transformation of real land into imperishable currency in the New World: 'Thus in the beginning all the World was *America ...*' (301).

3 It is important to note that Burke writes in *defence* of limited Catholic admission to the franchise; he qualifies his definition of virtual representation by stating 'But this sort of virtual representation cannot have a long or sure existence, if it has not a substratum in the actual. The member must have some relation to the constituent. As things stand, the Catholic, as a Catholic, has no *virtual* relation to the representative, – but the *contrary*' (293). Thus, though I am taking his definition as exemplary, I am far from intending to cite Burke as a dogmatic advocate of, or ideological believer in, the capacities of virtual representation.

4 See the Antifederalist paper published in the *Massachusetts Gazette*, 29 January 1788, which concludes: 'Let us not flatter ourselves that we shall always have good men to govern us. If we endeavor to be like other nations we shall have more bad men than good ones to exercise extensive powers' (reprinted in Lauter, 1994: 1206–8). Gordon Wood states more broadly of Antifederalist attacks upon elite governance: 'Thus the Antifederalists were not only directly challenging the conventional belief that only a gentlemanly few, even though now in America naturally and not artificially qualified, were best equipped ... to represent and to govern the society, but they were as well indirectly denying the assumption of organic social hegemony on which republicanism rested' (Wood, 1969: 492).

5 The term 'paranoia' has particular resonance in the context of Revolutionary fears of political conspiracy. See Wood's seminal article, 'Conspiracy and the Paranoid Style: Causality and Deceit in the Eighteenth Century'. Wood gives an invaluable survey of the evolution of 'paranoid' thought through the new republic until the emergence of new notions of social causality itself (Wood ends with Bentham), stressing the role of moral philosophy in the transfer of agency from God, to a mechanistic universe, to man's sometimes-rational 'psychologised' interiority.

6 See Michel Serres, 1982, 'Turner Translates Carnot'. Serres discusses, in particular, J.M.W. Turner's painting of the ship the *Fighting Téméraire* (1844) being towed to her berth to be destroyed. In Serres's words: 'Turner understood and revealed the new world, the new matter. *The perception of the stochastic replaces the art of drawing the form ...* The timber framework is dead. Statics is dead. Mechanics, geometry, the art of drawing vanish before the fire ... With Turner the furnace appears as the new model of the world' (58–61).

7 Foucault is discussing, of course, panopticism. The full citation is as follows: 'The body of the king, with its strange material and physical presence, with the force that he himself deploys or transmits to some few others, is at the opposite extreme of this new physics of power represented by panopticism; the domain of panopticism is, on the contrary, that whole lower region, that region of irregular bodies, with their details, their multiple movements, their heterogeneous forces, their spatial relations' (208). Foucault would seem here to be indebted to de Tocqueville.

8 Part One of Derrida's Otobiographies: *l'enseignement de Nietzsche et la politique du nom propre*, 'Déclarations d'Indépendance', was given as a talk at the

University of Virginia upon the occasion of the Declaration of Independence's bicentennial. The translations of Derrida are my own. Michael Warner, in The *Letters of the Republic: Publication and the Public Sphere in Eighteenth-Century America*, translates large passages from Derrida in his chapter on the Constitution, 'Textuality and Legitimacy in the Printed Constitution'.

9   Derrida is indebted to J.L. Austin's exhaustive account of the inadequacy of the constative vs. performative distinction in How *to do Things with Words*, particularly where Austin states: 'It is essential to realise that "true" and "false", like "free" and "unfree", do not stand for anything simple at all; but only for a general dimension of being a right or proper thing to say as opposed to a wrong thing, in these circumstances, to this audience' (145). See also Derrida's 'Limited Inc a b c...' for a long critique of Austin's legacy in speech-act theory.

10 Warner very clearly makes this opposition: 'The national community of the constitutional we is an aspect of the people's abstractness and may be contrasted with the intense localism of the popular assemblies which were its main rival for the role of the people' (112).

11 The displacement of the personal/local by print is the orienting theme of Warner's text, so it would be futile to attempt to cite pages. He also, it is worth noting, makes the homologous opposition of print to speech. Early in his text, he claims to reject the 'conventional distinction between oral and literate societies, in which oral means preliterate and innocent of the exploitation that comes through writing... as sentimental and ideological' (21). Here Warner explicitly aligns himself with Derrida's *Of Grammatology*. Yet later, in the discussion of the Constitution cited above, Warner will evoke that document as a threat to 'the voice of the people', its ultimate operation figured as the 'existence of the written text ceaselessly representing a silent people' (113). In this resonant evocation of the Constitution, Warner's terms are given their (moral) orientation by the very same Rousseauistic nostalgia that he has earlier dismissed as 'sentimental and ideological'. Even if invoked metaphorically – though given the stress Warner places upon the Constitution's historical rival, 'popular assemblies', this is not the case – the voice is still opposed to the written.

12 Warner deploys the Foucauldian concept of surveillance to thematise the political meanings of printedness in the new republic: 'Clearly, the assumption behind this concept of publication is the principle of supervision... the optic and spatializing metaphor of supervision became in eighteenth-century America the dominant way of conceptualizing the public... And it is the specificity of *reading* as the paradigmatic public action that lies behind the literalizing trope of supervision' (52).

13 The post-Enlightenment rise of 'indefinite' or panoptic discipline is evoked by Foucault in a passage that is worth quoting at some length:

> The general juridical form that guaranteed a system of rights that were egalitarian in principle was supported by these tiny, everyday, physical mechanisms, by all those systems of micro-power that are essentially non-egalitarian and asymmetrical that we call the disciplines... The real, corporeal disciplines constituted the foundation of the formal, juridical

liberties. The contract may have been regarded as the ideal foundation of law and political power; panopticism constituted the technique, universally widespread, of coercion. It continued to work in depth on the juridical structures of society, in order to make the effective mechanisms of power function in opposition to the formal framework that it had acquired. (222)

It is of interest that the disciplines which Foucault opposes to rights are, in fact, 'physical' and 'corporeal': in contrast to Warner's appropriation of his work, Foucault here defines discipline in its residual or dissimulated *corporeality*, not, as is frequently taken to be the case, in its invisibility or virtuality.

14 Wollstonecraft discusses the effect of educational strategies upon feminine access of rationality, suggesting that girls and boys be 'dressed alike' (168). This sartorial strategy of de-essentialism can be read in light of her earlier judgement: 'A man of sense may only have a cast of countenance that wears off as you trace his individuality, whilst the weak, common man has scarcely any character, but what belongs to the body' (18): here we might locate the final fantasy of a feminine 'man of sense,' whose body 'wears off' as (s)he gains access to the realm of sense.

15 There is no room left here, unfortunately, to explore how Wollstonecraft's model of gender might suggestively figure *every* national body. In its attempt to co-ordinate rational and embodied parts of the self, it meshes intriguingly with recent work on gender and sexuality (particularly that of Judith Butler) that stresses the constitutive instability of the philosophical/ historical imagining of a transparently rational self.

Works cited

Austin, J.L. 1962. *How to do Things with Words*. Cambridge, MA: Harvard University Press.

Bailyn, Bernard. 1967. *The Ideological Origins of the American Revolution*. Cambridge, MA: Harvard University Press.

Burke, Edmund. 1894. *The Works of the Right Honourable Edmund Burke*. Vol. IV. Boston: Little, Brown.

Derrida, Jacques. 1984. *Otobiographies: l'enseignement de Nietzsche et la politique du nom propre*. Paris: Galilée.

de Tocqueville, Alexis. 1835. *Democracy in America*. Vol. 1. Trans. Henry Reeve. New York: Vintage, 1945.

Foucault, Michel. 1979. *Discipline and Punish*. Trans. Alan Sheridan. New York: Vintage.

Lauter, Paul. ed. 1994. *The Heath Anthology of American Literature*. Lexington, MA: Heath.

Locke, John. 1690. *Two Treatises of Government*. Ed. Peter Laslett. Cambridge: Cambridge University Press, 1988.

Madison, James. 1787. *The Federalist*, No.10. Reprinted in *The English Literatures of America, 1500–1800*. Ed. Myra Jehlen and Michael Warner. New York: Routledge, 1997, 885–90.

Serres, Michel. 1982. 'Turner Translates Carnot'. In *Hermes: Literature, Science, Philosophy*. Trans. Josué Harari and David Bell. Baltimore: Johns Hopkins University Press.

Warner, Michael. 1990. *The Letters of the Republic: Publication and the Public Sphere in Eighteenth-Century America*. Cambridge, MA: Harvard University Press.

Wollstonecraft, Mary. 1792. *A Vindication of the Rights of Woman*. Ed. Carol Poston. New York: Norton, 1988.

Wood, Gordon. 1969. *The Creation of the American Republic, 1776–1787*. New York: Norton.

Wood, Gordon. 1982. 'Conspiracy and the Paranoid Style: Causality and Deceit in the Eighteenth Century'. *William and Mary Quarterly*, 39:3, 401–41.

Chapter 9

Spectres of abjection:
the queer subject of James's
'The Jolly Corner'

Eric Savoy

In his 1913 autobiography, *A Small Boy and Others*, Henry James produces the Gothic trope of the haunted text to explain his compositional process: 'To look back at all is to meet the apparitional and to find in its ghostly face the silent stare of an appeal. When I fix it, the hovering shade, whether of person or place, it fixes me back and seems the less lost' (James, 1913: 92). This figurative moment, which conflates prosopopoeia with chiasmus, represents the subject who obsessively haunts – and is haunted by – what James called 'the American past of a preponderant unthinkable queerness' (127), and it is typical of the Gothic *turn* in James's work that followed his *return* to the United States in 1904. The 'unthinkable queerness' of late Jamesian Gothic accrues in the interstices of the split or divided authorial subject: the magisterial James, architect of labyrinthine syntax, seeks out his apparitional double, his spectral other, in the rhetorical 'figures' of either his youthful self or a hypothetical American self whose development was foreclosed by his European sojourn. Such specular, spectral doubles – the real 'others' in *A Small Boy and Others* and such ghostly tales as 'The Jolly Corner' – are produced as signs, the import of which is simultaneously solicited and refused. As Donna Przybylowicz has argued,

> signification is rarely attained and fully mastered in James, for, even though the characters sense they have achieved a certain plateau of self-perception, ... one is left with the feeling that they are not quite satisfied at the end of the work and are still searching for the meaning of events, which suggests that the hermeneutic process is never finished in James.
>
> (Przybylowicz, 1986: 125)

The 'figure' of the apparitional other in Jamesian Gothic is, I argue, a sign that is queerly suspended between desire for, and repression of, signification. In the argument that follows, I explore the rhetorical operations of prosopopoeia (which I understand as the controlling trope of the 'ghost story'); I am particularly interested in its expressive or performative relation to the sexually ambiguous, 'queer' subject, and in the possibility of theorising a precise psychoanalytics of this uncanny trope. My intention here is to chart the overlaps or resonances among the rhetorical operations of this trope, its deployment within the parameters of Gothic narrative, and post-Freudian concepts of melancholia and abjection. Prosopopoeia, in late Jamesian Gothic, is the discursive field in which the Other is named, imag(in)ed, embodied: governed by the desire to make the absent, the dead, the abstract present and palpable, its Gothic potential is always latent; narrative turns toward the Gothic in proportion to the literalisation – itself, ironically, a figurative 'coming-to-life' – of this trope. To put this another way, the Jamesian ghost story acquires its Gothic horror by its ability to transform sign into fictional character. Such an operation is a response to the subject's complex desire to know the Other, yet such knowledge is inevitably horrific. The Gothic deployment of prosopopoeia, then, is an important dimension of James's celebrated complexity and ambivalence, and as such, is properly understood as a response to loss, an obsessive need to speculate about the lost or repressed Other.

According to Freud, melancholia – which arises when the trauma of loss cannot be resolved by the work of ordinary mourning – results in a splitting of the ego: 'one part of the ego sets itself over against the other, judges it critically' (Freud, 1917: 256); this 'critical agency' is similar to what Freud will later conceptualise as the super-ego. In melancholia, the ego establishes an identification with the lost object; 'thus, the shadow of the object fell upon the ego, and [it] could henceforth be judged by a special agency, as though it were an object, the forsaken object. In this way an object-loss was transformed into an ego-loss, ... a cleavage between the critical activity of the ego and the ego as altered by identification' (258). In Freudian theory, melancholia arises from the subject's ambivalent and unresolved relation with the lost object, and it is precisely this ambivalence – this 'shadow' cast by the critical superego upon the ego's identifications – that produces the abject. As Freud explains, 'if the love for the object ... takes refuge in [the ego's] narcissistic identification, then the hate comes into operation on this substitutive object, abusing it, debasing it, making it suffer and deriving sadistic satisfaction from its suffering' (260).

Crucial for my purposes is Freud's metaphor of 'the shadow of the object' that falls upon the ego, splitting its energies into identification and abjection. This metaphor recurs in Julia Kristeva's work: melancholia, she argues, can be broadly conceptualised as 'a sad voluptuousness, a despondent intoxication' emanating from 'the shadow cast on the fragile self, hardly dissociated from the other, precisely by the loss of that essential other'. It is the 'shadow of despair' (Kristeva, 1989: 5). Canonical American Gothic – at least in the nineteenth century – arises from the subject's traumatised sense of historical loss, a disconnection from the field of power where the subject wishes to locate or to construct a more authentic self. This impossible elsewhere is at once a ghostly terrain and the historically real; it finds representation in a speaking shadow whose function is less an ego-identification than a superegotistical alignment that abjects the subject. For example, in the semiotics of Hawthorne's Gothic historiography, melancholia – which is manifest as a form of romantic 'writer's block' – is occasioned by the loss of palpable connection to the Father; Hawthorne's writing, governed by a tropics of exhumation and a will-to-prosopopoeia, is haunted by the murmurings of 'one gray *shadow* of [his] forefathers the other' (Kristeva, 1989: 127). Hawthorne's Gothic melancholia explains the central problematic in his writing: the ambivalence between his subordination to the patriarchal project and his resentment of the father's tyranny. While James works within this American Gothic tradition of melancholy historiography, and while his fictional subject is similarly abjected by the shadowy voices from a hypothetical past, the structures of Gothic melancholia arise from a rather different traumatic occasion, and the reliance upon prosopopoeia, the trope of haunting, attempts a different and less successful resolution.

James's return to America in 1904 might usefully be characterised as a return of the repressed and the repudiated – what Spencer Brydon in 'The Jolly Corner' understands as 'all the old baffled forsworn possibilities' that are shadowed forth from 'that mystical other world' (James, 1908: 455) of the past. To understand precisely how such a return might have been the occasion of trauma, generative of melancholia, it is necessary to posit some plausible conception of James's ego investments and 'identity' that came under assault. Revisionist approaches to Henry James have presented solid arguments that James, in maturity, had moved toward consolidation of homosexual identity. (I would not argue that such a position was unproblematic – indeed, James's bachelor fictions tend cumulatively to suspend simple notions of 'identity' – but I agree entirely with Eve Kosofsky Sedgwick's assertion that in James's life 'the pattern of homosexual desire was brave enough and resilient enough to be at last biographically inobliterable' (Sedgwick, 1990: 197). The question of how Henry James explained himself *to* himself as a subject of desire is – and had better be – vexed.) My argument rests on two different but related occasions of likely trauma.

The first is the subject of James's autobiographical project, a reconstruction that is torn between embracing and repudiating childhood experiences of difference and stigmatisation that are 'shameful'. Sedgwick has argued that the 'chronically effeminate boy' is the *'haunting* abject of gay thought itself' (Sedgwick, 1994: 157); moreover, 'the eclipse of the effeminate boy from adult gay discourse' signifies the cir-. culation of 'the effeminate boy [as] the discrediting open secret of many politicized adult gay men' (158). It strikes me as entirely plausible that the authorial James sustains an ego identification with the abandoned child – the *deject*, the pale ghostly figure in the autobiographies – which prompts melancholic sorrow, as well as a superegotistical repudiation of this queer being, which is converted into an *abject*, and the occasion of punishment of the ego for its empathetic identifications. Julia Kristeva defines the abject as that which does not fit, and associates it with waste material or threshold substances that are neither inside nor outside, with things or states that lack clear conceptual boundaries. As Tilottama Rajan explains, the abject, 'as the site of some undefinable horror...must be expelled for the subject to constitute itself as a bounded ego. But the very term "abjection" resists such boundaries, intercontaminating self and other, act and affect...implicating the subject in what it rejects' (Rajan, 1994: 45). I am persuaded by Sedgwick's account of the effeminate childhood as the 'haunting abject' that has the potential to disrupt adult gay masculinities, and I suggest that this recuperation is traumatic for the mature James, and it may indeed explain the numerous instances of shameful confession or performance in the autobiographies.

Its interest, however, lies in its contextual relation to the second – the most strikingly Gothic – of James's representations of trauma. While the confrontation with a stigmatised childhood involves a return to the historically Real, its corollary involves James's speculations about the historically hypothetical: what would this boy have become in America? This is precisely the interrogation sustained by Spencer Brydon, James's autobiographical agent in 'The Jolly Corner', his most brilliantly complex Gothic tale in which the goal of the writing is to generate a 'figure' that will correspond to this hypothetical double, this unlived life. James writes,

> [Brydon] was wholly taken up with one subject of thought. It was mere vain egoism, and it was moreover...a morbid obsession. He found all things come back to the question of what he personally might have been, how he might have lived his life and 'turned out', if he had not so, at the outset, given it up.
>
> (James, 1908: 448)

Invoked by prosopopoeia, this apparitional figure is simultaneously desired and feared, is at once the object of identification and repudiation. Like the 'restless analyst' who narrates *The American Scene*, Spencer Brydon returns to New York and his childhood home on 'the jolly corner', appalled by the monstrous urban transformation and its obliteration of his personal past. In *The American Scene*, this loss is inscribed as psychic wound – 'I felt amputated of half my history', James writes – which gives rise to a ritualistically mournful text. I would argue that, despite its Gothic traces, the work of mourning is accomplished in *The American Scene* because the lost object is recovered, reconstituted in the Symbolic Order: this is the generic requirement of travel writing. Kristeva argues that the work of ordinary mourning accepts the loss of the object by recovering it again in signs; she personifies the subject's voice thus: 'I have lost an essential object...But no, I have found [it] again in signs, or rather since I consent to lose [it] I have not lost [it].' This, for Kristeva constitutes the fundamental negation of mourning, the negation of loss. Melancholics, on the contrary, refuse the consolations of the Symbolic: they 'disavow the negation, they cancel it out, suspend it, and nostalgically fall back on the real object (the Thing) of their loss...to which they remain painfully riveted' (Kristeva, 1989: 44–5).

As I have suggested, Spencer Brydon's return is a case history of such melancholy 'riveting' to an historically lapsed possibility which coalesces in the syntax of the past conditional: 'If he had but stayed at home...' (James, 1908: 440). Initially, Brydon attempts to mourn the loss of this hypothetical other self through the speculative production of specular figure, but this work of mourning becomes pathological exactly in proportion as the narrative turns toward the Gothic. Essentially, the ghostly double that haunts the house on the jolly corner is 'authored' as a sign – or more precisely, is co-authored by Brydon and his old friend, Alice Staverton, who represents 'their quite far-away and antediluvian social period and order' (439). The turn towards the Gothic is realised when this sign – specifically, the prosopopoeia that invokes the double – is literalised and materialises in the narrative only to prove inadequate to the resolution of mourning. Horrified by this figure – speculative, specular, spectral – and by its signification of what he would have become had he remained in America, Brydon constructs 'it' as the abject, that which must be refused and expelled to sustain the ego's coherence. Crucial to my argument is Brydon's repudiation of the prosopopoeial sign and its signification of otherness: the Gothic is most horrific, I would argue, *not* in the production of the ghostly sign that haunts Brydon's consciousness as well as the literal house on the jolly corner, but in the failure to accept the sign's adequacy merely as a sign, which suspends Brydon in the irresolutions of melancholia. Thus, he cannot recover the lost hypothetical identity, nor can he resolve its urgent imperatives; his melancholia is constituted, and interlined, by an abjection that will continue to haunt the margins of his 'identity' and thus prolong its traumatic unravelling. This crisis of identity might be conceptualised as an endemic state of gender and sexual panic, to which I shall turn after taking up the question of how the ghostly double is produced and the unspeakable otherness it comes to represent.

'The Jolly Corner' presents abundant connotative suggestions that Spencer Brydon has constructed an authentic, though highly discreet, homosexual identity, which has been made possible by the freedoms of 'Europe' (which, by this point in James's career, is always set within inverted commas to suggest 'something' tacit, something beyond the realm of the denotative). Living on the income from his New York real estate, he has devoted himself to pleasure: as he tells Alice Staverton, 'I know at least what I am … I believe I'm thought in a hundred quarters to have been barely decent. I've followed strange paths and worshipped strange gods; it must have come to you again and again … that I was leading, at any time these last thirty years, a selfish frivolous scandalous life' (450). While this speech may partake of Jamesian hyperbole, its connotative resonances with the modern stereotype of the homosexual role, especially in the wake of the Wilde Trials of 1895 – its associative cluster of aestheticism, dissipation, irresponsibility, self-indulgence, degeneracy – seem strikingly evident.

I contend that Brydon's 'morbid obsession' (448) with his hypothetical double generates a figure whose American life, whose interpellation within compulsory heterosexuality and narrow masculine roles, has required the repression of homosexual desire and identity. The abject double is the figure in the closet, a prosopopoeial 'figure' that, as we shall see, is figured in association with a strikingly literal closet in the house on the jolly corner. I am not suggesting a simple binary between

Brydon's 'uncloseted' identity and the wasting rigours of the closet of his 'heterosexual' double, for such a supposition would have been historically improbable. However, I do suggest that Brydon's closet is *logistical*, and circulates as the open secret in this narrative: 'I at least know what I am', he insists, whereas the closet of his ravaged ghostly double is primarily *epistemological*. This figure comes to signify, horrifically, the life without an identity, and is analogous to that of John Marcher in 'The Beast in the Jungle' – the man to whom nothing has happened. It is this dreadful 'nothingness' that is repudiated by Brydon.

The materialisation of Brydon's abject other, his ghostly double, requires not merely the exploration of 'a compartment of his mind never yet penetrated' (438) or the Gothic convention of the haunted house, but rather the literalisation of 'the queerest and deepest of his...most disguised and most muffled vibrations' (441): the emergence of a queer 'something' into consciousness, into the rhetoric of prosopopoeia, and finally into spectral form.

> It had begun to be present to him after the first fortnight, it had broken out with the oddest abruptness, this particular wanton wonderment: it met him there... *very much as he might have been met by some strange figure*, some unexpected occupant, at a turn of one of the dim passages of an empty house. The quaint analogy quite *hauntingly* remained with him, when he indeed didn't rather improve it by a still intenser form: that of his opening a door behind which he would have made sure of finding nothing, a door into a room shuttered and void, and yet so coming, with a great suppressed start, on some quite erect confronting presence, something planted in the middle of the place and facing him through the dusk. (441)

In James's tortuous syntax, the 'it' – the referent of which is Brydon's 'wanton wonderment' – receives several figurative reinscriptions, all of which are controlled by prosopopoeia: the 'it' is said to have 'met him there' (prosopopoeia number one), exactly *'as* he might have been met by some strange figure, some unexpected occupant' (simile and prosopopoeia number two); this 'occupant' is then refigured as a 'confronting presence...facing him' in the dusk of some empty room or closet (prosopopoeia number three).

In a subsequent conversation with Alice Staverton, Brydon claims that he had had no reason to remain in America – 'not the ghost of one' (446). Alice responds, ominously, 'Are you very sure the "ghost" of one doesn't, much rather, serve – ?' Brydon panics at Alice's aposiopesis, and rushes to finish her incomplete sentence 'between a glare and a grin: 'Oh ghosts – of course the place must swarm with them!' (446). I have already suggested that Jamesian Gothic is horrific not simply because of the appearance of the ghostly double, but rather the melancholic suspension that occurs when Brydon cannot accept its significance, and recoils in revulsion. Strictly in terms of the plot, this tale acquires its Gothic eeriness in proportion as it becomes clear that the ghostly double is not only produced discursively by both Alice and Spencer, but indeed is familiar to Alice, who sees it not as horrific but as an object of empathy, even desire. This suggests not merely that Alice and Spencer may be understood as 'co-authoring' the ghost, but, more importantly, that the ghost signifies Alice's role as agent of compulsory heterosexuality: the double is the version of Spencer Brydon who would have been available for marriage and middle-class domesticity. In the remainder of the narrative, Spencer Brydon tracks the ghostly *alter ego* – 'his other self...this ineffable identity' (461–2) – to a closet in the upper reaches of the house, and turns away in fear only to confront his double at the foot of the staircase. This 'penumbra, dense and dark, was the virtual screen of a figure' (475), yet this 'screen' is itself 'screened', or de-faced and disfigured: 'what made the face dim was the pair of raised hands that covered it and in which, so far from being offered in defiance, it was buried as for dark deprecation' (475). Brydon responds with 'revulsion' at the 'meaning' of the spectral double: 'he could but gape at his other self in this other anguish, gape as a proof that he, standing there for the achieved, the enjoyed, the triumphant life, couldn't be faced in his triumph' (476). Yet Brydon's grasp of the figure's 'meaning' is surely suspect: his repudiation, his abjection of this abject other, refuses its signification – that is, its connection to his own life as an entirely plausible, hypothetical other identity. In his panicked response, Brydon sees the 'it' as 'unknown, inconceivable, awful, disconnected from any possibility...such an identity fitted his at *no* point, made its alternative monstrous' (476–7).

'The Jolly Corner' is a tale of return, chiefly, the return of a hypothetical identity that had been forsworn and abandoned in order to consolidate 'identity' as choice. Speculation about the form of that identity – the 'figure' one would have cut in some other but entirely plausible life – prompts a mourning for this lost opportunity, which in turn generates a set of signs; yet when the import of these signs is refused as 'monstrous', the work of mourning cannot be resolved and degenerates into a melancholic pathology. Sustaining profoundly ambivalent relations with the monstrous other – a complex web of fascination and fear – the subject incorporates the lost object, constructs an ego identification that is refused by the superego. Brydon's suspension of identity occurs when his superego cannot dismantle the ego's uncanny and illogical affiliation with its hated other. In the final Gothic turn of the screw in this tale, Brydon seems doomed to abandon his hard-won 'European' identity and its homosexual implications, for James's closure implies that Brydon capitulates to heterosexual compulsion as Alice's prisoner, and in so doing will *become* the abjected other. The final irony is that Brydon, in refusing to 'know' the other, can no longer be said to 'know' himself, and this is what I mean by the suspension of identity in an endemic homosexual panic marked by a return to an epistemological closet. 'It's not me ... I was to have known myself' (482), Brydon insists, but Alice's eerie consolation is 'You couldn't' (482). Alice, whom we are to understand as *knowing* the ghostly double, defends him. While Brydon protests that 'He's none of me, even as I *might* have been', Alice responds, 'Isn't the whole point that you'd have been different?' (483). 'To me', she continues, 'he was no horror. I had accepted him ... And as *I* didn't disown him, as I knew him ... I pitied him ... He has been unhappy. He has been ravaged' (484–5).

The psychoanalytic dimensions of Spencer Brydon's monstrous other, his prosopopoeia-come-to-life, are explicable within the theories of gender regulation and identity formation advanced by Eve Sedgwick and Judith Butler. I want to chart a particular intersection between Sedgwick's work on homosexual panic and Butler's exploration of the melancholia of gender which has some bearing on the figurative operations of prosopopoeia, the master-trope of haunting that is crucial in the discursive production of the other in paranoid Gothic texts. Prospopoeia designates the figure that makes present to the senses something abstract and not susceptible of phenomenalisation (the lost object, the unnameable Thing). As Deborah Esch argues,

> in giving a face (*prosopon*) or the semblance of one ... to an entity that lacks a literal visage, prosopopoeia serves as a guarantor of its existence. According to Pierre Fontanier, prosopopoeia consists in 'staging ... the absent, the dead, supernatural beings, ... to make them act, speak, respond; or at least to take them for confidants, witnesses, guarantors, accusers, avengers, judges.'
>
> (Esch, 1983: 594)

The resonance between Fontanier's 1821 formulation of staging the hypothetical accuser, avenger or judge through this figurative turn and the role of Brydon's ghostly double suggests an obvious connection between prosopopoeia and the psychoananalytics of identification, of incorporating the shadow of the other into the ego, in the work of melancholia. If, in the paranoid Gothic, the ghost is the prosopopoeial allegorisation of the split subject, then Paul de Man's assertion that 'prosopopoeia is hallucinatory, [for] to make the invisible visible is uncanny' (De Man, 1986: 49) suggests not only that prosopopoeia is always already a Gothicised trope, but also that this trope is imbricated in a complex psychoanalytic of melancholia's need to figure forth the haunting other.

If Spencer Brydon may be understood as representing a coherent homosexual subject, then his double – who signifies the repression of homosexual possibility by heterosexual interpellation – is a striking figure of what Sedgwick has conceptualised as 'homosexual panic', by which masculinity is regulated, whose apparitional emergence is a traumatic assault upon – and indeed an 'undoing' or 'unbinding' of – Brydon's identity, which has been based on what Butler terms a 'foundational repudiation' of heterosexual possibility. In Butler's argument, *all* sexual 'identities' are predicated upon the exclusion of other possibilities, which are relegated to the domain of the abject, and as such haunt the permeable border of identity with subversive power: 'identity', she insists, is but another name for a profoundly melancholic relation with the repudiated abject. What, then, are the operations of gender melancholia within the regulatory operations of homosexual panic?

Sedgwick's entire mapping of male homosociality hinges upon her concept of how western culture consolidates control 'over the bonds of men who were not part of the distinctly homosexual subculture' (Sedgwick, 1985: 88). Because of the correspondences between the most sanctioned forms of male homosocial bonding and the most reprobated expressions of homosexual sociality, she argues, 'no man must be able to ascertain that he is not (that his bonds are not) homosexual' (Sedgwick, 1985: 89). The result, she concludes, is the 'blackmailability of western maleness through the leverage of homophobia', and such 'homosexual panic' is the 'most private, psychologized form in which [men] experience their vulnerability to the social pressure of homophobic blackmail' (Sedgwick, 1985: 89). It is important to emphasise that, in this theory, it is only the homosexual-identified man who is exempt from the ideological tentacles of homosexual panic; such panic is therefore instrumental in the construction of socially acceptable heterosexual masculine identifications.

Spencer Brydon, as a 'homosexual', is exempt from at least the epis-temological reaches of homosexual panic: his prosopopoeial double, however, whose conformity to American masculinity positions him within what Sedgwick calls 'the treacherous middle stretch of the mod-ern homosocial continuum' (Sedgwick, 1990: 188), signifies not only the heterosexual possibility that Brydon abandoned in his youth, but also the panic attendant upon such an identity. This goes far in explaining the abject performance of 'his other self in this other anguish', who literally cannot face the 'triumphant life' (James, 1908: 476) that Brydon has sustained in Europe. It is not surprising that the double *performs* as abject since his very status, his significance, is the identity that Brydon has long rejected and abjected but now, sum-moned up by the curiosities that shape his return, comes back to haunt the margins of his subjectivity. Moreover, this haunting abject emerges initially as a desired object, an object of ego identification, arising from Brydon's melancholic fascination with what he had foreclosed so long ago.

According to Judith Butler, the subject acquires gender and sexual identity through what she terms an 'exclusionary matrix': identifica-tion, she argues, takes place through a repudiation which produces a domain of abjection, a repudiation without which the subject cannot emerge. That which is refused, excluded, abjected from the subject's identification constitutes a 'zone of uninhabitability', a site of a dreaded identification against which the domain of the subject will circum-scribe its own claim to autonomy and to life. 'In this sense, then', she writes, 'the subject is constituted through the force of exclusion and abjection, one which produces a *constitutive outside* to the subject, an *abjected outside*, which is, after all, 'inside' the subject as its own found-ing repudiation' (Butler, 1994: 3). Moreover, this repressed identifica-tion, while 'outside', comes to 'haunt' the boundaries of identity 'as the persistent possibility of their disruption and rearticulation' (Butler, 1994: 8). It seems to me that Butler's concept of identity founded on an abjected 'other' is a useful, even necessary, supplement to Sedgwick's argument that homosexual panic is a 'psychologized' response to the 'social pressure of homophobic blackmail' (Sedgwick: 1985, 89). Moreover, Butler's figuration of the abject as 'haunting' the domain of the subject suggests the plausible emergence of this abject in Gothic representation, particularly through the discursive operations of such specular tropes as prosopopoeia and their ghostly literalisation.

My entire argument about the significance of Spencer Brydon's apparitional other, and the grounds for its emergence, is guided by a corollary to Butler's theory: if the subject is constituted through a matrix of exclusion, a 'foundational repudiation' of an unthinkable otherness, then this abjected and hypothetical otherness haunts the subject precisely as the Freudian shadow of the lost object in the pathology of melancholia. Indeed, Butler suggests that the melancholia attendant upon repudiation is the 'law of desire', the structuring principle of *all* identities, both prescribed and proscribed. Following Freud, who argues that the lost object becomes internalised as ego identification, Butler theorises heterosexuality as 'the melancholic answer to the loss of the same-sexed object', by which the 'subject is required to incorporate, and indeed to become that object through the construction of the ego ideal' (Butler, 1990: 63). Subsequently, 'all identification constructed through the exclusion of a sexuality…puts those identifications into question' because 'the excluded term of the binary continually haunts and disrupts the coherent posturing' of the ego's identifications; the 'excluded sexuality…contests the self-grounding pretensions of the subject' (Butler, 1990: 66). Moreover – and this is crucial for understanding the Spencer Brydon's impulse to call up the abjected other in 'The Jolly Corner' – the melancholic structure of gender and sexual identifications is applicable to both homosexuals and heterosexuals. 'Clearly', Butler writes, 'a homosexual for whom heterosexual desire is unthinkable may well maintain that heterosexuality through a melancholic structure of incorporation, an identification and embodiment of the love that is neither acknowledged or grieved' (Butler, 1990: 70).

I have long been fascinated by Sedgwick's observation that, in the nineteenth century, the troubling of gender and sexual identification is most evident, most clearly traumatic, in Gothic narrative. My interest is not in psychoanalytics of melancholia and abjection as such, but rather in the *writing* of Gothicised trauma, the possibility that the characteristic rhetorical devices of the Gothic might be said to have a precisely psychoanalytical grounding. 'The Jolly Corner' strikes me as an exemplary narrative of the unbinding of coherent sexual identities because James's psychological interests are intricately related, and may indeed arise from, the potentiality of Gothic tropes. Spencer Brydon's melancholy fixation upon a hypothetical, heterosexual other suggests that his double emerges from a long-repressed desire for the consolations of normative American identification – that it has long constituted the abjected 'outside' of his homosexual positioning. If it returns in the discursive production of prosopopoeia, the trope of haunting, it may also be understood as *allegorising* the melancholic structure of gender and sexual identification, as well as the unbinding of identificatory coherence. The Gothic extreme of James's narrative is not only that Brydon's repudiated 'heterosexual' other *returns*, but rather that it returns to perform, to signify, the panic that has prompted the ghostly double to *negate* Brydon's achieved identity in its own hypothetical 'life'. The Gothic horror is, I would say, *doubled* when Brydon, in his recoil from this monstrous other, is incapable of reading it simply as a sign. This failure to read what he has 'written' – what he has produced discursively – results in the undoing of his precarious homosexual identity, his inevitable *identification* with that excluded, abjected other. We leave Brydon in the firm control of Alice, who is properly understood not simply as co-author of the ghostly double, but as the agent of heterosexual compulsion; what his life will be with Alice, in his embodiment of this long-repudiated otherness, is a matter for speculation: and *this*, I suggest, is the Gothic nightmare of 'The Jolly Corner'. The effect of Brydon's Gothic melancholia, his extreme psychosis, is that he cannot accommodate difference or plurality. If, as Donna Przbylowicz has argued, this tale enacts 'a quest for signification', Brydon negates the possibility of having comprehended the signified' (Przbylowicz, 1986: 122). This negation of the signifier, its ghostly warning, suggests that Brydon 'negates the existence the other as part of himself and manifests an illusory return to unity whereby desire is repressed, thus reinstating the myth of the overtly coherent and centered self' (123–4). Because he cannot know the abject in its status as excluded other, his melancholia knows no resolution except an ironic identification with it. This is the punishment in late James for not knowing how to read, for mistaking the Gothic figure for literal reality. The Gothic excesses of 'The Jolly Corner', in the psychoanalytics of the discursive production of the abject double, reveal the peculiar modernity of the Gothic mode, as well as the indebtedness of emergent psychoanalysis to such cultural production.

Works cited

Butler, Judith. 1990. *Gender Trouble: Feminism and the Subversion of Identity.* New York: Routledge.

Butler, Judith. 1994. *Bodies that Matter: On the Discursive Limits of 'Sex'.* New York: Routledge.

De Man, Paul. 1986. *The Resistance to Theory.* Minneapolis: University of Minnesota Press.

Esch, Deborah. 1983. 'A Jamesian About-Face: Notes on "The Jolly Corner"'. *ELH* 50, 587–605.

Freud, Sigmund. 1917. 'Mourning and Melancholia'. In *On Metapsychology and the Theory of Psychoanalysis*. Trans. James Strachey. Ed. Angela Richards. London: Pelican, 1977, 245–68.

Hawthorne, Nathaniel. 1983. *The Scarlet Letter*. In *Novels*. Ed. Millicent Bell. New York: Library of America.

James, Henry. 1908. 'The Jolly Corner'. *New York Edition of the Novels and Tales of Henry James*.Vol. 17. New York: Scribner's, 435–85.

James, Henry. 1913. *A Small Boy and Others*. New York: Scribner's.

Kristeva, Julia. 1989. *Black Sun: Depression and Melancholia*. Trans. Leon S. Roudiez. New York: Columbia University Press.

Przbylowicz, Donna. 1986. *Desire and Repression: The Dialectic of Self and Other in the Late Works of Henry James*. University of Alabama Press.

Rajan, Tilottama. 1994. 'Mary Shelley's Mathilda: Melancholy and the Political Economy of Romanticism'. *Studies in the Novel* 26, 43–68.

Sedgwick, Eve Kosofsky. 1985. *Between Men: English Literature and Male Homosocial Desire*. New York: Columbia University Press.

Sedgwick, Eve Kosofsky. 1990. *Epistemology of the Closet*. Berkeley: University of California Press.

Sedgwick, Eve Kosofsky. 1994. *Tendencies*. Durham, NC: Duke University Press.

Part IV
Europe: dimensions of the body

The Gothic and the 'Otherings' of ascendant culture: the original *Phantom of the Opera*

Jerrold E. Hogle

> Let us examine anti-Semitism. It is not enough to say that we must liberate ourselves of so-called 'anti-Semitic prejudices' and learn to see Jews as they really are – in this way we will surely remain victims of these so-called prejudices. We must confront ourselves with how the ideological figure of the 'Jew' is invested by our unconscious desire, with how we have constructed this figure to escape a certain deadlock of our desire.
>
> (Slavoj Žižek, *The Sublime Object of Ideology*)

Especially over the last two decades, we have come to understand much more about the cultural drives underlying the European 'Gothic' fiction and drama that reached one apogee in the conflicted era still called 'Romantic' and then achieved a later effulgence at the next turn of the century (1885–1914), another tumultuous period of social transition, this one sometimes labelled the time of 'Decadent Romanticism'. Thanks to Leslie Fiedler, David Punter, Franco Moretti, Kate Ferguson Ellis and others in their wakes, we now see that it is in the Gothic, since the later eighteenth century, that 'the middle class displaces the hidden violence of present social structures, conjures them up again as past, and falls promptly under their spell' (Punter, 1980: 418). The Gothic enables a growing bourgeois hegemony to be both haunted by and protected from the 'hidden barbarities' (Punter, 1980: 419) that have helped make it possible, and hence the repressed uncertainties it feels about its own legitimacy, by recasting such anomalies into the horrors of old and seemingly alien spectres, buildings, and crypts. Indeed, as the Anglo-European-American Gothic progresses from *The Castle of Otranto* (1764), *The Mysteries of Udolpho* (1794), and *The Monk* (1796) to *Frankenstein* (1818), 'The Fall of the House of Usher' (1839),

Jane Eyre (1847), *Dr Jekyll and Mr Hyde* (1886), *Dracula* (1897) and *The Turn of the Screw* (1898), it keeps facing the middle-class reader and class-shifting protagonists with relocated, 'othered', monstrous, and/or spectral forms of the contradictions – and hence the potential dissolutions – that threaten, and threaten to expose, the unstable and mixed foundations of the cultural positions that such authors, characters and readers want to secure for themselves. This encounter is usually constructed so that the middle-class subject can be kept from beholding the contradictions directly by the extreme 'strangeness' or ghostliness of their Gothic reincarnations (see Moretti, 1988: 104–8). Albeit in different and changing ways, the Gothic author, hero(ine) and spectator thereby re-enact the cultural process that Thomas Pfau has seen in the treason trial rhetoric of early Romantic England:

> In order to compensate for the fundamentally unbearable knowledge of their historical instability, and so as to suspend the consciousness [that] a non-contradictory and fully aligned 'self' and 'culture' [are] irremediably illusory, [mostly middle-class] subjects tend to represent their historical knowledges in prosecutorial form, namely, by projecting them as malignant intentions onto [an] Other.[1]

The problem is that the 'Other' in the Gothic, which can disembody and conceal what it also incarnates and represents, has often become 'the unconscious' in too simple a sense, sometimes in the initial renderings or adaptations of Gothic works and quite frequently in the dominant ways of explaining or reusing the Gothic for most of the twentieth century. To be sure, the cultural process that helped generate Gothic fictions – the displacement of older aristocratic and priestly authority by an increasingly capitalist control of the economy that longed for the powers and features of what it had overcome – produced a 'dread of the [avenging] super-ego' from the patriarchal past 'whose splendid battlements [had] been battered but not quite cast down' and turned the hollowed-out 'shell[s] of paternal authority' (castles, abbeys, crypts) into dark locations of lost origins and primordial longings, whereupon a 'maternal blackness' was retrojected into them by middle-class desires both to repossess and to escape a predetermining past (Fiedler, 1966: 134). From this spatial and emotional configuration developed, in conjunction with other discourses, the Freudian ideological scheme of a buried, sequestered and archaic personal unconscious filled with ghostly memory traces of longings for the mother's body and repressed erotic and aggressive (even death-seeking) drives for the resatisfaction of those longings through above-ground substitutes that are dragged backward and downward toward this 'underground' or *anderer Schauplatz*. The Gothic thereby helped to provide some of the spacialisations of desire basic to what has since become a revealing way to interpret it. Even the increasingly female writers and protagonists of many Gothic fictions, prompted by the post-1750 ideology of the biological mother as more and more central to the nuclear family and home,[2] found themselves pulled back towards depths that contained the 'spectral presence of the dead-undead mother' (Kahane, 1985: 336).[3] There these women, like some male Gothic characters too, felt both longing and loathing at the prospect of being reabsorbed into the dead or dying maternal body, including all the repressions of drives and potentials by which that body had been confined to the depths of houses by the patriarchal schemes of the past and especially the present. What has become the psychoanalytic narrative of both seeking and trying to escape the inaccessible mother (the locus of birth by emergence *and* death by reabsorption) has governed and confined even proto-feminist moments in some Gothic works and readings of them. It seems as though one or another psychoanalytic plot were nearly always the essential Gothic plot, however much the Gothic precedes psychoanalysis in history and whatever the basis of the Gothic's psychological schemes in a larger cultural project of enacting and disguising social inequities and anxieties.

It should hardly be surprising, then, that some of the most advanced work on the Gothic over the last decade has suggestively connected its monstrous or ghostly 'others' to the process of 'abjection' and the figure of 'the abject' as defined in Julia Kristeva's highly neo-Freudian *Powers of Horror*.[4] Kristeva sees the primordial 'maternal blackness', dimly remembered in the body language or somatic memory of everyone, as a desired *and* feared state of utter betwixt-and-betweenness: the condition of being partly inside and partly outside the mother's body at the moment of birth and thus of emerging out of death (prenatal non-existence) and starting to live towards death (the end-point of the 'want' that begins at birth) all at the same time. This liminal situation is the radical heterogeneity, the difference of the self from itself at the start of its being, from which a person is never entirely removed, yet must work to 'feel separated', as Kristeva puts it, 'in order to be' a bounded, coherent individual able to be identified according to categories in the cultural-Symbolic order. The separation can seem to occur only if the individual carries out the literal meanings of 'ab-ject'. He or she must 'throw off' the original inside/outside and living/dying multiplicity (including the bisexual condition of a male child at that point of still being partly in the mother) and simultaneously 'throw [it] down and under', cast it off into a symbol, an 'other', that can be subjected to, and read as repugnant within, the Symbolic order apparently governed by the cultural Law of the Father rather than the Body of the Mother.

By such a construction, this act of 'abjection' produces 'otherings' that embody 'the abject' by being contradictory in themselves (death in life/life in death, ambisexual, infantile/adult, marginalised/centralised, fragmentary and whole) so that the observing 'subjects' can seem to be completely different from, and thus seem to have more identity than, those 'ugly' or 'buried' conditions. The Gothic, seen in this way, allows readers who have all 'abjected' in their own fashions both to confront and to keep othering the abject forcefully in antiquated, grotesque, and/or ghostly-cadaverous forms: in the bleeding and fragmented effigy-ghost in *The Castle of Otranto*; the shape-shifting boy-vixen Rosario/Matilda – or the highly Germanic, living/dead 'Wandering Jew' – in *The Monk*; the man-child yellow-black 'monster' brought to life from pieces of decaying bodies in *Frankenstein*; the necrophilial and incestuous embrace of Roderick and the encrypted Madeline in 'the House of Usher'; the swarthy, sexually voracious and multi-racial Bertha Rochester (the madwoman in the attic) of *Jane Eyre*; the infantile, external/internal, high-class/low-class, possibly heterosexual/homosexual 'angry man' in *Dr Jekyll and Mr Hyde*; the undead aristocratic-capitalist patriarch who can maternally feed his vixens from his breast (while still having a mostly 'child-brain') in *Dracula*; and the ghosts of forbidden, class-crossing sex that are undecidably 'out there' and 'all in the mind' for the governess in *The Turn of the Screw*.

But this reading of the Gothic, like more generally Freudian ones, valid though they often are up to a point, can be taken in even more revealing *or* in repressive and deceptive directions. The result depends on the degree to which we connect psychological repression with the cultural ways of constructing coherent senses of 'self' that initially made, and still make, the very concept of repression conceivable. Kristeva herself shows both the possibilities of seeing and the problems of not really exploring these links in the parallels we can find between abjection in *Powers of Horror* and her sense, in *Strangers to Ourselves*, of how and why we Westerners view or construct various kinds of 'foreigners'. On the one hand, she shows in *Strangers* how French abjections are bound up with a centripetal, 'compact social texture' that tries to establish an order of 'values' that remains 'sheltered from great invasions and intermixing of populations' (Kristeva, 1991: 38). On the other hand, 'the fascinated rejection that the foreigner arouses in us' for Kristeva is ultimately, in its 'uncanny strangeness', a reflection of 'our infantile desires and fears of the other – the other of death, the other of woman, the other of uncontrollable drive'. The foreigner is thus always 'within us', always a sign that 'we are fighting our unconscious', that otherness within ourselves, whenever we fear or disparage someone 'other' than ourselves (Kristeva, 1991: 191). The first cause for cultural conflict is personal and psychological and universally so, it seems, as though the construction of what is 'personal' or 'psychological' were not itself a product of cultural interactions, of attempts to fashion grounds for group identities (such as the 'self-determined psyche' of bourgeois ideology) over against some 'other' of those grounds that seems culturally foreign to them.

To fall back thus on a universal human nature, albeit an otherness from the self in the self, is to cover up and distract attention from the cultural othering that allows any construction of a human 'essence' to situate itself in contrast to a 'nature' different from its own. Worse yet, to find only a universality of human self-division within the Gothic interplay of forms is doubly deceptive. That sort of reading, when too exclusive, ignores both the priority of cultural over psychological othering and the fact that the figures for the abject in the Gothic, as in the 'monsters' listed above, are all anomalies within standards of cultural wholeness. They are crossers of boundaries between the 'normal' separations of classes or genders or races or states of existence and so are 'other' because they violate by combining differentiations that hegemonic culture would like to keep distinct. We should continue to explore the psychoanalytic 'abjections' in the Gothic, then, but mainly as they interact with and manifest the 'throwings down and under' of attempts at cultural distinction. Struggles for cultural definition are what clearly haunt the Gothic most in its anomalous monsters and spectres, as well as the desires of its heroes and heroines, and are in fact what brought the Gothic about as a mixture of waning aristocratic and rising bourgeois discourses.[5]

Unfortunately, too many modern interpretations of the Gothic, outside certain restricted circles of authors, readers and academicians, allow a reductive version of the psychoanalytic view, or sanitised forms of it that are even more reductive, to wrest Gothic materials into safe manifestations of predictable, commodifiable, middle-class emotions that suppress and ignore the cultural power-plays being acted out – and sometimes exposed – in Gothic abjections. Nowhere has this 'whitewashing' been more apparent than in the most successful revival of a

European Gothic story in the last decade: the musical stage version of *The Phantom of the Opera* by Andrew Lloyd Webber, Charles Hart and Richard Stilgoe, which debuted in London in 1986, opened on Broadway in New York in 1987, and is still playing to capacity houses in several fixed and touring productions around the world. Although it returns more than some earlier adaptations to aspects of the original French Gothic novel written by Gaston Leroux and published in Paris in 1910, this *Phantom* plays heavily on the subterranean 'ghost's' initial disguise as the 'Angel' whose coming to the young singer-heroine, Christine Daae, backstage at the Paris Opera seems to fulfil the promise of her now-dead violinist-father 'to send the Angel of Music to you ... When I'm in heaven.' The Lloyd Webber phantom calls erotically to Christine from behind the mirror in her dressing-room as a Music Master/Voice of the Father singing 'inside [her] mind' and soon draws her hypnotically with him to the 'labyrinth underground', especially to his medievalised lair (complete with portcullis) on one shore of the lake over which the Opera was built. There he offers to be the male ful-filment of 'all [her] fantasies' – clearly Freudian fantasies of feminine desire for the father – while revealing himself as seeking a substitute in her, her voice and 'the music of the night' for the mother who turned from him in 'fear and loathing' when his face failed to change from its deformed condition at birth (Perry, 1987: 145–6, 165).

This emphasis, complicated by very little other personal history in this version, unabashedly carries through the principal reduction of Leroux's story that begins with the Lon Chaney silent film, resplen-dently produced by Carl Laemmle in 1924–5, and continues in Universal's sound and full-colour remake (with Claude Rains) in 1943, as well as in most subsequent filmings. As James Twitchell has shown,[6] the general pattern of adaptations takes what is already the very French tale of Beauty and the Beast, itself an allegory about the threat of incest (where the Beast takes the place of Beauty's father as the master of her new home), and turns it into a challenge to the young to be tempted by, but then to reject, the necrophilial seductiveness of the already-dead or 'underground' father-figure – or, in the phantom's case, the mother-figure – and to prefer, instead of such 'bestiality', a more proper, exogamous love: the Vicomte Raoul de Chigny for Christine, her childhood sweetheart in the Leroux and Lloyd Webber versions (Twitchell, 1985: 279–87).

The musical's final scene, unlike the endings of the Universal films, even offers the double satisfaction/renunciation of Christine kissing the unmasked phantom full on the lips *in order to secure* her and

Raoul's freedom to leave together. This 'climax' allows all the conflicting main fantasies to be fulfilled at once within precise limits of conscious acceptability. 'Daughter' kisses 'father' specifically for the sake of choosing exogamy (as finally happens with Beauty and the Beast); the 'son' is finally embraced (though not for too long) by the 'mother' so that he at least feels less rejected; and Christine and Raoul are liberated to marry by the heretofore threatening 'father', who must then determine the mode of his own disappearance for having almost insisted, Beast-like, on a form of incest. All these prospects stay neatly within the confines of the bourgeois, nuclear 'family romance' ideology as possibilities it encourages us first to pursue and then to sublimate, deny and even punish vicariously. They are also played out, not just in spaces of illuminated conscious performance haunted by masked figures from an 'underground' *Schauplatz*, but amid a splendour of dazzling production values that offers and markets the illusion of middle-class access to spectacles available only to the wealthy, the position of being 'invited backstage at the Opera' to which the audience (like the phantom) aspires, sometimes by paying the highest London or Broadway prices for 'popular musical theatre'.[7]

Such recastings of the Leroux novel, while they occasionally offer glimpses into its cultural acts of 'casting out and down', suppress most of the abjections that the book carries out. To counter this excessively comforting concealment of what really makes the story most frightening and to show how the tale both resists and empowers that very concealment, I want to look more closely at Leroux's *Fantôme de l'Opéra*. Indeed, I want to show how much it is a 'Decadent Romantic' culmination, in fact an astonishing and unsettling effulgence, of the cultural othering that develops and accelerates in the Gothic generally, particularly at the turn of the nineteenth into the twentieth century. The original *Phantom*, I would argue, written by a journalist-novelist manifestly steeped in the Anglo-European and American Gothic (among many other discourses), shows the enormous range of cultural abjections that Gothic constructions make possible at a time of great social upheaval and consequent attempts at re-establishing national, class, racial, gender and city/country distinctions. Moreover, by taking these tendencies in the Gothic to such extremes, the original *Phantom* comes to expose the basic nature of the culturally determined 'deadlock of desire', the social and *then* psychological instability that perpetually threatens the dissolution of the middle-class 'fragmented subject'.[8] It is *this* betwixt-and-between condition, both half-revealed and half-concealed in Leroux's *Phantom*, that leads to the Gothic process (and other processes) of cultural 'othering', to its concealment within the ideologies of the personal unconscious and the nuclear family romance (and thus within purely psychological notions of 'abjection'), and to the effort in nearly all the adaptations to keep us safe from the phantom's greatest threats.

Granted, Leroux's novel was written in the midst of widespread French interest in the new Freudian psychoanalysis, fairly public debates about its connections to and differences from the dynamic psychiatry of Charcot and Janet, and the consequent increase in middle-class and journalistic uses of the libidinal/primitive/infantile/mother-seeking unconscious to explain anarchist uprisings, foreign rebellions against European imperialism, and the causes of increased urban criminality, as well as publicised cases of female hysteria, incest, infidelity and homosexuality – all contributors to a *fin de siècle* fear of European cultural degeneration and decadence.[9] Consequently, the original *Fantôme de l'Opéra* encourages the more sanitised Freudianism of many adaptations by making its title figure, Erik, draw Christine down to an extremely maternal, and phallically maternal, underground/unconscious. The chamber in which he keeps her at the heart of his very *non*-medieval lair is an exact duplicate of his mother's exceedingly 'bourgeois' bedroom furnished from the Louis Philippe era (the 1830s–1840s) – 'all that remains for me of my poor, miserable mother' – and one distinctive feature of this room is a small hanging sack, 'the little pouch of life and death'. (Leroux, 1910: 471, 416).[10] The pouch contains two keys that Christine may use to turn either of two phallus-shaped figures of bronze, a 'scorpion' or a 'grasshopper', one of which will initiate a flooding 'rocket of water' and the other a massive explosion of powder at the depths of the Opera that would like, officially, to pretend it is not grounded in such orgasmic possibilities for its own destruction (Leroux, 1910: 463). It would seem that Erik is almost asking a mother-substitute to put the fragmented parts of male genitals, apparently castrated ones, back together and thus to be the locus, the maternal bed, of the phallus he wants her (and himself in her) to have. But the phantom really seeks a more complete, and less simply sexual, satisfaction, and that is what diffuses his aggressions at the original novel's climax. Leroux's Christine does not kiss Erik (nor does she help admit his destroyers, as in other versions) but instead holds him tenderly at breast level in the mother's bedroom underground and weeps copiously so that her 'tears flow onto [his] forehead', into his eye sockets, even 'into [his] mouth', all now unmasked (Leroux, 1910: 480). This moment is a combination of *pietà* pose (with Erik soon to die), quasi-feeding at the breast, and the infantile face awash in clear maternal fluid, as at the moment of birth itself (or, in this case, a reversed birth, a partial re-entry into the birth canal). In the true Kristevan sense, Erik, half-inside/half-outside the mother, becomes a locus of the abject, especially at the instant when the boundaries of self and other seem almost to dissolve between Erik and Christine.

The actual nature of Erik's horrific face, as rendered by Leroux, seems only to add to this blatant Freudian symbolism. From birth that face has been a nearly naked skull, one with deeply recessed eyes and paper-thin skin as yellow as parchment. Despite Leroux's debts to Victor Hugo's *Nôtre Dame de Paris* (1831), the original phantom is not the merely deformed, Quasimodo-like figure that appears in all the film and stage versions, even the ones where some characters have the momentary impression that he looks like a skull.[11] For Leroux he is not wearing a skull-mask (as one of his many masks) when he appears as Edgar Allan Poe's 'Red Death' at the *bal masqué*, a frequently adapted scene. The skull is his face. He is the only figure at the ball in the novel who enters *un*masked, and the effect of his face on its beholders, even before they have fully seen it, is to pull them towards the state of death it suggests, as when 'a cadaverous pallor spread itself over Christine's face [and] her eyes developed circles around them' at Raoul's mere mention of his having overheard the voice of 'the other' (*l'autre*) behind her dressing-room door (Leroux, 1910: 109–10). Leroux's Erik is the haunting of death and the death-drive from the depths of the unconscious (perhaps the ultimate Other),[12] even as he also embodies the degeneration and decadence that many feared they would find beneath the surface of *la belle époque* in France. Most especially, he is a figure of the abject, where death is coterminous with birth and life proceeds from and towards death from the start (so much so that the mother-substitute can become the object of desire *as* death). After all, the phantom's face can suggest both an aged death's-head and the state of the head at birth during that brief extra-uterine time when the skin seems barely to cover the skull. It would seem that Erik both masks and incarnates the drive towards and away from being-in-the-mother and the drive away from and towards death itself, all of which must be 'thrown down and under' for consistent selves to be distinct from such inconsistent states.

To leave Leroux's *Phantom* at such levels, though, however flagrantly (indeed, *too* obviously) they announce themselves, is to ignore all that these images are connected to in the novel – and thus the full range of what is really being symbolised and abjected there. By 1910, the 'underground' face as skull, for one thing, was already laden with extensive cultural baggage. Leroux points to some of it when he connects his skeletal anti-hero to the mental condition of a 'veritable child', much as Bram Stoker's ancient Dracula was given a 'child-brain', and when he has his phantom confront the Persian, the former policeman from Mazanderan who knows Erik's history better than anyone, with the 'air' of a 'fatal rock' which can also stand 'upright at the back of [his] boat and sw[i]ng about with the balance of a monkey' before disappearing into the lake beneath the Opera (Leroux, 1910: 387, 389). Such pointed additions allude to the skull as it frequently appears in post-Darwinian criminology, where it is used to represent the still-primitive lurking in man, the childhood of the race remaining as a potential in its unconscious, that is supposedly revealed in criminals (like Erik – or the 'troglodytic' Mr. Hyde) who show that humankind can *de*volve and degenerate back towards the simian and savage states from which it has supposedly evolved. Cesare Lombroso had reasserted, just before Leroux began *Le Fantôme*, that the quite distinct skull of the criminal, as though social difference were identical with biological destiny, clearly reveals 'an atavistic being who reproduces in his person the ferocious instincts of primitive humanity and the lower animals' (in Nye, 1984: 99).

Leroux tacks this Darwinian regression onto Freudian regression (or vice versa), using both to link his phantom to the class and culture implications not so very hidden in Lombroso's sense of the 'lower'. *Le Fantôme* juxtaposes Erik's extraordinary knowledge of classical music and feel for high-class opera with the relative illiteracy of his 'bizarre' notes to the Opera managers. The result is a skull-faced phantom who can restyle Mozart's *Don Giovanni* into his own 'Don Juan Triumphant' and yet 'has not yet learned to join his letters' at the level of rudimentary middle-class penmanship (Leroux, 1910: 250, 63). Especially since he turns out to be the son of an entrepreneurial mason from Rouen (Leroux, 1910: 494), Leroux's Erik is a grotesque combination of the 'highbrow' and the 'lowbrow'. He crosses and blurs a line of social differentiation that had become increasingly vital to the rising middle classes and the new or surviving aristocracy (the audience, management and patrons of the Opera). That line was based precisely, Erik's face reminds us, on the phrenological distinction between 'highbrowed' and 'lowbrowed' races which frequently employed skulls to demonstrate the difference. A vivid example is this illustration from *Coombs' Popular Phrenology* of 1865, which blatantly contrasts a symbol of European 'high culture' (the high-browed head of William Shakespeare) against a slant-browed, skeletal representative of 'low', non-European, pre-civilised existence (the disinterred skull of a New Zealand aborigine).[13] Leroux's Erik-skull, by this standard, may not be 'Deficient in…all the Intellectual Organs' the way the New Zealand chief is said to have been, but it clearly pulls high culture towards that other extreme to such a degree as to threaten the dissolution of a hierarchy basic to the cultural position of the Opera and its subscribers.

Moreover, the skull-faced phantom is just as threatening as an 'other' of indistinction who shifts between racial, sexual and political positions. The yellowness of his thin epidermis, along with his years in Mazanderan and his knowledge of the Punjab rope trick from India, *orientalises* Erik. He is wrapped, despite being a native-born Frenchman, in Western misconstructions of 'the Orient', a less than fully civilised otherness that supposedly stretched from Africa and the Middle East all the way across southern and eastern Asia.[14] Indeed, Erik's capacity to become racially other has the widest possible range, even to the point of extending beyond the genus of upright mammals. He can appear to Raoul like 'certain albinos' noted for having 'the eyes of a cat at night' or

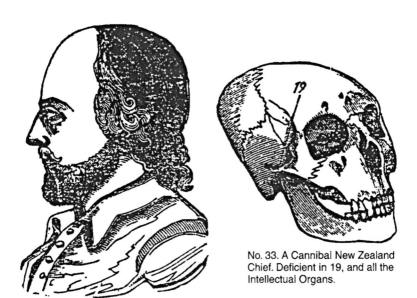

No. 33. A Cannibal New Zealand Chief. Deficient in 19, and all the Intellectual Organs.

No. 32. Portrait of Shakespeare.

Figure 10.1   First published in *Coombs' Popular Phrenology*, 1865, reproduced in Lawrence W. Levine, *Highbrow/Lowbrow: The Emergence of Cultural Hierarchy in America* (Cambridge, MA: Harvard University Press, 1988).

can become the most attractive he ever seems to Christine by dissolving completely into the role of Verdi's Otello behind a 'black mask' as they sing together underground (Leroux, 1910: 295, 252–3). He can disappear into a radically (and racially) other self far more than opera singers are supposed to do when they are a 'Carlotta' or 'Christine' *singing* Gounod's Marguerite rather than *becoming* that character. This range of racial possibilities is matched by the extraordinary six-octave range of Erik's singing voice, which in turn allows him to appear to change genders, particularly when he disguises himself as *la Sirène* singing a femininely 'sweet and captivating harmony' through a reed and does so from the depths of the lake beneath the Opera to tempt unwanted invaders into the waters of indistinction (Leroux, 1910: 384–5).

Meanwhile, since Erik builds his hidden passages and parts of his lair from the remnants of the Paris Commune (which occupied the unfinished Opera for three months in 1871),[15] he explicitly recalls the 'skeleton' that workmen 'uncovered' in what had been Commune dungeons under the Opera and that Paris 'newspapers' had claimed to be 'a victim of the Commune', despite what Leroux considered insufficient evidence (Leroux, 1910: 15). Leroux turns this ambiguous skeleton into a skeletal 'phantom' who, on the one hand, seems a Communard rebel to authorities partly because he still occupies Commune space and, on the other, behaves like a class-climbing, bourgeois entrepreneur and stockholder, acquiring and investing massive capital (20,000 francs a month from the Opera management) for the sake of taking over and expanding the Commune infrastructure. Rebuilding and extending his original bourgeois home underground, Erik aspires to the high-culture status, wealth and dress of those who occupy boxes at the Opera, such as his reserved Box Five (Leroux, 1910: 63). As we have seen, previous Gothic monster/ghosts have been the 'others' into which several social, as well as personal, inconsistencies – and anxious feelings about them – have been abjected. But few have been layered with as many betwixt-and-between and shifting cultural positions and roles as Leroux's original phantom of the Opera.

The great irony in this novel is that the Paris Opera, the most centralised and official institution of high culture and the supreme announcement of French 'imperial power … and the participation of the urban middle-class audience in the imperial enterprise',[16] is entirely dependent on the multiple transgressions abjected into its underground 'opera ghost', as Leroux suggests by making Erik one of the Opera's original (if unsung) builders as well as the perpetual caretaker of its deepest (if most hidden) foundations (Leroux, 1910: 497). The Opera cannot conquer and contain, let alone 'other', the 'Orient' as it does in its interior design resembling a 'Turkish bath' (as Debussy claimed) or its several operas on 'exotic' oriental subjects (ranging from *Otello* to Massenet's *Roi de Lahore*, both mentioned in the novel) unless these different cultures can truly intersect and the 'Oriental' can pull the 'Occidental' towards itself.[17] Nor can there be the gender-crossing and role-playing essential to many operas (as when Christine sings the young man 'Siebel' in her first Gounod role) unless Erik's quasi-transvestism and ability to become black are possible (as it was possible for Leroux to disguise himself as an Arab to report on riots in occupied Morocco).[18] The Opera cannot be a monument to rising high culture, and hence the epitome of class-climbing acquisition, unless it can set itself against more primitive, 'low-brow', provincial, even criminal counterparts, all that Erik embodies alongside his own, more naked class-climbing. Then, too, the operas staged in this cultural centre cannot ultimately subject women, the handicapped, foreigners and the old to religious, state-based, usually Caucasian, and middle-aged (or younger) patriarchal dominance, the way Catherine Clement has shown them to do, unless the subjected figures can all be ideologically linked to 'the forces of the night' and the desire for that night connected, at least in women, to a pre-conscious longing for the patriarch himself (Clement, 1988: 22).[19] Erik incarnates all these necessary – but also necessarily denied and hidden – possibilities upon which high culture constructs its façades and self-stagings. He consequently threatens to expose their actual, mixed foundations and basic drives and so must be demonised, criminalised and reduced, even by sympathisers, to those parts of him that are aberrant, low-brow, 'foreign', childish, and grotesque in their cultural, sexual and artistic hybridity. As the native-born 'foreignness within' the very centre of cultural nationalism, he represents the intertwined multiplicities within culture that must be abjected, both visibly and invisibly, before there can be institutions that propose and promote entirely psychological abjections.

The most shocking threat that Leroux's Erik presents to Opera high culture, though – and ultimately the novel's greatest threat to a simply psychoanalytic reading of it – is his extensive connection with and prodigious display of the carnivalesque. The phantom's famous projection of a toad's 'Couac' into the mouth of the prima donna Carlotta during a performance of Gounod's *Faust* stops the action for several pages prior to Erik's dropping of the chandelier, pages that dwell on the opera audience's utter 'consternation', the 'sort...they would have felt if they had been present at the catastrophe that broke off the arms of the Venus de Milo!' (Leroux, 1910: 153). The most 'classic' of high-culture icons (either the Opera or the most famous Greek statue in the Louvre) is viewed as grossly violated, not just by the intrusion of an animal into a human voice, but by its source in a trick of country-carnival ventriloquy learned by Erik, along with many other feats of lower-class 'magic', in his younger days as a circus freak made 'to traverse Europe from fair to fair' (Leroux, 1910: 153). As Peter Stallybrass and Allon White have shown, carnival was turned into 'trade shows' and then totally suppressed in the streets of Paris from the 1870s through to 1910–20 (the exact time-frame of *The Phantom*) as 'the emergent bourgeoisie' deliberately *'made* carnival into the festival of the Other', even in such well-controlled events as the Opera's *bal masqué*, in order to define itself as the conqueror of "base" languages' precisely in such institutions as the Paris Opera (Stallybrass and White, 1986: 177–81). For the phantom to invade the Opera with carnival and for him to be carnival unmasked at the masked ball is for him to be, very literally, the 'return of the repressed' from a mixed-class social cacophony that has had to 'go underground' or stay outside the city as the most 'lowbrow' and 'childish' theatrics of all – though again a theatrics quite basic to many of the devices in opera.

In fact, Erik is not the father or the son in a subterranean quest for the paternal or maternal, nor can he construct the bag and the bronze switches in his counterfeit of his mother's *boudoir*, until he has first become what he has been much longer: a builder of carnival funhouses and (later) Persian 'magic box' variations on them. Aspects of these, after all, appear in his construction of much of the Opera, as well as in the little 'palace of illusions' (or hexagon of twisting mirrors) crafted to drive invaders mad right behind the underground bedroom (Leroux, 1910: 494–6, 433). The psychoanalytic scenario of Christine and Erik's journey to the depths, like the Paris Opera, is built on the foundations and from the materials of carnival first. Even for Christine to see Erik as in some ways equivalent to her father is to recall that old Daae, before his death and his promise of an 'Angel of Music', was a country fiddler 'going from fair to fair' much as the phantom did (Leroux, 1910: 97). Christine herself is thus a 'lowbrow' carrier of the carnivalesque into the Opera, especially as she is drawn more into its depths. It is therefore the betwixt-and-betweenness of the carnivalesque, epitomised in the ways Erik straddles the borderlines of many distinctions, that must be abjected within and beneath the Opera before the resulting 'abject' figures can incarnate any maternal inside or outside, any paternal incest or any buried condition of living from and for death.

Leroux's novel confirms Stallybrass and White's startling reminder to us that the verbal renderings of many hysterical symptoms by Freud and his mainly bourgeois patients, and hence the larger constructions of the unconscious by psychoanalysis, were frequently composed from 'broken fragments of carnival'. These had 'suddenly reemerge[d] in the heart of bourgeois life', like a phantom in the Opera, and made that life the 'site of [a] potential neurosis' born from the ascendant class's 'phobic alienation' from and lingering desire for carnival. 'By forcing [this] threshold and interrogating the liminal position' of this alienation and desire, Leroux's *Phantom of the Opera*, recalling some tendencies in 'bourgeois romanticism and its modernist inheritors, stage[s] a festival of the political unconscious and reveal[s] the repressions and social rejections which formed it', even as the novel eventually falls back on the fading of this kind of 'abject' (Erik's willing of his own death and burial) in the wake of a psychoanalytic resolution that seems to offer a return to immersion in the fluid of the mother (Stallybrass and White, 1986: 171, 180–2).

As much as or more than *The Monk*'s Wandering Jew, Frankenstein's creature, Poe's Ligeia, Charlotte Brontë's Bertha Rochester, Dr Jekyll's Edward Hyde and Stoker's Dracula, the original 'opera ghost' of Leroux incarnates what Stallybrass and White call 'the 'Other' of a defining group or self' by being 'a boundary phenomenon of hybridisation and inmixing, in which self and other become enmeshed in an inconclusive, heterogeneous, dangerously unstable zone' (Stallybrass and White, 1986: 193). Indeed, by serving as such a figure of the 'abject', the phantom of the Opera brings the Gothic interplay of discourses to an unusually direct, though never head-on, confrontation with an historical process in which the Gothic has always participated, knowingly or unknowingly. Stallybrass and White define the process thus:

> When the bourgeoisie consolidated itself as a respectable and conventional body by withdrawing itself from the popular, it constructed the popular as grotesque otherness; but by this act of withdrawal and consolidation it produced *another grotesque*, an identity-in-difference which was nothing other than [the bourgeoisie's] fantasy relation, its negative symbiosis, with that which it had rejected in its social practices... The 'poetics' of transgression reveals the disgust, fear and desire which inform the dramatic self-representation of that culture through the 'scene of its low Other'.
> (Stallybrass and White, 1986: 193, 202)

Leroux's phantom, who is many aspects of the 'popular' turned into a single incarnating 'other', is clearly a supreme Gothic example of that 'other grotesque' which can be ideologically (and poetically or dramatically) constructed by this mode of cultural production. An 'other grotesque' is not simply 'the popular othered' but a symbolic distancing of that process from those who perform it. In operating so 'away from us' and 'down there', it is also a partial disguise/partial revelation of how the 'othering' of the hybrid/carnivalesque creates both an 'abject' of revulsion and an object of desire, a horror cast off *and* wanted – as the often attractive, enticing 'other' – by the culture that needs this otherness in order to seem itself by contrast. The partial desire for that other and the prohibition of that desire, sometimes combined in a pitying of the othered figure, as happens with Christine and the narrator by the end of *Le Fantôme* (Leroux, 1910: 481, 497–8), are essential components of the ascendant culture's establishment and governance of both itself *and* what it 'throws off'.

At the same time, just as Leroux's novel incorporates the phantom into the 'undergrounds' and 'backstage' of the Opera, the ascendant culture 'produces [its supposed] domain [of mastery] by taking into itself as *negative introjections* the very domains that surround and threaten it' (Stallybrass and White, 1986: 89). In this fashion all that is jointly 'othered' can be both basic to and excluded from – and thus 'abjected *in*' – the constructed 'centre' of dominant culture, particularly at a time of transition in Europe when those producing that centre wanted to re-establish control over the exclusions that made the dominant order what it seemed to be by being at once subsumed within and cast outside it. This duplicity of containment and exile is even enhanced by the way its middle to upper-middle-class schematisation takes its negative introjections of hybridity and transforms them into purely subjective phobias and fascinations, some of them acceptably 'conscious' and some of them repressed into an 'unconscious' that can declare its most basic drives only in disguised manifestations of them – much as this whole scheme is a disguised manifestation of the drives for cultural distinction that are quite basic to it. Leroux's novel, while portraying the cultural 'abjection' of betwixt-and-between 'carnivalesque' conditions and the 'return of the abject' in what wants to subsume these, is itself betwixt and between in both playing out theatrical and fictional exaggerations of this process and reflecting the psychoanalytic drive towards rendering that process as a dream-like, subjective struggle of desires for the mother, the father and death. That hybridity in the original *Phantom*, which parallels its condition as partly 'highbrow', partly 'lowbrow' (the condition of many Gothic novels), is what most basically sets the stage for both its misreading by and its difference from its adaptations.

Still, Leroux's book does manage to resist its sanitised versions in one especially important way, and this resistance points back to the deeply cultural 'deadlock of our desire' that the middle-class Gothic, as well as *The Phantom of the Opera*, has always been about to some extent. The Erik–Christine relationship, as Leroux renders it in 1910 – that of an older, obsessed, apparently demonic, yet highly skilled music master hypnotically teaching a young woman to sing with great brilliance – alludes immediately to the figure of Svengali, the Austrian Jew often called 'the German', who mesmerises the title character into becoming a dazzling singer in George du Maurier's novel *Trilby* (1894). This English literary sensation by a French expatriate was very quickly adapted for the stage, adding to Svengali's notoriety. One of the most anti-Semitic creations in literary history, Svengali far outdistances Shylock, Fagin *and* the Wandering Jew in his ugly and lascivious conniving. Given Svengali's passion for travelling in 'the poisonous East', much like Erik's, and his ability to frighten his love-object into looking like a 'stupid empty skull' (du Maurier, 1894: 337, 105), foreshadowing Christine's imitation of the death's-head quality of Erik's face, it is impossible for Leroux's phantom to avoid at least some of the associations attached to Svengali's Jewishness. In fact, his having travelled throughout Eastern Europe, Persia, India and even southern Russia before his return to France lends Erik some aspects of the turn-of-the-century reconstructions of the Wandering Jew. Inspired by the flood of Jewish immigrants into Paris which stemmed mostly from the Russian pogroms of 1881 (about the year of *The Phantom*'s main events), this constructed figure was partly the creation of French psychiatrists, who attributed the 'nomadic proclivities' of Jews to a mental condition of the race which, as with Erik, 'made great intellectual powers and cerebral debilities intersect' (Goldstein, 1985: 535, 543).[20]

Yet even as Leroux plays with these associations, he is clearly anxious to dissociate Erik from Judaism *per se*. This is the same Gaston Leroux, we should recall, who was already known as a journalist for his ringing indictments of anti-Semitism in his reports on the retrial of Alfred Dreyfus for *Le Matin* in 1899.[21] Svengali's most specifically Jewish traits are therefore left out of Erik, by and large, and the European part of the phantom's 'foreignness' is connected only to those aspects of him that seem Germanic: his adopted name, his special affinity for Mozart and his attempted seduction of Christine with a dish marinated in Tokay wine 'from the cellars of Koenigsburg' (Leroux, 1910: 248–50). After all, the demonisation of the German, and even the Scandinavian, was *de rigeur* in Paris by 1910, given the increasing tensions with Germany

and the fear of German infiltrators which would soon climax in World
War I, the anger still seething over the German-Prussian invasion of
Paris in 1870–1 (the time when the phantom supposedly begins working on his parts of the Opera), and the near-total ban on German compositions at the Paris Opera itself, even in the Gounod version of *Faust*,
which Frenchifies the heroine (turning Gretchen into Marguerite) and
damns her still-German hero-seducer, precisely as Goethe, Gounod's
main source, would not finally do.[22] With this 'otherness' added to his
many 'others', Leroux's Faustian 'Erik' becomes a mixture of French/
Germanic and Gentile/Wandering Jew-ish origins, as well as a being who
is civilised/troglodytic, ageing adult/young child, highbrow/lowbrow,
occidental/oriental, male/female, white/'coloured', social-climber/com-
munard and operatic/carnivalesque, not to mention lover/father and
living/dead. And all the while, his most expressed desire is to emerge out
of these multiple conditions, through his several class-climbing efforts,
so as 'to live as everyone in the world does' above ground – to abject all
of his otherness, as 'normal' people do, and not *be* abject/abnormal –
even if that means inventing 'a mask that makes [him] the figure of just
anyone' (Leroux, 1910: 411). Erik's eagerness to don a mask is made
highly ironic by the perspective of Leroux's narrator, whose most direct
and judgemental intrusions into the narrative make it clear that he
regards the above-ground world Erik seeks as a gallery of deceptive simulacra where a 'person will never be Parisian who has not learned to wear
a mask'. In 'Paris, one is always at a masked ball' (Leroux, 1910: 54–5).
Even to be 'just anyone' is to be masked in some way, whether one is
inside or outside the Opera and its *bal masqué*.

Given this irony, Erik's demonised, 'othered' and abjected complex
of contraries becomes a frightening symptomatic reference to the
potentially irresolvable slippage between possible states of existence
that underlies the ideology of the bourgeois subject who strives to rise
above such a morass from within it. This terrifying threat of dissolution is at the root of the 'deadlock of our desire' suggested by Žižek in
my epigraph – and a key motivator, I would claim as well, for the
process of 'othering' throughout the middle-class Gothic, a othering
brought to a revealing, if momentary, climax in the original *Phantom of
the Opera* far more than in any of its adaptations. As both Žižek and
Leroux demonstrate in their different discourses, contradictory or
repugnant states are not 'othered' into races of people (such as Jews or
Germans or 'Orientals') or other kinds of scapegoats simply because
some of us refuse to see 'what those beings are really like'. Such throw-
ings-down-and-under occur because any attempted ideology of definite

selfhood, especially the bourgeois ideology (the ideology that Erik is ultimately trying to suit), misrepresents, even in claiming to represent, the 'antagonism', the 'traumatic social division' that leads to competing ideologies, from which presumptive identities try to emerge by casting this antagonism off (Žižek, 1989: 45).[23]

To image or articulate this antagonism, which encompasses a welter of social possibilities difficult to separate *or* reconcile, is immediately to cover it (as Erik keeps doing and cultured Paris does too) with an ideological mask that at once confronts a 'deadlock': its inadequacy to its amorphous 'object', its claim of desired certainty that is really uncertain of its historical foundations and sanctions. Bourgeois capitalist thinking only compounds this problem in the 'contradiction' basic to it 'between the [actual] social mode of production and the [supposedly] individual, private mode of appropriation' that has to misrecognise and abject its multiple social underpinnings (Žižek, 1989: 52). The negativity and the disruption of a desired coherence in this contradiction can be overcome only if the inconsistency can be embodied in an 'other' – for self-deceiving Aryans in the 'traumatic figure of the Jew' or African or Oriental – that seems to both incarnate and sequester the contradiction (allowing it to live as dead in a certain sense) while thereby becoming, as hegemony's apparent negation, the 'positive condition' of a 'higher culture' identity (Žižek, 1898: 176). In that way the projectors of this alterity, to recall Pfau's words, can 'compensate' for the 'unbearable knowledge of their historical instability', the sort of knowledge with which the class-crossing and death-bound phantom confronts his observers. They can 'represent [such] historical knowledge' as an Other's 'malignant intentions', as though, by contrast, there could be, aided by the ideological mask of a psychoanalytic subjectivity, 'a non-contradictory and fully aligned "self" and "culture"', the illusion that covers over the actual antagonism of basic social existence and of the subjective and the social in bourgeois ideology.

The full realisation of this process, towards which Leroux's *Fantôme* draws us while offering us ways to evade it, is ironically re-embodied in another neo-Freudian concept, even though this very notion might be used to conceal the truth once more if the concept is interpreted too much as a purely subjective figure. I refer to Nicolas Abraham's notion of 'the phantom' in his and Maria Torok's 1970s 'complement' to Freudian psychology. There is a parallel between this idea and the original 'phantom of the Opera', although not the one that strict Freudians might expect. Leroux's Erik, enveloped as he is by cryptic maskings of his foundations including concealments of his own father's station and his connection to the social roots of Christine's father, anticipates Abraham's sense that many evasions in the 'cryptonymic' figures emerging into conscious speech from the unconscious are actually indicators of a 'phantom', ghostly signs of a 'gap that the concealment of some part of a loved one's [earlier] life [has] produced in us' (Abraham, 1987: 75). This encrypting of what a predecessor's unconscious has attempted to hide within or eject from itself – 'the burial of an unspeakable fact *within the loved one*' (Abraham, 1987: 76) – can be taken in a Freudian, strictly familial direction with Leroux's book if one forces it, against any clear evidence in the text, to suggest a dark, perhaps incestuous secret in the younger lives of Christine's or Erik's fathers, ones that might explain (say) the former's amazing vocal gifts or the latter's 'defective' birth as the figure of death. But what is most unspeakable and unconscious in what we know of the fathers of Erik and Christine in the novel is what happens within and behind their class shifts, either in the oscillation between sheer mason and entrepreneur in Erik's otherwise unmentioned father or in the sudden decision of old Daae, upon the death of his 'invalid' (*impotente*) wife, to sell his peasant land-holdings and 'seek [musical] glory [for Christine and himself] in Upsala', where 'poverty' forces him back into the state of a fiddler wandering 'from fair to fair' or seeking a bourgeois patron and thus initiates a see-saw existence between country and city life that finally leaves others unable to 'comprehend anything about this violinist who roamed the countryside with this beautiful child who sang so well' (a role the phantom replays in several different guises) (Leroux, 1910: 97–9). When Christine and Erik both extend and surpass these 'incomprehensible' movements of their parents to the point of sublimating them, even leaving them behind, partly through the more 'sublime' figure of the 'Angel of Music' (who is also a death's head) *inside* the Paris Opera, they are, like patients haunted by Abraham's 'phantom', repeating and disguising the ghosts of paternal misrepresentations, in which the parents (and now the children even more) strive to mask the social divisions and slippages in their own foundations. The 'phantom' that haunts the two main characters in Leroux's *Fantôme* is like Abraham's precisely because it is the skeletal vestige of a class-crossing effort prior to them. This effort has already performed a cultural repression and abjection, already tried to silence the basis of itself, leaving such processes to be reannounced as even more 'thrown down' by the heirs to such counterfeitings of identity.[24]

Leroux's *Phantom of the Opera*, I contend, points more directly at this social history than most Gothic novels, while also enacting its partial suppression by Freudian schemes that work to affirm the bourgeois subjectivity so basic to the adaptations, especially the recent musical. The original phantom, after all, is both the 'abject' Other who embodies numerous social antagonisms and at the same time the supreme performer of bourgeois aspiration who works to maintain his petit bourgeois roots in parts of his lair while also striving far beyond them in his effort to be the supreme wealthy investor, opera-goer, composer, aristocratic seducer and impresario all at once. He incarnates the full range of the bourgeois contradiction, in other words, including the suppression of that range behind the mask of recovering Mother and seeking death by way of substitutes in *ein anderer Schauplatz*. In doing so, Leroux's Erik brings out in one figure what the fundamental struggle usually is in the Gothic, ever since *The Castle of Otranto*, between heroes or heroines and the monster/ghosts that embody and abject the unsettled inconsistencies in the historical and cultural conditions giving rise to both sets of characters. What Gothic protagonists face, sometimes within their own bodies, in their often fragmented, anamorphic, boundary-crossing 'others' (sometimes their 'phantoms') is the drift among different class-based possibilities for the grounds of the self that Gothic protagonists, authors, and readers want to face *and* deny in order to reenact their self-definitions. By going back to the original *Phantom of the Opera*, we affirm that such is the Gothic project underlying the more strictly psychological abjections that are also played out in such works. As the final sentence of Leroux's novel restates, Erik's is 'no ordinary skeleton' (Leroux, 1910: 498). It is the skeleton in the closet of the Gothic that reminds us what the Gothic really does.

Acknowledgement

My deepest thanks to William Veeder, Elisabeth Bronfen, Joan Dayan, Mary Beth Callie, Allan Lloyd Smith, Victor Sage, David Punter and Robert Miles for their helpful suggestions about this essay.

Notes

1 Pfau, 'Paranoia Historicized: Legal Fantasy, Social Change, and Satiric Metacommentary in the Context of the 1794 Treason Trials', in *Romanticism, Radicalism, and the Press*, ed. Stephen C. Behrendt, forthcoming, Wayne State University Press. My thanks to Professor Pfau for sending me an advance copy of this essay.
2 The best accounts of the growth of this ideology in relation to the Gothic and the Romantic are in Ellis, 1989: 3–31, and Gelpi, 1992: 35–82.

3 This pull is discussed most thoroughly, however, by Bronfen, 1992.
4 See the definitional sections of *Powers of Horror*, especially 3–55, from which I draw in what follows. See also Gordon, 1988; Hogle, 1988; Williams, 1991, 1995; Rajan, 1994; and Hurley, 1996, especially 3–12 and 42–45.
5 The best study of the Gothic as rising from and acting through conflicting modes of discourse is Miles, 1993, especially 1–48.
6 Twitchell's reading of Beauty and the Beast is based on Bruno Bettelheim's throughly Freudian approach in *The Uses of Enchantment*, 1976: 303–10.
7 Very public assertions and displays of production values have always been associated with film or stage adaptations of *The Phantom*. Laemmle's 1925 silent production was the most lavish film (including two colour sequences) made by his studio up to that time and was advertised as 'Universal's Masterpiece'; the 1943 remake won Academy Awards for colour cinematography and interior decoration; and the musical is always presented with programmes that detail its many expensive technical achievements, down to the 6,000 beads, 35 to a string, in the chandelier which is raised over the audience and made to fall to the stage, via unseen wires, as the First Act ends. See Perry, 1987, 46–50, 56–9 and 93.
8 This phrase signals my general agreement with Robert Miles that 'the Gothic is a discursive site [and] "carnivalesque" mode for representations of the fragmented subject' (Miles, 1993: 4).
9 See Ellenberger, 1970: 749–803, and Showalter, 1990: 1–18, 76–126 and 169–84.
10 Translations from Leroux are my own.
11 Such a sighting of the phantom is mentioned in the fifth scene of the 1925 silent movie, despite the only somewhat cadaverous face of an escaped homicidal maniac that Lon Chaney's Erik turns out to have in the released film, and that scene is briefly duplicated in Act I, Scene 7 of the Lloyd Webber musical, even though the Phantom's face there has gnarled distortions and slightly cut-away skin on only one side. No dramatised version duplicates the skull that is the phantom's real face in the novel. See Perry, 1987: 50–5, 147, and *The Phantom of the Opera* dir. Rupert Julian, with Lon Chaney, Mary Philbin and Norman Kerry, Videocasette (Video Yesteryear, 1982).
12 To be sure, Freud had neither developed nor announced his concept of the death-drive by the time Leroux's *Fantôme* appeared. But the idea of the beginning and goal of life as death, prior to and beyond consciousness, was a European notion in wide circulation by 1910, among not only followers of Schopenhauer but French enunciators of decadence. See Ellenberger, 1970: 205–6, 261, 275, 280–4 and 514–15. The desire for and avoidance of the death in the 'other' is also basic to the Gothic tradition from Mary Shelley and Edgar Allan Poe to Bram Stoker.
13 Cited in, and copied here from, Levine, 1988: 222. As Levine further notes (on 221–2), 'highbrow' as a term of cultural superiority came into use in the early 1880s (the decade in which Leroux's novel is set), and 'lowbrow' became common for naming a deficiency in cultural acquisitions soon after 1900 (the decade in which *Fantôme* was written).
14 After all, as Edward Said reminds us, 'Paris was the capital of the Orientalist world' in the West for much of the nineteenth century – in other words,

the cultural centre of an imperialistic styling and mythologising of an Occidental construct called 'the Orient' (Said, 1978: 51).

15 See Leroux, 1910: 354; Perry, 1987: 13–14; and Williams, 1969: 5–7.

16 A reference directly to the Paris Opera in Lindenberger, 1984: 238.

17 On Debussy's statement, see Mayer, 1972: 61. See also Leroux, 1910: 37.

18 See Leroux, 1910: 146, and, on Leroux's inter-racial disguise (one of his many famous deceptions when he was a reporter) see Perry, 1987: 24–5.

19 I do not quite agree, however, with Clement's brief reading of *The Phantom* (26–7) as simply duplicating the Death-and-the-Maiden pattern of standard opera without any critique of the pattern's foundations.

20 The final quotation here is drawn by Goldstein from Henry Meige's 'La Juif-errant à la Salpêtrière'.

21 See one of his statements for *Le Matin*, 19 August 1899, in Olivier-Martin, 1981: 160.

22 See Perry, 1987: 12; Mayer, 1972: 62–3; and Cross, 1985: 228–35.

23 Žižek's sense of the unrepresentable 'kernel' or Real as 'antagonism' is indebted to Laclau and Mouffe, 1985. As it happens, too, Žižek discusses Leroux's *Phantom* in portions of 'Grimaces of the Real, or When the Phallus Appears'. He takes this particular analysis, though, in a very Lacanian direction which sees the phantom as a prime example of numerous 'monsters' that invade the Symbolic order and subjectivity with many symptoms of the 'nonsensical', primordial Real or Thing (the unmeaning welter, the maternal phallus, the Body of the Mother in its most amorphous sense) which no verbal or subjective representation can encompass. This is a rich extension of the Freudian reading I have rehearsed already. But I have sought to explore, more than Žižek does, what he notes when he briefly sees the phantom as a '*fetish* that stands in for the class struggle ... by combining into one two quite different elements that undermine the established bourgeois order' (1991: 62). In fact, I do not see the 'two' (or even *just* two) exactly as Žižek describes them, and I cannot finally agree with him that the stand-in's effort to 'render invisible the actual contours of social antagonism' (63) is but one symptomatic indicator of the far more basic personal *and* cultural effor to keep misrecognising the 'inaccessible Thing' (66).

24 This kind of cover-up in the phantom-ised father and his son (the patient) is the very sort that Abraham uses as his primary example–an effort 'to hide the degrading fact' of the father being socially illegitimate (Abraham, 1987: 76–7).

Works cited

Abraham, Nicolas. 1987. 'Notes on the Phantom: A Complement to Freud's Metapsychology'. Trans. Nicholas Rand. Rpt in *The Trial(s) of Psychoanalysis*. Ed. Françoise Meltzer. Chicago: University of Chicago Press, 1988: 75–80.

Bettelheim, Bruno. 1976. *The Uses of Enchantment: The Meaning and Importance of Fairy Tales*. New York: Knopf.

Bronfen, Elisabeth. 1992. Over *Her Dead Body: Death, Femininity, and the Aesthetic*. Manchester: Manchester University Press.

Clement, Catherine. 1988. *Opera, or the Undoing of Women*. Trans. Betsy Wing. Minneapolis: University of Minnesota Press.

200   *Jerrold E. Hogle*

Cross, Milton. 1985. *The New Complete Stories of the Great Opera*. Rev. ed. Ed. Karl Kohrs. New York: Doubleday.

du Maurier, George. 1894. *Trilby*. London: Everyman, 1931.

Ellenberger, Henri F. 1979. *The Discovery of the Unconscious: The History and Evolution of Dynamic Psychiatry*. New York: Basic Books.

Ellis, Kate. 1989. *The Contested Castle: Gothic Novels and the Subversion of Domestic Ideology*. Urbana: University of Illinois Press.

Fiedler, Leslie. 1966. *Love and Death in the American Novel*. New York: Dell.

Gelpi, Barbara Charlesworth. 1992. *Shelley's Goddess: Maternity, Language, Subjectivity*. New York: Oxford University Press.

Goldstein, Jan. 1985. 'The Wandering Jew and the Problem of Psychiatric Anti-Semitism in Fin-de-Siècle France'. *Journal of Contemporary History* 20, 521–52.

Gordon, Marci M. 1988. 'Kristeva's Abject and Sublime in Brontë's *Wuthering Heights*'. *Literature and Psychology* 34, 44–58.

Hogle, Jerrold E. 1988. 'The Struggle for a Dichotomy: Abjection in Jekyll and his Interpreters'. In *Dr Jekyll and Mr Hyde After One Hundred Years*. Ed. William Veeder et al. Chicago: University of Chicago Press, 161–207.

Hurley, Kelly 1996. *The Gothic Body: Sexuality, Materialism, and Degeneration at the fin de siècle*. Cambridge: Cambridge University Press.

Kahane, Claire. 1985. 'The Gothic Mirror'. in *The (M)other Tongue: Essays in Feminist Psychoanalytic Interpretation*. Ed. Shirley Nelson Garner et al. Ithaca: Cornell University Press: 334–51.

Kristeva, Julia. 1982. *Powers of Horror: An Essay on Abjection*. Trans. Leon S. Roudiez. New York: Columbia University Press.

Kristeva, Julia. 1991. *Strangers to Ourselves*. Trans. Leon S. Roudiez. New York: Columbia University Press.

Laclau, Ernesto and Chantal Mouffe. 1985. *Hegemony and Socialist Strategy*. London: Routledge.

Leroux, Gaston. 1910. *Le Fantôme de l'Opéra*. Paris: Le livre de poche, 1959.

Levine, Lawrence W. 1988. *Highbrow/Lowbrow: The Emergence of Cultural Hierarchy in America*. Cambridge, MA: Harvard University Press.

Lindenberger, Herbert. 1984. *Opera: The Extravagant Art*. Ithaca: Cornell University Press.

Mayer, Tony. 1972. 'L'Opéra Paris', in *Grand Opera: The Story of the World's Leading Opera Houses and Personalities*. Ed. Anthony Gishford. New York: Viking.

Miles, Robert. 1993. *Gothic Writing, 1750–1820: A Genealogy*. London: Routledge.

Moretti, Franco. 1988. *Signs Taken for Wonders: Essays on the Sociology of Literary Forms*. Trans. Susan Fischer et al. London: Verso.

Nye, Robert A. 1984. *Crime, Madness, and Politics in Modern France: The Medical Concept of National Decline*. Princeton: Princeton University Press.

Olivier-Martin, Yves. 1981. 'Chronologie de Gaston Leroux'. *Europe* 59, 158–65.

Perry, George. 1987. *The Complete Phantom of the Opera*. New York: Henry Holt.

Punter, David. 1980. *The Literature of Terror: A History of Gothic Fictions from 1765 to the Present Day*. London: Longman.

Rajan, Tilottama. 1994. 'Mary Shelley's *Mathilda*: Melancholy and the Political Economy of Romanticism'. *Studies in the Novel* 26, 43–68.

Said, Edward. 1978. *Orientalism*. New York: Pantheon.

Showalter, Elaine. 1990. *Sexual Anarchy: Gender and Culture at the Fin de Siècle*. New York: Viking.

Stallybrass, Peter, and Allon White. 1986. *The Politics and Poetics of Transgression*. London: Methuen.

Twitchell, James. 1985. *Dreadful Pleasures: An Anatomy of Modern Horror*. New York: Oxford University Press.

Williams, Anne. 1991. '*Dracula*: Si(g)ns of the Fathers'. *Texas Studies in Literature and Language* 33, 445–63.

Williams, Anne. 1995. *Art of Darkness: A Poetics of Gothic*. Chicago: University of Chicago Press.

Williams, Roger, ed. 1969. *The Commune of Paris, 1871*. New York: John Wiley.

Žižek, Slavoj. 1989. *The Sublime Object of Ideology*. London: Verso.

Žižek, 1991. 'Grimaces of the Real, or When the Phallus Appears'. *October* 58, 44–68.

Chapter 11

Heiner Müller's Medea: towards a paradigm for the contemporary Gothic anatomy

Barnard Turner

Medea that ungracious Imp, King Aetas wicked chylde,
Yet hath not from our careful realme her lingring foote exilde.
Som naughty drift she goes about, her knacks of old we kno,
Her jugling arts, her harming hands are known wel long ago.
From whom will shee withhold her harme? whom will this cruel beast
Permit to live, from perrill free, in quietnesse and rest?

(Seneca, *Medea*, in the 'Tudor translation' of John Studley)

Heiner Müller (1929–96) is arguably Germany's leading contemporary (post-Brecht) dramatist and a major figure of the international post-modernist avant-garde. With a notable and lasting output of creative work himself, his collaborations were extensive, from Brecht of course to perhaps, most famously, Robert Wilson in the *CIVIL warS* project; conversely, his work has inspired wide-ranging responses, including an opera by Wolfgang Rihm and a recording by Einstürzende Neubauten, a gripping video-film by Dominik Barbier of the Paris-based Fearless Evil Productions, and Andrzej Wirth's Brecht/Müller/ Wilson 'Inter-face'. His creative work for the theatre stretches from the 'Production Plays' of the 1950s through the reworkings ('copies') of other people's plays (including the two *Shakespeare Factory* volumes) of the 1970s to perhaps his most familiar plays in the Anglophonic world: *Hamletmachine* (1977) and *Despoiled Shore Medeamaterial Landscape with Argonauts* (1982), to which I shall later return.

As may then already have been inferred from these titles, it has often been noted that Müller's work mediates between Classicist realism and neo-Romantic fantasy, all set within a general postmodernist context. It is this 'New Classicism', to borrow Charles Jencks's familiar term, which makes Müller's take on the postmodern singular in European literature. If, that is, as Allan Lloyd Smith argues, the postmodern is cross-hatched with Gothic preoccupations in 'its populist tendency, its lurid, low-rent sensationalism and exploitation of affect, its opening up of tabooed realms', 'its embrace of the fragmentary' and 'use of paranoia' (Smith, 1996: 15), all of which catalogue Müller's plays quite well, his work escapes typical postmodernist nominalism by being inextricably grounded in the historical realia of Germany's birth, death and rebirth as an historical nation over the past two centuries or so. A telling example of this is the presentation of the Prussian state, as in *Gundling's Life Frederick of Prussia Lessing's Sleep Dream Scream* of 1976, or the 'Brandenburg Concerto 1' section of *Germania Death in Berlin* (1956/71), in which a *revenant* Frederick the Great appears in a comic interlude between two 1949 episodes; in this scene, the realities of German neo-Classicism (Frederick's love of French, his ascription as 'the first servant of his state') are presented as a Gothicised, but equally politicised pointer to the 'return of the [nationalist] repressed'.

I do not, however, want in this context to read Müller's Gothic in exclusively sociohistorical terms, particularly since this has been ably done in an essay by Hans-Thies Lehmann, who reminds us of the use of 'spectres' and ghosts in the rhetoric of historical and dialectical materialism from Marx to Derrida. Unlike Marx, Lehmann argues, and like Derrida in his *Spectres of Marx* volume, Müller does not wish to 'exorcize' the spirits of alienated (and thus 'ghostly') labour, but to accept their place in economic reality, which is one of the inevitable loss of the object according to the processes associated with its exchange value. The 'self-presence', to use Lehmann's words (Lehmann, 1995: 93), of Marxist ideology, of a holistic life of reciprocal use-value, is an illusion, for the demands of the future require that surpluses be prepared in the present, and for this to occur something must always be held back, out of circulation, unused but exchangeable according to a specific future need. As with an economic storehouse, so with cultural capital, which is never exhausted because it is never at any one moment fully present; to paraphrase Brecht, what begins as tragedy ends as farce, a point I shall consider in more detail later. Therefore, the old dichotomy between 'neo-Classicism' (or, in this context, socialist realism) and the 'Gothic' (or the much despised by socialist pundits 'fantasy' literature) is dubious, since the former were always ready to decompose into the latter, and it is thus possible to read Müller's peculiar version of the contemporary Gothic as the return of that which, quite literally, neo-Classicism (or, in his case, the 'spectre' of socialist realism) is said to have repressed: the ghost of the Shakespearean macabre or unruly, its mixture of styles and genres from which arises its dubious moral stance, and which has its origins (as does in a sense the Gothic itself) in that which the Elizabethan period had itself repressed in the Greek and Roman classics: that touch of violence which it sites in the feminine and which patriarchy finds both bewitching and repulsive, to which it therefore reacts either in the laughter of Aristophanes or Theocritus's Simaetha poem, or in the circumscribing *Verfremdungseffekt* of madness and/or witchcraft, as in Euripides's Bacchae or in the Medea of Euripides, Seneca or Ovid.

The well-known inscription of 'Shakespearean negotiations' is apparent both at the generally accepted origins of the Gothic, Walpole's Prefaces to *Otranto* (even if this be taken 'ironically', as David Punter suggests it should [Punter, 1980: 51]), and in its most recent criticism (for example, the papers by Hogle and Clery in the Smith/Sage conference volume, *Gothick Origins and Innovations*). It is not then just for its female writers, as Susan Wolstenholme suggests, that the Gothic constitutes an act of '(Re)Vision'. More particularly then, it need not be emphasized here that what the writers of the early literary Gothic found so appealing in Shakespeare was perhaps also precisely that which he found so beguiling in Seneca and other playwrights of the classical period, and what Müller brings to the surface of his own work: the combination of the irrational and the inevitable, finding its expression in what the Greeks termed *Até*, the feminine personification of the divinely inspired frenzy of retribution. So inspired, people become merely instruments (but necessary ones, a fact which separates this more Gothic force from the essentially demonic Eumenides or the more divine Fates) rather than agents of their own desire (such is the case with Müller's Medea, as I shall contend later). This frenzied state is both longed for (as putting an end to torment and its expectation) and feared; in short, then, it shares certain qualities, in very general terms, with the more localised, desecrated form of the Freudian *unheimlich*. 'I am Revenge, sent from th'infernal kingdom', proclaims one of the earliest female Goths – literally speaking – in English literature, the 'displaced' (and thus in a sense *unheimlich*, or at least *unheimisch*) Tamora of Shakespeare's *Titus Andronicus*, a play incidentally which Heiner Müller 'anatomised' in his *Anatomie Titus Fall of Rome*, first performed in 1985, and which appears after his version of *Hamlet* in the *Shakespeare Factory 2* volume.

I do not, however, wish to reinscribe Müller's take on the Gothic within the formalist lines of the Freudian *unheimlich* – even if these be updated in the light of more recent work – not only because, of course, this has already been achieved (as far as it is possible), but also because

Freud's *unheimlich* is, even in his own terms, a supremely overdetermined concept, as is the Gothic itself; and, even if it could be restricted to a certain play of meaning, this would still require, as Freud himself notes, that the *aesthetic* dimension be distinguished from the *psychoanalytical*. One might, therefore, contend in this regard that far from the specific concerns of the Freudian paradigm, the Gothic (in very general terms) becomes 'uncanny' because it revolves around two fundamentally literary questions which realist modes (and particularly, one might add, in the context of a paper on Heiner Müller, socialist realist modes) seek to ignore: 'When is now?' and 'Where is here?' Forces from the past act undeniably but inexplicably on the present, and one is compelled to acknowledge one's ignorance with respect to one's 'place', whether this be regarded as one's habitation or, more generally, one's social position. The remote and the familiar must thus be juxtaposed, or, as Elizabeth MacAndrew notes, the Gothic brings back 'out of the wilderness … symbolic figures and landscapes from the dark, irrational past' (MacAndrew, 1979: 48). In this regard, the Gothic as it has been traditionally con- and re-ceived has much in common with that 'return of the repressed' as presented in social realist (and now 'classic') Scandinavian theatre, in such plays as Ibsen's *When We Dead Awaken* or *Ghosts* or even, in more otherworldly yet still minimally realistic fashion, Strindberg's *Ghost Sonata* or *Dream Play*.

Moreover, one cannot simply suggest that every literary expression of the *unheimlich* is equal to a Gothic moment, since the former can be inspired in various ways without recourse to the familiar Gothic attributes, settings, etc., which Maurice Levy, in his contribution to the Smith and Sage volume, quite rightly regards as indispensable to the definition of the Gothic. The Greek formulation of *Até*, however, in certain guises at least, is helpful in circumscribing the Gothic past and present, in that it is contextualised in precisely those areas which are integral to it: it gives rise to and is propelled by the *literal* (and not only the Freudian) sense of 'displacement' ('homelessness') which roots the *unheimlich*, that sense of transgression, of moving outside the bounds of the known, which Todorov cites as one of the main provocations of the uncanny (Todorov, 1975: 48). This in turn is developed by recourse to the sense of living in premises guarded by spirits and enveloped in laws that, as a newcomer, one finds bewildering and intimidating, and against which one's struggle can appear to take only the form of madness.

One would like to suggest that it is this *cultural* sense of the *unheimlich* which has attracted marginalised writers to it: Scottish and Irish writers, for example, or those more generally caught between two (or more) cultural formations (*Vathek*, for example) or cultural codes (the relatively large percentage of female writers, and the [needless to say, *male*] 'analogy between physical darkness and femininity' to which Wolstenholme refers [Wolstenholme, 1993: 23]). It is this sense which may indeed account in part for its survival, particularly within the contemporary context of the decentering of the vectors of cultural power; the marginal now is everywhere and the centre indefinite.

It is not just then Joyce's Stephen Daedalus whose tools are 'silence, exile, and cunning', as these form the necessary cultural baggage of all cultural wanderers, whose sense of being 'guests' can so easily turn to that of being 'ghosts', strangers in a strange land, invisible men and women. Which brings me back, at last, to Heiner Müller and his 'Gothic anatomy', *Medeamaterial* (the central part of his *Verkommenes Ufer* [*Despoiled Shore*] triptych, 1982). Cutting up and across cultural traditions and stereotypical gender roles, interspersing the irrational with the fitting (the 'proper') and the timely (the *kairos*), destroying the house which the literary tradition has built as a defence against Medea's inexplicable, irreducible and unparaphrasable magical language and sentiment, Müller's text shows how the Gothic in contemporary terms can both be true to its roots and interrogate them, resuscitating the old horror for a world whose core text, as he puts it in his 'autobiography' *Krieg ohne Schlacht* [*War without Battle*, to my knowledge as yet untranslated], is Eliot's (equally 'anatomical') *Waste Land* (Müller, 1994: 320). No doubt unconsciously – but this is the best, and for Jungians at least, perhaps the only way – Müller has dug deep into the resources of the Gothic, exhuming, however, more sense than sentence, not confining himself to direct transmission but more to a reincorporation of its particular perspective into his own politicized dramatic project (here Todorov's notion of Gothic 'transgression' can be seen in a more pointed, ideological light).

How Müller draws upon a full range of Gothic resources in *Medeamaterial* can be initially considered by taking a short extract from the play, which takes place during the initial confrontation of Medea and Jason:

Medea   I
             Am not welcome here Would a death take me away
             Thrice five nights Jason have you not
             Called for me Not with your voice
             And not with a slave's voice nor
             With hands or gaze

Jason	What do you want
Medea	To die
Jason	I've heard that often
Medea	Does this body mean
	Nothing more to you Do you want to drink my blood
	Jason
Jason	When will this end
Medea	When did it begin Jason
Jason	What were you before me woman

(Müller, 1984: 129; here as elsewhere later, I have modified Weber's translations.)

[*Medea*	Ich
	Bin nicht erwünscht hier Daß ein Tod mich wegnähm
	Dreimal fünf Nächte Jason hast du mich
	Verlangt nach mir Mit deiner Stimme nicht
	Und nicht mit eines Sklaven Stimme noch
	Mit Händen oder Blick
Jason	Was willst du
Medea	Sterben
Jason	Das hört ich oft
Medea	Bedeutet dieser Leib
	Dir nichts mehr Willst du mein Blut trinken Jason
Jason	Wann hört das auf
Medea	Wann hat es angefangen Jason
Jason	Was warst du vor mir Weib (Müller, 1983: 93)]

A catalogue of Gothic effects and resources is here apparent. Medea conceives of death as a translation, a seizure or kidnapping, rather than as sheer annihilation or ascension. Here the echoes of Hades and Persephone would be pertinent, were it not that Müller has already subverted this by the reference to 'a death', rather than its personification. What Medea has in mind, of course, is death in the plural, that of Jason's apparent new love, then her own murders of her sons with him, acts followed lastly no doubt by her own suicide. Jason conversely indulges in typical Gothic male fantasies, not only the obvious vampirism Medea ascribes to him ('Do you want to drink my blood Jason'), but also the view of the female as a male creation ('What were you before me woman'), who is valuable as a 'body' ('Leib') only (a view which Medea has seemingly internalised), on which violence can be enacted at will. That such violence is seen more in the neglect which

instigates Medea's growing hysteria ('Thrice five nights…') itself produces a familiar Gothic *topos*, here again given a certain new resonance: the imprisonment of the female, not entirely literally (although
it must be remembered that she could easily be so confined if her plots
against the Corinthian royal house became known), but more as a consequence of her psychological inability to envisage life without Jason,
for whom she has given up so much. Without him, she wishes but 'to
die' ('Sterben'), and here the echoes of Petronius' version of the
Cumaean Sibyll (familiar as the epigraph to Eliot's *Waste Land*) are rein-
forced by Medea's ability to make herself live through her dying, to
which I shall return later.

Although such catalogues of Gothic imagery could be multiplied at
will through Müller's play, one might summarise an already lengthy
argument by suggesting that what makes his work particularly resonant for the Gothic in general is his recourse to the classics of the irrational, notably to the work of Shakespeare, Euripides and Seneca, as a
springboard towards a post-Brechtian German theatre. What more particularly now he finds in them are expressions of his own fascination
with death as motif and horizon, a presence in the face and defiance of
which the artwork is constructed. Thus Hamlet's 'undiscovered country' becomes visible in his texts, even if only for a fleeting instance, as
in the confusing, paradoxical stream of images which constitute his
text 'Bildbeschreibung' ('Description of a Picture'), which describes, as
its footnote proclaims, 'a landscape on the other side of death' (Müller,
1985: 14; 1989a: 102). As provocation to the imagination to which it is
closed, death figures as the once and future ground of *ex nihilo* literary
creation (compare, of course, Frankenstein). As Müller's Medea herself
puts it, 'Death is a gift' (Müller, 1984: 132; 'Der Tod ist ein Geschenk'
[Müller, 1983: 97]), as its sense of loss presents at once both the first
impulse and the ultimate provocation to the imagination. Müller's
Hamletmachine then reinscribes Hamlet's problem by regarding death
as comedy; its third act, curiously named a 'scherzo', takes place in the
'University of the Dead', where gravestones are used as lecterns, dead
philosophers throw their books at Hamlet and dead women tear the
Prince's clothes from his body. Shakespeare's outcast Eumenides, whose
parts are never filled in his work, here haunt his most famous creation.
For Müller, then, as he puts it in a provocative 1990 interview,
'Necrophilia is Love of the Future', 'art originates and is rooted in the
communication with death and the dead. The point is to find a place
for the dead. That's what culture really is' (Müller, 1991: 23). Later, he
claims: 'One must accept the presence of the dead as partners in or

impediments to dialogue – the future arises only out of the dialogue with the dead' (31). In true Romantic fashion, familiar to any reader of Shelley, Goethe or Hölderlin, he holds that 'whoever does not die, does not truly live' (70); this will come as no surprise also to a certain Transylvanian count or to Connor MacLeod of the Clan MacLeod.

What, in Müller's play, however, prevents such a contention of life/death continuum and interchange from becoming just another vapid reinscription of German Romantic Idealism (Goethe's 'stirb und werde') is its intersection with the feminine as dynamic, yet thanaturgic principle, and thus as the spirit of both the revolution and annihilation. It is quite frequent to come across critical articles on Müller with titles like 'Death is a Woman' (Schmidt/Vaßen, 1993: 138); and Hendrik Werner, in a review of a 1988 book by Carlotta von Maltzan, comments that her claim that 'presentations of revolution almost always appear in connection with female figures' in Müller's work is common enough to have already been suggested by critics like Genia Schulz and Helen Fehervary (Schmidt/Vaßen, 1993: 361). Such figures are thus frequently endowed with the capacity to destroy the house that patriarchal domestication of the female has built; in Müller's work, Coventry Patmore's 'Angel in the House' most clearly often becomes a demon, who 'possesses' it in more ways than one, and whose paradigm, in this (literally) unsettling gesture of the *unheimlich/unheimisch*, is of course Medea.

As many other female figures do in Müller's texts, Medea focuses one's attention on the fissures in the social fabric, the parts of the economies of value and exchange (the domestic and political 'economy' or literally 'household accounts') which do not quite add up; 'Today', she says, 'is pay-day', and Jason owes her a brother (Müller, 1984: 97). Thus, in the light of the above, one can suggest that Medea localises within the socio-economic sphere the close connection between the Gothic and anatomy (literal or literary) as theme and/or background, which has been reasonably well documented (for example, by Tim Marshall in the Smith and Sage volume).

More widely considered, dissection as theme surfaces for example in Müller's short, Beckettesque 'Herzstück' ('Heart-piece') of 1981, which begins with the line 'May I lay my heart at your feet', and which ends with the ('animistic'?) comment that the heart is a brick which 'beats only for you' (Müller, 1983: 7). Medea says that she wants to cut her children out of her heart, practising thus the anatomy on herself, and giving a suggestion that the violence she enacts on them is the reversed vector of the same strategy which she would otherwise enact on herself.

An even more telling example for the Gothic of this 'anatomy' is found at the end of 'Death notice' ['Todesanzeige'], the occasion of which is grounded in the repeated attempts at suicide by Müller's wife, and their eventual success. Here the ambivalence between the *heimisch* and the *unheimlich*, which Freud notes in his piece on the uncanny, is achieved by the destruction of the home as patriarchal nexus by the negative power of female power turned inwards and against itself. Here the suicide sets off the dream of entering a ruin, a haunted, derelict house, which has become part of the landscape with trees growing within it, and ascending a staircase over which hangs a huge, naked woman, into whose pudenda ('Schamlippen') the protagonist is drawn, along the lines of the Freudian fantasy of 'the entrance to the former *Heim* [home] of all human beings' (Freud, 1985: 368). One might, at a stretch, relate this episode to the *vagina dentata* motif (the stairs being the teeth), but other Gothic motifs intrude: the zombie-like nature of the protagonist, who suffers no anxiety at the occurrence of seemingly being devoured; and the equivalent nature of the hanging woman, who is of course dead. So one is left with a wider point, away from the specifics of Freud or Klein, but still consistent with the Gothic: that which has given life can give death also, until eventually all independent, rational being is subsumed into one's final dwelling, the halls of death.

Müller comments in his 'autobiography' that he is 'a cave-dweller, or nomad', and prefers his ex-GDR high-rise apartment in the unfashionable Berlin-Friedrichsfelde because 'it revokes ["aufhebt"] the concept of "dwelling"' (Müller, 1994: 308). As the Gothic had long ago acknowledged, ruins – houses an-atom-ised – are perhaps in some cases easier to live with (and in), as they replace the illusion of perpetual domestic bliss with their own *momento mori*. 'Death notice' therefore anatomises domesticity as a self-contained, self-perpetuating holism ('the nuclear family') by showing the destruction of its constituent parts: the female *genius loci* and the very fabric of domesticity itself, the house. The text therefore cannot be but *unheimlich*, whether this be for its strict Freudian analogues, or for its more literal ('aesthetic') Gothic sensibility.

As I have noted briefly above though, Medea deflects this destruction of her (royal Colchian house) outwards, towards an external opponent (Creon's daughter Creusa, whom Jason will marry, and also to her own children by him). Yet even here we can detect another Gothic motif, for the new bride is but a version of the old, a 'Doppelgängerin', or lifeless unit of exchange, in Jason's war of position, as he is once more marrying only for personal advantage, to further his own hidden agenda of which Medea, as wise woman, is only too aware. Thus she has her old bridal robe, now imbued with a fatal poison, delivered to Creusa as a gift for the new marriage; as her 'second skin', the robe thus permits Medea to be 'close to [Jason's] love' and 'far away' from herself (Müller, 1983: 96; Müller, 1984: 131). It is this second self which she destroys, as she destroys also her grounding in her temporal being with Jason by the murder of their offspring.

Yet all this is becoming more 'classic' than 'Gothic', and might generally be considered under the heading of the 'know thyself and kill it' theme were it not the case that Müller's Medea is consistent, finally, with another integral feature of the Gothic, evident to all readers of *Vathek* (one of the funniest stories I have read): what Victor Sage in *Gothick Origins* calls 'the peculiarly close relationship between horror and humour' (Smith and Sage, 1994: 190). Fred Botting, in a similar vein, underlines 'the capacity of Gothic formulae to produce laughter as abundantly as emotions of terror or horror' (Botting, 1996: 168), an ambivalence that is particularly pronounced in contemporary variants with their 'spilling over of boundaries' (167). Such cross-generic transgression would be expected from a postmodernist writer like Müller, but here the ambivalence takes on a particularly Gothic tinge, as Medea's murderous actions, appearing as tragic to many in the auditorium (both on stage and off) and to the pervasive tradition, appear comic to herself. Whatever pain she is suffering through being scorned and consequently exiled, she is able to convert into laughter; she kills for revenge of course, but perhaps more because she simply just enjoys it. Her power over Creusa's death is but an extension of that control she has extended over Jason's life (by allowing him to obtain the fleece, evade capture in Colchis and by obliging him to bring her to Corinth). Thus the rationality of revenge is deflected into the irrationality of misrule, where her knowledge of the 'Doppelgängerin' and thus of the interchangeability of all roles ('You're actors' [Müller, 1984: 132]; 'Schauspieler seid ihr' [Müller, 1983: 97]) leads her to specify her particular play as a comedy.

And why should it not be a comedy when it revolves around the farcical situation of the Corinthian version of the preference for the rich bimbo over the woman of power, the (perhaps literally) archetypal 'witch' ('a barbarian witch, a prey to her excessively violent emotions', as Hugh Lloyd-Jones calls her [Lloyd-Jones, 1980: 442])? Such oft-repeated situations, as Brecht suggests, return eventually as farce, the ultimate alienation effect which signals the imminent arrival of the new (in this case, the murders and renewed exile which signal the break with what is rapidly becoming Medea's past in Corinth). So, addressing maybe anyone within earshot, including no doubt the audience who have come to see a modern version of a classical tragedy, Medea cries out:

> Are you laughing I want to see you laugh
> My play is a comedy Are you laughing

> (Müller, 1984: 132)

> [Lacht ihr Ich will euch lachen sehen
> Mein Schauspiel ist eine Komödie Lacht ihr

> (Müller, 1983: 97)]

The fear of death is here transmuted into the comic perception of the meaninglessness of life, where values, purposes, and social and emotional stability are at the mercy of expediency; in such a world, to be strong is to laugh, as, in Ted Hughes's 'Examination at the Womb-Door' poem, Crow does, another example of the Gothic (e.g. Poe's Raven) turning to laughter in the latter half of the twentieth century.

To create herself, then, to give herself the free room in which to move to the destruction of her other, her second self whom Jason is to marry, Medea has to kill herself as figure of revenge – acting for human motives of scorn, resentment, and so on – and create herself anew as irrational grotesquerie, neither human nor beast, neither man nor woman, but in a transitional state with qualities of both, and thus of neither. She looks into a mirror and comments that what is reflected in it 'is not Medea' (Müller, 1984: 93) (so much for the 'mirror stage'!). Thus the counterpart to Creusa as Medea's 'Doppelgängerin' in the victim position is the view of a second Medea as instrument of destruction. Medea, therefore, shares a typical position of characters in Müller's drama, of wishing to be withdrawn from her position in the network of power, and thus able to act unnoticed, even by herself; as Müller's Hamlet, in a similar position states: 'My place, were my drama still to happen, would be on both sides of the front, between the fronts, over and above them' ['Mein Platz, wenn mein Drama noch stattfinden würde, wäre auf beiden Seiten der Front, zwischen den Fronten, darüber' (Müller, 1984: 94)]. Medea thus shares with other zombies of the Gothic a sense of indifference to the human need of having a home, in contrast to her considerable anxiety about it which shores up her actions in earlier versions (in Euripides' version, for example, she does not act until she has been virtually assured a shelter in Athens). Dislocated by her indifference to domesticity then, this 'mad' woman is here no longer kept in the attic, but is staring the male in the face and abrogating his power. Medea herself comments:

> Would that I had remained the beast that I was
> Before a man had made me his woman
> Medea the Barbarian
>
> (Müller, 1984: 132)
>
> [Wär ich das Tier geblieben das Ich war
> Eh mich ein Mann zu seiner Frau gemacht hat
> Medea Die Barbarin
>
> (Müller, 1983: 97)]

Here we would note the familiar Gothic motif of lycanthropy, but this is not all; before Medea's carnage can begin, she must first transmute herself into an epicene being, thus anatomising gender-based distinctions:

> I want to break mankind into two parts
> And live in the empty middle I
> No woman no man
>
> (Müller, 1984: 132)
>
> [... will ich die Menschheit in zwei Stücke brechen
> Und wohnen in der leeren Mitte Ich
> Kein Weib und kein Mann
>
> (Müller, 1983: 97)]

(Here one may note in passing that another *unheimlich* characteristic of Müller's texts is the frequency of stylistic parataxis, as here, which makes the plays remarkable and rather 'out of place' in contemporary German; if one then concedes Todorov's point about the centrality of transgression in the definition of the uncanny, this feature can be located in Müller's work at the stylistic level also. Further, one could argue that it is partially this stylistic feature of Shakespearean diction, and the range of rhythmic possibilities in any one line, that made his plays so unacceptable to the much more limited, rigid alexandrines of French neoclassical playwrights.)

Yet Medea's wish to be removed from such a 'real' gendered, political context is impossible, as the Althusserian Ideological State Apparatus or Benthamite/Foucauldian network extends to every aspect of one's life; one should not forget that this is a play designed for performance in the now defunct, yet somewhat mourned and still spiritually present GDR. In any case, to wish to seal oneself off from the social is to be metaphorically and politically dead, to become a social zombie. Even in her closing moments on stage, when she appears to reassert her identity ('Oh I am clever I am Medea' (Müller, 1984: 133) ['O ich bin klug ich bin Medea' (Müller, 1983: 98)]), she is no longer the living scorned wife but the figure of legend, the woman who has dared to transgress and by this violence has claimed her place in history. Jason, in contrast, the male hero-turned-victim, is now, she thinks, to be forgotten. As he seeks to frame the imminent violence by intercession of patriarchal logic (which takes up some considerable part of earlier versions), he is only able to utter Medea's name before she curtails his speech, and the scene itself, by her asking the nurse: 'Do you know this man' ('Kennst du diesen Mann'). (The lack of a question mark here might be thought indicative of her indifference to the answer were not such omissions normal for the text as a whole, as in certain of the quotations above.)

Thus, in Müller's play, the Medea who commits the atrocities is already, and paradoxically, disembodied and undead, in her body but no longer the agent of its actions, working through but not for it. She is thus mere instrument, devoid of reason, and so becomes truly dangerous and uncontrollable. She acts then for what legend has, in her mind, already demanded of her: she acts as a ghost from the future performing a rite which, from its perspective, has already been performed in the past. One might here, as a socio-historical parallel (in our age of continuous threat, be it of nuclear, environmental or biological extinction, and their frequent use as tools of social legislation), be reminded of Brecht's famous lines from the *Fatzer* fragment, which, Müller says in a 1990 speech in Munich when he received the Kleist Prize, he 'could not get out of [his] head':

WHILE, EARLIER, SPIRITS CAME FROM THE PAST
SO NOW FROM THE FUTURE JUST THE SAME

[WIE FRÜHER GEISTER KAMEN AUS VERGANGENHEIT
SO JETZT AUS ZUKUNFT EBENSO

(Müller, 1991: 60)]

With her self-conception as already dead then, Medea can act without considerations of her bodily location in time/space and of her self-identity, and the realistic framework of cause and motive is abandoned: she may have been impelled to act as she does because of Jason's imminent desertion, but this only gives her the awareness that she can do so. To become Medea – our Medea, the one to whom the literary tradition refers and with which Müller here plays – Müller's character must undergo a familiar Gothic process (an 'anatomy') of dehumanisation: first into a beast, which she had already been before Jason had 'domesticated' her by bringing her Greece, and then into a zombie, an undead creature ('created' perhaps by a patriarchal literary tradition which had need of incorporating its deepest fears of the irrational in the visible, and thus ostensibly controllable guise of the feminine). Yet even this reading must be positioned within a wider socio-historical context if it is to be consistent with the true significance of Müller's revitalisation of certain Gothic motifs for our time, Benjamin's 'age of mechanical reproduction', where the real 'marriage', as Müller suggests in the 'Necrophilia' interview, is that between 'people and machines' ('die Hochzeit von Mensch und Machine' [Müller, 1991: 18]), where everything, in Baudrillard's terms, becomes no more than a 'simulacrum' (one of whose meanings is the more familiar Gothic device of the 'ghost'). Yet in this process, as in cyberspace, in the wish-fulfilment nightmare of *Star Trek*'s Borg or as from the air-conditioned cockpits of the Gulf War, one would kill the real with impunity, as Medea wishes she could do.

Works cited

Botting, Fred. 1996. *Gothic*. London: Routledge.
Freud, Sigmund. 1985. 'The 'Uncanny'. In *The Penguin Freud Library*. Vol. 14. Ed. Angela Richards and Albert Dickson. Harmondsworth: Penguin, 336–76.
Lehmann, Hans-Thies. 1995. 'Heiner Müller's Spectres'. In *Heiner Müller: ConTEXTS and HISTORY*. Ed. Gerhard Fischer. Tübingen: Stauffenburg, 87–96.
Lloyd-Jones, Hugh. 1980. 'Euripides, *Medea* 1056–80'. *Greek Epic, Lyric, and Tragedy*. Oxford: Clarendon Press, 1990.
MacAndrew, Elizabeth. 1979. *The Gothic Tradition in Fiction*. New York: Columbia University Press.
Müller, Heiner. 1983.*Verkommenes Ufer Medeamaterial Landschaft mit Argonauten. Herzstück*. Berlin: Rotbuch, 1983 [*Despoiled Shore Medeamaterial Landscape with Argonauts*. Hamletmachine *and Other Texts for the Stage*].
Müller, Heiner. 1984. Hamletmachine *and Other Texts for the Stage*. Ed. and trans. Carl Weber. New York: PAJ Publications.
Müller, Heiner. 1985. *Shakespeare Factory 1*. Berlin: Rotbuch.

Müller, Heiner. 1989a. *Explosion of a Memory*. Ed. and trans. Carl Weber. New York: PAJ Publications.

Müller, Heiner. 1989b. *Shakespeare Factory 2*. Berlin: Rotbuch.

Müller, Heiner. 1991. *Jenseits der Nation*. Berlin: Rotbuch.

Müller, Heiner. 1994. *Krieg ohne Schlacht: Leben in zwei Diktaturen. Eine Autobiographie*. 2nd ed. Cologne: Kiepenheuer und Witsch.

Müller, Heiner. 1997. *Germania Tod in Berlin* [*Germania Death in Berlin*]. Berlin: Rotbuch.

Punter, David. 1980. *The Literature of Terror: A History of Gothic Fictions from 1765 to the Present Day*. London: Longman.

Schmidt, Ingo and Florian Vaßen, eds. 1993. *Bibliographie Heiner Müller*. Bielefeld: Aisthesis.

Seneca, Lucius Annaeus. 1581. *Medea*. Trans. John Studley. In *Seneca: His Tenne Tragedies Translated into English*. Ed. Thomas Newton. *The Tudor Translations: Second Series*. Ed. Charles Whibley. Vol. 12. London: Constable, 1927.

Smith, Allan Lloyd. 1996. 'Postmodernism/Gothicism.' *Modern Gothic: A Reader*. Ed. Victor Sage and Allan Lloyd Smith. Manchester University Press, 6–19.

Smith, Allan Lloyd and Victor Sage, eds. 1994. *Gothick Origins and Innovations*. Amsterdam: Rodopi.

Todorov, Tzvetan. 1975. *The Fantastic: A Structural Approach to a Literary Genre*. Trans. Richard Howard. Ithaca, New York: Cornell University Press.

Wolstenholme, Susan. 1993. *Gothic (Re)Visions: Writing Women as Readers*. Albany: SUNY.

Part V
Contemporary (re)versions

Chapter 12

Deaths in Venice: Daphne du Maurier's 'Don't Look Now'

Avril Horner and Sue Zlosnik

In spite of the enduring popularity of Hitchcock's 1940 film, most people recognise *Rebecca* (1938) as a Daphne du Maurier novel. Fewer people know that du Maurier wrote the short story 'Don't Look Now' on which Nicholas Roeg's 1973 film – described in *The Second Virgin Film Guide* as one of his 'finest and most accessible' works – is based (Monaco, 1993: 220). The story, published in 1971, is economically plotted. It opens with a conversation between John and his wife, Laura, who have come on a short holiday to Venice; they are there in order to try to recover some sense of normality following the loss of their five-year-old daughter, Christine, who has died from meningitis. John and Laura meet Scottish twin sisters in their sixties, one a retired doctor, the other blind, who are also tourists in Venice. The blind sister is psychic and claims to have had a vision of the couple's dead daughter, which she communicates to Laura. Laura believes her and gains comfort and happiness from it; John is annoyed and upset by the claim. A strange incident occurs: one evening, walking in the narrow streets of Venice, they hear a strangled cry; John then catches sight of what looks like a little girl, wearing a pixie-hood, who seems to be trying to escape from something or someone by jumping from boat to boat in the canal. Unnerved by this, and made anxious by the sisters, John tries to engineer their outings so that they avoid the two women, but, by coincidence, it seems, they keep meeting them in Venice. The couple receive a telegram from their son's school, informing them that he has suspected appendicitis and may have to be operated upon; Laura catches a flight to Gatwick; the plan is that John will follow her by car and boat. After seeing his wife safely off in the airport launch, however, John thinks he sees her, looking distressed, travelling on a vaporetto with the two sisters. Convinced that she has been abducted by the women, he reports his wife as a missing person to the police in Venice. Whilst at the police station he learns that two murders of a particularly horrible nature have recently been committed. Later, telephoning his son's school in England, he discovers that his wife has arrived there safely. Meanwhile, the two sisters have been arrested for the abduction of his wife. He makes a formal apology to both the police and the two sisters, at which point the psychic sister goes into a trance-like state. Returning from the police station to his hotel, John loses his way amongst the labyrinthine streets of Venice and comes upon the pixie-hooded figure he saw earlier. Again she seems to be running for her life; this time he follows her, assuming she is fleeing from the murderer since he spots a man in pursuit. Anxious to protect her, he follows the child into a room in a building and locks the door behind him, against the pursuing male. He turns to reassure the 'child'; her pixie-hood falls away from her head and he is faced with the unveiled, monstrous spectacle of a 'thick-set woman dwarf' (du Maurier, 1973: 55) with long grey hair and a huge head who draws a knife on him. The story closes with his consciousness fading as the blood runs from his body, the knife having pierced his throat.

The setting for du Maurier's short story follows the conventions of the classic Gothic tale which frequently uses Italian cities as sites for the exotic, the sinister and the transgressive. The Venice of du Maurier's story represents the precariousness of 'normality': a holiday resort, it is nevertheless haunted by death. In 'Don't Look Now' the city appears warm and sheltered by day, but this 'bright façade' (25) gives way to an 'altogether different' place at night with the long narrow boats on the dank canals looking 'like coffins' (19). Indeed, John himself perceives it as a dying city, sinking down into its own waters, doomed to become eventually 'a lost underworld of stone' (26). Like the city of Thomas Mann's *Death in Venice*, it is a site of death, decay and degeneration. Yet as a place famous for its tradition of masquerade, Venice is also associated with carnival. However, the festive inversions typical of carnival survive in this story only in grotesque form in the figure of the dwarf-woman murderess who dresses as a child; correspondingly, the city's very brilliance is predicated upon a dark underside which invites a descent into horror, suggested by the labyrinth of narrow canals which John negotiates so well at first but in which he eventually loses his way and, finally, his life. In her short story, du Maurier seems to draw on both the Venetian tradition of carnival and, more generally, the post-Enlightenment fascination with masquerade itself. Terry Castle suggests that it was 'the Enlightenment rigidification of conceptual hierarchies and atomized view of personal identity' that made masquerade so popular in – and so unsettling to – eighteenth-century England. She continues:

> With its shocking travesties and mad, Dionysiac couplings, the masquerade represented a kind of 'uncanny space' at the heart of eighteenth-century urban culture: a dream-like zone where identities become fluid and cherished distinctions – between self and other, subject and object, real and unreal – temporarily blurred.
>
> (Castle, 1995, 17)

Like many recent critics, then, Terry Castle sees the Enlightenment as necessarily *creating* its own darkness and uncanny spaces: arguably, Romanticism further developed this culturally created sense of the uncanny in its rendering of the Gothic, whilst Freudian discourse later duplicated its narrative and epistemological strategy by confining the unconscious to the dark attic and backrooms of the otherwise well-lit house of the post-Enlightenment mind.[1] Correspondingly, du Maurier's tale draws on both Freudian discourse and a post-Romantic sense of the grotesque as strange and uncanny. This mode of the grotesque, as Mary Russo points out, 'is associated with Wolfgang Kayser's *The Grotesque in Art and Literature*, with the horror genre, and with Freud's essay "On the Uncanny"' (Russo, 1994: 7). In differentiating between the comic grotesque (associated with carnival) and the grotesque as uncanny, she asserts that the latter

> is related most strongly to the psychic register and to the bodily as cultural projection of an inner state. The image of the uncanny, grotesque body as doubled, monstrous, deformed, excessive, and abject is not identified with materiality as such, but assumes a division or distance between the discursive fictions of the biological body and the Law.
>
> (Russo, 1994: 9)

'Don't Look Now', we suggest, both presents and implicitly interrogates a Freudian analysis of an identity in crisis. It also sets up the uncanny figure of the dwarf as polymorphous and multivalent; in so doing, it constructs the dwarf as a 'perfect figure for negative identity' (Halberstam, 1995: 22). Through this character du Maurier is able to explore yet again her interest in the nature of identity, a preoccupation which had informed her long writing career.[2]

A Freudian analysis illuminates some aspects of the story. In its use of eyesight/blindness and fear of madness as recurrent motifs, du Maurier's tale, like E.T.A. Hoffmann's *The Sandman*, lends itself to a Freudian approach which reads such motifs as expressing fear of death and castration. Like Hoffmann's story, du Maurier's tale is concerned to explore estrangement and alienation; it is, ironically, John's fidelity to the realm of 'everyday legality' or the Law (represented in 'Don't Look Now' by the discourses of medicine and patriarchy) which prevents him from understanding Venice and its signs, and which leads, arguably, directly to his ghastly death in a room somewhere in the back alleys of the city. As the place of escape from death and self-interrogation, Venice becomes the location of John's confrontation with both. Because he refuses the latter, he invites the former.[3] However, integral to this process of denial is the role played by the elderly twin sisters, whose 'uncanniness' is linked to both the everyday unusual (they are identical twins) and the 'supernatural' (the blind twin is 'psychic'). Their physiological 'doubleness' which disturbs the eye (and the 'I' of John) is offset, though, by the differences between them: one sister, rather masculine in dress, is a retired doctor who practised in Edinburgh and is often described as 'active'; the other is blind, psychic and invariably passive except when she goes into trance or pronouncement. They both are, and are not, 'identical': one appears to suggest the *heimlich*; the other the *unheimlich*. John's reaction to these sisters veers between extremes: sometimes he credits them with evil power (at one point he perceives the blind sister as a Gorgon-like figure who fixes him with her sightless eyes [14]); at other times he dismisses them as merely eccentric and interfering. His rejection of the sisters can be read as a rejection of death itself; his inability to accept fully his daughter's death is signalled, correspondingly, by the fact that his attempts to return life to 'normal' are fated to failure, indicated by his 'seeing' the dwarf woman as a five-year-old girl. His efforts to make the hotel room like home – an assertion of the *heimlich* in the face of the unknown – involves the repression of his and Laura's experience of death and suffering. However, the repressed, as Freud argued in his essay 'The Uncanny', has a habit of returning. Consequently, even within the supposedly safe confines of the hotel room, the radio song 'I love you Baby...I can't get you out of my mind' evokes the presence of the dead daughter. Further, John's determination to avoid meeting the sisters leads him, uncannily, to the very restaurant near the church of San Zaccaria where the sisters have also chosen to eat. Explained in terms of Freud's repetition-compulsion principle, this element of *unheimlich* in du Maurier's story signals repression – in this case the repressed fear of death – which John projects onto his environment. John's tendency either to dismiss or domesticate the strange can be seen as a denial mechanism; this, in turn, leads him into errors of judgement, the most grave of which brings about his own death. Such an interpretation of 'Don't Look Now', of course, turns John into a case study of psychological malfunction and the story into a cautionary tale in which the elements of Gothic and masquerade can best be interpreted through the discourse of Freudian psychoanalytic theory.

This reading, however, also constructs the sisters as merely an adjunct to the central story of John's psyche and its mechanisms of repression. The text itself, though, allows the sisters to function in a much more complex way than this might suggest; its meaning(s) cannot be contained by the Freudian frame. Within its first few pages the tale allows the women a multiplicity of imaginary roles. '"Don't look now", John said to his wife, "but there are a couple of old girls two tables away who are trying to hypnotise me"' (7); Laura and John then amuse themselves, barely suppressing their hysteria, by speculating on what the twins might 'really' be. The list includes middle-aged transvestites, murderers, hermaphrodites, retired schoolmistresses and lesbians. John, relieved that his wife is smiling and laughing again, recognises this fantasising as a healing process which has 'temporarily laid' the 'ghost' of their dead daughter (8). Within the first few pages, then, the story both appropriates and travesties the transgressive and supernatural elements found in Gothic writing. However, what the reader is soon allowed to see, which John cannot, is that his own 'psychic' powers, perceived by the blind twin, which he refuses to acknowledge, mark him as the third 'weird' sister. This denial of supra-rational knowledge, outside the realm of 'everyday legality', goes hand in hand with a denial of that side of himself which he perceives as 'feminine'; for example, he finds it difficult to handle his emotions on hearing his wife's voice on the telephone from England – 'shame upon shame, he could feel tears pricking behind his eyes' (44). Laura's natural wish to grieve for her daughter and to preserve her memory (even through the agency of the sisters' psychic powers) is deflected by her husband's supposedly superior knowledge of what is best for her in her current emotional state of mind, but the story itself shows this knowledge to be both fallible and inadequate in the face of death.

John's 'superior' knowledge emanates from a subject position constructed through age, nation, class and gender. His confidence that he is right derives from his identity as a well-educated upper-middle-class

English male of the mid-twentieth century, and he dislikes or dismisses anything that threatens that sense of self. He is part of an episteme which frames 'knowledge' within certain accredited discourses; he negotiates Venice by map; he accepts his doctor's medical opinion of what Laura 'needs'; he is deeply suspicious of anything beyond the rational and the logical: 'There was something uncanny about thought-reading, about telepathy. Scientists couldn't account for it, nobody￼ could' (13). This sense of identity valorises and defines itself *against* the feminine. So John perceives women and children as needing his protection; to a certain extent he infantilises his wife (offering, for example, to buy her things to cheer her up) and seems to concur with their doctor's advice, the language of which construes women as 'other': 'They all get over it, in time. And you have the boy' (10). He deals with his wife's very different approach to life largely by ignoring it: 'John *knew* the arrival of the telegram and the foreboding of danger from the sisters was coincidence, nothing more, but it was pointless to start an argument about it' (27; emphasis added). John's rationality is, then, based on what feminist theorists have defined as an exclusion model: 'reason, conceptualized as transcendence, in practice (comes) to mean transcendence of the feminine, because of the symbolism used' (Whitford, 1991b: 58). It is also typical of Enlightenment epistemology which, as Terry Castle suggests, defines itself through a 'rigidification of conceptual hierarchies and [an] atomized view of personal identity'.

However, the sisters impinge upon John's confidence in himself and provoke an ambivalent reaction: he thus describes them variously as 'the old dears' (13), 'two old fools' (14), 'frauds' (23) and 'a couple of freaks' (24). His attitude to them derives from a construction of masculinity which is complemented by its binary opposite of a weak and dependent femininity and which consigns the older woman to the category of the grotesque – a category which is, nevertheless, as Mary Russo has pointed out, 'crucial to identity-formation for both men and women as a space of risk and abjection' (Russo, 1994: 12). John thus finds the masculine appearance and apparent self-assuredness of one of the sisters threatening to his own 'manhood': 'He had seen the type on golf-courses and at dog-shows – invariably showing not sporting breeds but pugs – and if you came across them at a party in somebody's house they were quicker on the draw with a cigarette-lighter than he was himself, a mere male, with pocket-matches' (9). The blindness of the other sister, then, symbolically demonstrates the fear of castration which John feels in the presence of the twins. Dismissive of the sisters' 'knowledge' of his child's death at first, John's confidence in his ways of 'knowing', and hence in himself, is gradually undermined as the sisters appear to be more in the right as the story proceeds; he correspondingly demonises them, referring to them at one point as 'those diabolical sisters' (39). He is finally thrown into crisis by the fact that they are proved publicly right and he is proved wrong (they have not abducted his wife; she is safe in England). Significantly, it is at this point that his feelings of paranoia and hysteria (respectively indicative in classic Gothic texts, according to Eve Kosofsky Sedgwick, of masculine and feminine anxiety) force him to reflect on the fact that he might be going mad (Sedgwick, 1980: v–xiii). He is at that moment of hesitation diagnosed by Tzvetan Todorov as central to such literature: 'either he is the victim of an illusion of the senses, of a product of the imagination – and laws of the world then remain what they are; or else the event has taken place, it is an integral part of reality – but then this reality is controlled by laws unknown to us' (in Williams, 1995: 95). Rejecting his vision of the vaporetto (and with it the possibility of 'reading' the uncanny and 'laws unknown'), John chooses to 'contain' the experience within the discourses he recognises as valid: 'The only explanation was that he had been mistaken, the whole episode an hallucination. In which case he needed psychoanalysis, just as Johnnie had needed a surgeon' (45). Typically, then, John pathologises a state of consciousness (even his own) which is outside the scheme of everyday legality, just as he goes on to pathologise the blind sister's trancelike state as epilepsy. Du Maurier's story thus throws into doubt the adequacy of a Freudian psychoanalytic reading, since John himself, in recognising that he might be a suitable case for such treatment, thereby defines it as a dominant discourse which is part of the very episteme the tale sets out to destabilize. In this sense, the story accords with Jacqueline Howard's definition of Gothic writing as a 'metadiscourse' which works 'on prior discourses which embed values and positions of enunciation of those values' (Howard, 1994: 45).

The horror of the tale's end revives certain Gothic conventions in such a way as to confirm the reader's sense, set up by the text's insistent reference to his mistakes, that John is constantly prone to error. The most chilling example of this occurs when the dwarf's pixie-hood, misconstrued by John as a child's garment, drops to reveal a 'creature' of 'hideous strength':

> The child struggled to her feet and stood before him, the pixie-hood falling from her head on to the floor. He stared at her, incredulity turning to horror, to fear. It was not a child at all but a little thick-set

woman dwarf, about three feet high, with a great square adult head too big for her body, grey locks hanging shoulder-length, and she wasn't sobbing any more, she was grinning at him, nodding her head up and down... The creature fumbled in her sleeve, drawing a knife... (55)

The veil which obscures the beauty of the eighteenth-century Gothic heroine is here grotesquely travestied. In fact, the 'pixie-hood' bears more resemblance to the sinister cowl of Gothic fiction which often drops to reveal a similarly murderous intent, as in Ann Radcliffe's *The Italian*:

The monk... advanced, till, having come within a few paces of Vivaldi, he paused, and, lifting the awful cowl that had hitherto concealed him, disclosed – not the countenance of Schedoni, but one which Vivaldi did not recollect ever having seen before!... the intense and fiery eyes resembled those of an evil spirit, rather than of a human character. He drew a poniard from beneath a fold of his garment, and, as he displayed it, pointed with a stern frown to the spots which discoloured the blade...

(Radcliffe, 1797: 318)

The puzzling 'doubleness' of the twins, then, gives way finally to the sinister 'doubleness' of the dwarf whose childish clothes veil an aged murderess. John has fled from a male figure who, it turns out, was probably a policeman chasing the murderess, when he should have fled the female dwarf – an interesting variation on the classic Gothic 'pursuit' scene.

The figure of the dwarf woman is richly suggestive and one which enables du Maurier to explore powerful emotions such as intense fear and the desire for revenge. As a focus for revenge, the dwarf-as-child can be read as problematising twentieth-century sentimental narratives of the nuclear family. Certainly, in metaphorically presenting the 'child' as dangerous, du Maurier's story is typical of many mid-twentieth-century Gothic texts which interrogate the parent/child relationship and the 'innocence' of the young. Seen as a child (which is how John sees her, to his cost), she acts out the daughter's repressed feelings of hatred for the father within the family romance. She is both the unspoken narrative of Christine's (the dead daughter's) tale and, arguably, the avenging daughter of the father/daughter dyad within the modern family. It is perhaps worth noting at this point that the father/daughter romance significantly informed du Maurier's own life as well as her early fiction.[4] 'Don't Look Now' is one of several stories in the Gollancz 1971 collection (originally published as *Not After Midnight*) which suggest the author's continuing interest in the family romance; 'A Border-Line Case', for example, is a disturbing tale which deals with a young woman's brief love affair with an older man who turns out to be her father.

If, however, we adopt an Irigarayan perspective, the dwarf woman can be interpreted more broadly as an avenging figure who emerges from the dark corners of the Platonic cave or the well-lit Enlightenment mansion. Marianne DeKoven, summarising Irigaray's work, notes that in 'its compulsion to repress the maternal origin, masculine (self-) representation defines (refines) itself in opposition to maternal materiality as pure intellect, ideality, and reason' (DeKoven, 1991: 30). As we have seen, John does indeed define his identity in this way, in opposition to both the superstition and irrationality that the twin sisters seem to represent and his own wife's 'emotional' nature. In this light, John's death in the labyrinthine ways of Venice may be read as a manifestation of patriarchal anxiety: John is killed by the 'phallic' mother.[5] That is, John is killed by what has been repressed within Western culture, a system whose values have constructed his own. According to Irigaray, the symbolic order involves a failure to represent the mother tantamount to matricide. In 'Women-mothers, the Silent Substratum of the Social Order', Irigaray states:

> And once the man-god-father kills the mother so as to take power, he is assailed by ghosts and anxieties. He will always feels a panic fear of she who is the substitute for what he has killed. And the things they threaten us with! We are going to swallow them up, devour them, castrate them ... That's no more than an age-old gesture that has not been analysed or interpreted, returned to haunt them.
>
> (Whitford, 1991a: 49–50)

Du Maurier's association of women in 'Don't Look Now' with intuition, emotion and the uncanny is not, therefore, any more than is Irigaray's philosophy, a repetition of the classical equation that the feminine *equals* the irrational and the emotional; nor is it a prescription *for* female irrationality. Rather, as Margaret Whitford suggests in discussing the work of Irigaray, 'to say that rationality is male is to argue that it has a certain structure, that the subject of enunciation which subtends the rational discourse is constructed in a certain way, through repression of the feminine' (Whitford, 1991b: 53). What Irigaray explores in her work, and what, one might argue, is implicit in du Maurier's story, is a proposal for 'the *restructuring* of the construction of the rational subject' (Whitford, 1991b: 53); like Irigaray's work, 'Don't Look Now' can be read as exposing the supposedly neutral discourses of science and medicine as discourses of the *masculine* subject.[6] Read in this manner, the dwarf woman's act of plunging a knife into John's throat takes on an interesting intertextual dimension: it can be seen as retribution for the death of an old woman in du Maurier's *The Flight of the Falcon*, published in 1965. For in that novel Marta dies twice: she is stabbed to death in the streets of Rome, but her illegitimate son's refusal to recognise her existence as his mother, as he later acknowledges to his brother, has also 'killed' her.

However, the dwarf, like Venice itself, is a site of shifting meaning. She represents fear and terror as well as an avenging horror. For not only can she be read as representing the ultimate nightmare of patriarchy – the death-dealing figure of the avenging mother – but she may also be seen as representing a masculine revulsion from the ageing female body, a culturally constructed revulsion internalised by women as a terror of the ageing process itself. For the 'child' of John's imagination transmutes, in an instant, into the shrunken crone, with shoulder-length 'grey locks', who grins at her victim. The dwarf, in this reading, is a cackling hag whose physical presence bespeaks the horrors of old age for the woman writer and reader. Du Maurier was 63 years old when she wrote 'Don't Look Now' (the same age as the twin sisters in the tale); her anxiety about ageing is apparent in a letter written to Oriel Malet in 1965:

Kits, when he was here, took some photographs of me, and also a proper photographer came from St. Ives to do me too...But they make poor Tray look just like an old peasant woman of ninety – far older and more wrinkled than Lady Vyvyan, and I nearly cried when I saw them. I know I am lined, but I had not realized how badly! And the awful expression on my face, like a murderess...

(Malet, 1993: 194)[7]

There is here an echo of another du Maurier work, *The Scapegoat* (1957), in that the author sees herself as 'an old peasant woman of ninety', although in the earlier text this image of ageing is presented more positively – as a metaphorical transition into a way of life that is simple materially and based on moral integrity. In a novel published a year after 'Don't Look Now', du Maurier again managed to construct the ageing process optimistically. *Rule Britannia* (1972) is dominated by the character of an unconventional octogenarian, a retired actress named 'Mad' (short for 'Madam') who rules over an equally unconventional household comprising six adopted unruly boys and her granddaughter, Emma.[8] Supposedly based on the actress Gladys Cooper, Mad, who wears a Chairman Mao cap and who strides about the Cornish countryside, in fact bears a close resemblance to du Maurier herself who, in her seventies, 'looked eccentric and sometimes, in spite of her frailty, a touch threatening', according to Margaret Forster (Forster, 1993: 382, 412). She would, apparently, eat her meals quickly, 'then was capable of leaving the table abruptly and marching off. In her thick jacket and the postman-style cap to which she had become attached she looked as though she had settled into one last part and didn't care what anyone thought' (412). Comic and resolutely non-Gothic, *Rule Britannia* is an entertaining but odd and unconvincing work, 'the last and the poorest novel [du Maurier] ever wrote', in Forster's opinion (383). It is, nevertheless, interesting when read as an almost jaunty attempt to construct old age as a positive phase in a woman's life. In her darker moments, however, du Maurier saw old age in entirely negative terms. In a letter written to Oriel Malet in 1956 (when she was only 49 years old), du Maurier refers to herself as 'your foolish old Granny Tray' (Malet, 1993: 80). Fifty-eight years old and postmenopausal when she wrote the letter concerning her appearance to Oriel Malet, she saw herself as ageing rapidly.[9] Known for her beauty and vitality when young, she now felt herself to be asexual and potentially monstrous ('like a murderess'). The very grounds of her identity seemed to be shifting beneath her. In this, she was not unusual. Simone du Beauvoir, born a year after du Maurier, records in her book *Old Age* (*La Vieillesse*), published in 1970, how common it is for old people to have a distorted view of their body image, seeing themselves as grotesque or even as subhuman. She suggests, for example, that Swift projected his disgust at his ageing body onto the Struldbugs, and notes that Picasso portrayed himself when old as 'a withered shrunken old man or even a monkey' (de Beauvoir, 1970: 340, 374). This de Beauvoir attributes to the low status accorded to the old in modern Western societies.

On the one hand, then, 'Don't Look Now' can be seen as expressing not only a masculine revulsion from the older woman, but also the feminine fear of *becoming* that grotesque figure. On the other hand, du Maurier's tale becomes a warning against a gender-based complacency, vindicating as it does the wisdom of 'old women' (the twins) rather than that of its more youthful male 'hero' through whom all the events of the story are focalised. Thus du Maurier's story perfectly captures the precarious status of the aged woman in Western society as one which slides between that of wise seer and death-dealing grotesque: the dwarf woman, like the freak of Russo's enquiry, 'can be read as a trope not only of the "secret self", but of the most externalized "out there", hypervisible, and exposed aspects of contemporary culture and of the phantasmatic experience of that culture by social subjects' (Russo, 1994: 85). Noting that old people often dissociate their 'real' selves from their mirror reflections, de Beauvoir describes old age as having 'an existential dimension' since 'it changes the individual's relationship with time and therefore his relationship with the world and with his own history' (de Beauvoir, 1970: 15). The 'real' 'self', at such a time, can seem to become an 'Other' which is trapped within a decaying husk of a body which strangely continues to identify the individual; correspondingly, the body itself may be perceived as monstrous and 'otherized' as irrelevant to the 'real' 'self'. This experience seems to be one that du Maurier suffered in old age, and her fears and anxiety transmute themselves into Gothic tropes and motifs in her later work. Only her writing seemed to guarantee the continuance of an 'authentic' identity.

Yet the work itself was becoming increasingly difficult to sustain. In the absence of fresh inspiration, du Maurier turned from fiction to biography, writing two books on the Bacon brothers, which were published in 1975 and 1976. After the mid-1970s the only works to appear until the time of her death were reprints and newly edited collections of stories and autobiographical pieces written years earlier. The final and tragic subtext of 'Don't Look Now' is, then, the decline and death of the creative self. For with the death of John, we see also the death of du Maurier's writing persona, that 'masculine' side of herself which she associated with mental energy and the creative imagination – an aspect of her identity which she referred to in letters and autobiographical writing as the 'boy-in-the-box'.[10] John's psychic powers, perceived by others but unacknowledged by himself, can be seen to represent the writer's intuitive understanding of life. In this bleak reading, the hideous figure of the dwarf is a grotesquely parodic version of the bent and shrunken older woman who kills the 'boy-in-the box'. Age destroys not only youth and beauty, but mental ability and imaginative gifts – or so it seemed to du Maurier. Yet the 'boy-in-the-box' has, in this narrative, a feminine side – for John's psychic gifts are associated with that repressed imaginary identified with the feminine by Irigaray. In what is probably her last successful piece of writing, du Maurier interrogates the nature of that inner self, so vital to her sense of identity, and destabilises those boundaries which had for so long separated her 'masculine' writing persona from her social and public identity as a woman. Faced, however, with the death of that inner self, du Maurier seemed to lose the will to live and went into a long decline, dying in 1989.[11]

As in her most successful works, then, such as *Rebecca* and *The Scapegoat*, du Maurier uses Gothic conventions in 'Don't Look Now' to explore not only the notion of the supra-rational but also the social construction of identity. In this complex short story, du Maurier uses the Gothic tropes of the monstrous body, veiling, freakishness and masquerade in order to interrogate the uncanny nature of identity itself. A story based on *mistaken* identity, it can be read as interrogating gender as a form of masquerade, old age as a culturally constructed state of 'freakishness', the happy nuclear family as anodyne myth and rationality as a post-Enlightenment mental straitjacket. As such it is a classic piece of Gothic writing, emblematic of modernity in its anguished engagement with ways of knowing and ways of being.

Notes

1 Compare Anne Williams's work on the relationship between the Gothic, the Enlightenment and the uncanny in her *Art of Darkness*, 1995.
2 See our *Daphne du Maurier: Writing, Identity and the Gothic Imagination*, 1997, for a fuller exploration of this topic. This essay is a slightly amended version of the second part of Chapter 6 of that book.
3 Roeg's film emphasises this by adding a scene in which John almost falls to his death while working on a restoration project in a Venetian church.
4 See Chapters 1 and 2 of our *Daphne Du Maurier* for a fuller analysis of this aspect of du Maurier's life and work.
5 We are grateful to Clare Hanson for pointing out this connection to us.
6 This reading, whilst drawing on the work of Luce Irigaray, clearly refutes Jacqueline Howard's recent assertion that French feminist interpretations of Gothic fiction tend to collapse women's writing into *écriture féminine* (Howard, 1994: 55) and that they fail to acknowledge how differently individual women write; it also counters her complaint that feminist readings of Gothic works tend to universalise women as victims (56).
7 'Tray' was one of du Maurier's several nicknames; Lady Vyvyan was a neighbour in Cornwall.
8 *The Scapegoat* and *Rule Britannia* were published by Victor Gollancz in 1957 and 1972 respectively. Both novels are still in print and are published by Arrow.

9 Several letters in this volume refer to 'C. of L.' (an abbreviation for 'the change of life' or menopause) and its effects on du Maurier's sense of self.
10 See our *Daphne du Maurier*, Chapter 1 in particular, for a fuller discussion of how du Maurier perceived her creative imagination as a 'boy-in-the-box' and as a 'disembodied spirit'.
11 See Forster's biography, Part 5, 'Death of the Writer', for an account of this period of du Maurier's life.

Works cited

Castle, Terry. 1995. *The Female Thermometer: Eighteenth-Century Culture and the Invention of the Uncanny*. New York: Oxford University Press.
De Beauvoir, Simone. 1970. *Old Age*. Trans. Patrick O'Brian. Harmondsworth: Penguin, 1977.
DeKoven, Marianne. 1991. *Rich and Strange: Gender, History, Modernism*. Princeton: Princeton University Press.
Du Maurier, Daphne. 1973. *Don't Look Now and Other Stories*. Harmondsworth: Penguin.
Forster, Margaret. 1993. *Daphne du Maurier*. London: Chatto and Windus.
Halberstam, Judith. 1995. *Skin Shows: Gothic Horror and the Technology of Monsters*. Durhams NC: Duke University Press.
Horner, Avril and Sue Zlosnik. 1997. *Daphne du Maurier: Writing, Identity and the Gothic Imagination*. London: Macmillan.
Howard, Jacqueline. 1994. *Reading Gothic Fiction: A Bakhtinian Approach*. Oxford: Clarendon Press.
Malet, Oriel. 1993. *Daphne du Maurier: Letters from Menabilly*. London: Weidenfeld and Nicolson.
Monaco, James, James Pallot and BASELINE. 1993. *The Second Virgin Film Guide*. London: Virgin.
Radcliffe, Ann. [1797], 1991. *The Italian*. Oxford: Oxford University Press.
Russo, Mary. 1994. *The Female Grotesque: Risk, Excess and Modernity*. London: Routledge.
Sedgwick, Eve Kosofsky. 1980. *The Coherence of Gothic Conventions*. London: Methuen, 1986.
Whitford, Margaret, ed. 1991a. *The Irigaray Reader*. Oxford: Blackwell, 1994.
Whitford, Margaret 1991b. *Luce Irigaray: Philosophy in the Feminine*. London: Routledge.
Williams, Anne. 1995. *Art of Darkness: A Poetics of Gothic*. Chicago: University of Chicago Press.
Williams, Linda Ruth. 1995. *Critical Desire: Psychoanalysis and the Literary Subject*. London: Edward Arnold.

Chapter 13

Dr McGrath's disease: radical pathology in Patrick McGrath's neo-Gothicism

Christine Ferguson

Patrick McGrath is not the first, nor will he be the last, of the Gothic writers to display a fascination with images of pathology and mental dissolution. These grim motifs have populated the genre since its inception, their prevailing popularity attributed alternately to the modern malaise of *Schadenfreude*, or their symbolic significance as the radical antagonists of constrictive convention and order. An advocate of the latter theory, Linda Bayer-Berenbaum proposes that 'a fascination with disease and decomposition represents a liberation from the confines of beauty' (Bayer-Berenbaum, 1982: 28), a symptom of the insurgent *topos* which she ascribes to Gothicism as a whole:

> Gothicism allies itself with revolutionary movements because it cannot tolerate any restriction of the individual, and thus Gothicism is not merely revolutionary but anarchic in its sympathies. As all forms of order disintegrate, the Gothic mind is free to invade the realms of the socially forbidden. (43)

The term 'Gothic', as any student of the genre is aware, has a theoretical richness and complexity which defies monolithic definitions. That being said, Bayer-Berenbaum's alliance of Gothic pathology with the anti-establishment is none the less provocative and provides an interesting catalyst for our discussion. She is, of course, speaking of the first wave of modern literary Gothicism pioneered by the now canonical figures of Beckford, Lewis and Walpole, fiction which allied itself with insurgency by challenging the *ethos* of such hallowed contemporary institutions as church and class pedigree. De Sade was but one of the few to interpret the Gothic as 'the inevitable product of the revolutionary shocks with which the whole of Europe resounded' (in Fairclough,

1986: 14). Can we still confidently attribute the rhetoric of subversion to the madmen and terata of Gothicism's more recent literary incarnations? In this era saturated with media images of emerging disease epidemics and 'bizarre' forms of criminality, it appears that the deviant subject represents not the hidden, but rather the mundane. If traditional Gothic characters such as the madman and the contagious patient have arguably become clichéd through media proliferation, how can one evaluate their continued presence in the work of recent Gothic writers such as Patrick McGrath as anything less than anachronistic? For the insane and contaminated anti-heroes of new Gothicism to maintain the *ethos* of radicalism associated with their earlier eighteenth-century predecessors, it is essential that they have a different rhetorical purpose than simply to pose as the shocking antithesis of twentieth-century popular culture.

'My father would have liked me to become a doctor, but what growing up in Broadmoor gave me, that glimpse of the limits to which men and women can be driven by psychotic illness, has stimulated instead the writing of fiction' (McGrath, 1989a: 62), notes McGrath of his childhood at Britain's most notorious repository for the criminally insane, where his father served as Chief Superintendent. This was a strange environment indeed in which to spend an adolescence, and one which has contributed immeasurably to the formation of the author's literary sensibilities. All of the author's novels to date feature, in addition to a liberal use of Gothic landscape and imagery, protagonists of unstable psychology who habitually flit in and out of 'a false world of shadows and phantoms' (McGrath, 1993: 108). McGrath's capricious heroes in *The Grotesque* (1989), *Spider* (1990) and *Dr Haggard's Disease* (1993) all speak in the first person as they document their attempts to establish an objective, ordered version of truth in the face of ever-increasing pathological confusion. Some, such as Clegg in *Spider*, suffer simply from a psychiatric disorder, while Sir Hugo Coal in *The Grotesque* and Edward Haggard in *Dr Haggard's Disease* are also afflicted with somatic ailments. In each case, the reader is constantly aware of the deleterious effects of trauma upon the speaker's testimony. One might argue that McGrath has indeed followed in his father's footsteps, devoting a career to the observation, documentation and attempted explication (for do not all acts of fiction constitute acts of explication?) of mental disease. It would be a grave mistake, however, to equate the purposes of scientific examination with those of aesthetic exploration. Implicit in the clinical study of mental illness, as Sander Gilman and Michel Foucault point out, is a desire to render the chaos of aberration subject to classification under the sanitising tenets of Western science, to place the fruits of tainted reason in the defining context of the *scalae naturae* where their volatility may be mitigated through order. Medicine regards illness from the comforting vantage of health. In McGrath's fiction, however, this paradigm is reversed; it is the world of health and reason which becomes subject to the scrutinising gaze of madness. In combining the use of first person form with the choice of blatantly diseased narrators, his novels direct the reader into an uneasy communion with the 'truth' of an ailing mind and body. And rather than being overwhelmingly alien and outlandish, the psychological landscapes of McGrath's mental cripples are symptomatised by astonishing instances of order and logic.

> It was as though a huge bite had been taken out of the back of the house. The back porch, the back kitchen, the scullery, the kitchen itself – the rooms above – utterly destroyed. The blast had knocked the wall out and sideways. Small fires burned here and there. Strange thing, the way the unconscious mind works, for I perceived not wreckage but fragments of order.
>
> (McGrath, 1993: 182)

These thoughts come to Dr Edward Haggard, titular hero of McGrath's 1993 novel, during a nightmare in which he imagines the whole of his seaside practice to have been destroyed during a German air raid. When ruin and decay are the normal, Haggard muses, it is order which becomes aberrant and exotically distinct. Such a sentiment forms the governing trope of the author's Gothic discourse. The fictional milieux into which McGrath draws us, like the haunting vistas invoked by Haggard's subconscious, create an expectation of domestic degeneration and havoc; all else appears alien and bizarre. In the opening lines of *Spider*, Dennis Clegg remarks, 'I've always found it odd that I can recall incidents from my boyhood with clarity and precision, and yet the events that happened yesterday are blurred, and I have no confidence in my ability to remember them accurately at all' (McGrath, 1991b: 9). Here the speaker's pathologically induced bias, instead of being guarded as a trump card to be played only at the text's conclusion, is boldly advertised as the *sine qua non* of his history. So it is in both *Dr Haggard's Disease* and *The Grotesque*; Edward Haggard in the former freely admits that his rational faculties have been severely tainted by morphia addiction; Sir Hugo Coal in the latter concedes that his once-sharp wits have withered drastically since his paralysis.

'The scientific attitude to which I have for decades been faithful, with its strict notions of objectivity, etc., has come under heavy assault since the accident,' he states. 'Cracks have appeared, and from out of those cracks grin monstrous anomalies. I cannot subdue them' (McGrath, 1989: 145).

Paradoxically, the context and style of these admissions undercuts their intended meaning. In *Disease and Representation*, Sander Gilman notes that 'the language of madness has long held centre stage as that quality of the insane which defines madness in and of itself' (Gilman, 1988: 243). A tainted mind, in other words, manifests itself through tainted diction and form. If 'proper' language is indeed the shibboleth of sanity, then the voices which McGrath creates for his protagonists, with the possible exception of Dennis Clegg, mark them as healthy and rational men. Their diseased histories are told not through stream of consciousness cant nor eclectic vernacular, but through elegant phrases, precise grammar and causal plot progression. McGrath's pathological discourse comes not in the form of a terrifying howl, as John Hawkes suggests (McGrath, 1991b: Flyleaf), but in that of a logi-cal, well-mannered argument. 'You must forgive me if I appear at times to contradict myself, or in other ways violate the natural order of the events I am disclosing' (McGrath, 1989: 145), apologises Sir Hugo in a gentlemanly fashion during a period of mid-story confusion. Were it not for such frequently repeated admissions and apologies, one might well be swayed into crediting the narrative voice with the *ethos* of objective truth. For far from being antithetical to the mainstream, the mellifluous voices of McGrath's protagonist patients appropriate and mimic the decorum of the centre from which their disease appar-ently excludes them. The articulation of their sickness is not, as Bayer-Berenbaum might anticipate, in contradiction with principles of 'order, balance and proportion' (Bayer-Berenbaum, 1982: 39), but in alliance with them. The implications of this strategy are of crucial importance in understanding McGrath's relationship to the Gothic corpus.

We should note here that there is, of course, nothing necessarily new nor unique in the conceptual coupling of lunacy and order. In *Madness and Civilization*, Foucault talks about the so-called 'marvellous logic of the mad which seems to mock that of the logicians because it resem-bles it so exactly, or rather because it is precisely the same', and con-cludes that the 'ultimate language of madness is that of reason, but the language of reason enveloped in the prestige of the image, limited to the locus of appearance which the image defines' (Foucault, 1973: 95). There is little precedent for such an alliance in the traditional Gothic, however, which has preferred to revel in deviance's union with status (the mad despot, the corrupt Monk) rather than reason. McGrath's fiction also concerns itself with class, and does occasionally feature narrators whose language is as broken as their minds. For the most part, however, he chooses to focus upon characters who at once perpetuate and are enslaved by logic. This choice is indicative of a literary sensibility which has little interest in perpetuating traditional Gothic binaries of health and monstrosity. Another relationship between the apparently disparate worlds of mainstream normality and alien eccentricity is being formulated.

Not only is the language of McGrath's narrators incongruous with the conceit of their pathology, but the rhetorical foundation of their delusions blatantly contradict traditional models of the 'uncontrolled' mad (Gilman, 1988: 4). At the opening of *The Grotesque*, Sir Hugo Coal comments,

> disease, infection, rot, filth, faeces, maggots – they're all parts of life's rich weft and woof, and anyone with a properly scientific outlook should welcome such phenomena as facets of Nature every bit as wonderful as golden eagles and oak trees and great rift valleys and the like.
>
> (McGrath, 1989: 5)

This statement, although uttered before the onset of his severe illness, exemplifies the thinking that characterises its later manifestation. This invocation of the ranks of nature is not intended to display the egalitarianism of the speaker (for Sir Hugo is an overt, Social-Darwinist snob), but rather to convey his deep conviction that even the most foul and scatological of nature's offerings can be rendered subject to the powerful dominion of that impartial monarch, Science. As a self-declared 'empiricist', Sir Hugo is a devout disciple of that faith which bears as its credo the tenets of superior detachment, induction and objectivity. Even at the moments of greatest distress, such as the incident in which he realises that one of the men he is sharing a pint with has absconded with the corpse of his daughter's fiancé, he fails to abandon his empiricism to the base instincts of panic and fear. 'I did not get any further with my speculations that night', he remembers, 'I decided to suspend my hypothesis for the time being, and await new facts. This is the inductive method; it had guided my thinking for over thirty years' (McGrath, 1989: 106). He is, in all appearances, a very reasonable man. There is, however, something disturbingly unsatisfying in this phlegmatic reaction, as there is in all Hugo's applications of scientific principle to experience throughout the novel. Is it not shocking that a man should jeopardise the safety of his family out of adherence to inductive principle, and would refrain from taking action against his allegedly homicidal butler, Fledge, simply because he had not as yet formed a 'satisfactory plan' for 'getting back at him' (106)? The capriciousness of the protagonist is made most obvious when he indulges in fits of extravagant scientific reason, trumpeting proudly his detachment from sexual desire and the company of his fellow human beings and insisting obsessively that the reader must be able to see for themselves, through observation and induction, the truth of his version of events. Hugo is indeed a psychologically damaged man, and it is when he is most ill that he displays in extreme the traits which have come in Western society to be associated with rationalism, logic and 'healthy' thinking. The sleep of reason engenders monsters indeed.

Similar patterns emerge in McGrath's other novels. In *Spider*, Dennis Clegg constantly curses his terror of envelopment and his compulsive need to categorise history into rigid boxes of memory:

> But what is wrong with me, that in order to save my life I must bury it within wheels, wheels strung on radials forming compartments – allotments! containing only dead things…What sort of life is it, that can only take its existence at the hub of this ragged, wheel-like structure of empty cells?
>
> (McGrath, 1991, 136)

This pathological urge to categorisation is an ironic exaggeration of the scientific method advocated by Francis Bacon in his great mandate of empiricism, *Thoughts and Conclusions*. 'The kingdom of nature is like the kingdom of nature, to be approached only by becoming like a little child', writes the great philosopher. 'A great storehouse of facts should be accumulated… Further, the material collected should be sorted into orderly Tables, so that the understanding may work upon it and thus accomplish its appropriate task' (in Winsor, 1993: 178). Tables, allotments, radials and compartments – units of taxonomic control used by both the diseased and healthy mind alike. What does it mean when opposing poles in a binary are characterised not by contradictory but identical needs and principles of order, when the allegedly impenetrable barrier between health and insanity is shown to be flimsy and penetrable? It is just such a dilemma which lies at the very heart of McGrath's Gothic constructions.

In order to appreciate the meaning behind this dilemma, we must first understand what it *does not* mean. McGrath's fusion of the *topoi* of insanity with that of reason is not simply a clichéd affirmation of the age-old platitude that 'Great genius is to madness close allied, and thin partitions do these rooms divide.' No matter how much the author's characters seem to mimic the conventions of mainstream normality, they never quite manage to shirk the stigma of 'Otherness'. Haggard, for all his scientific training and noble sentiments, is unable to escape the intensifying dementia of his erotic metempsychosis; Clegg, while intent on mastering control, continuity and truth, cripples his *ethos* in articulating the vain fancies of his illness as fact. In one such instance, he recounts:

> I found a bottle of milk by the canal and in it was the putrefying corpse of a man my father had murdered the night before, and I opened it up and drank the milk. Another time I found a baby with a hole in the top of its head, and through the hole I sucked up and swallowed everything in the baby's head until it collapsed like an empty rubber mask. Later I remembered that this was how spiders devoured insects.
>
> (McGrath, 1993: 169)

These are the musings of madness indeed: not a gentle, interpretative madness which knocks at the door of reason, but one which is utterly alien, apart and divorced from all notions of the possible. McGrath is clearly not interested in subsuming disease within the nobler 'room' of health. Such a pursuit is antithetical to the Gothic dialectic; without the essential tension between abnormality and orthodoxy the genre would lose its fundamental framework. Gothicism cannot survive the humanisation of its monsters nor the reduction of its terata to the merely mundane. It is a form which needs the Other to remain other. McGrath does not challenge this paradigm by unifying the diseased and the pure into a bland homogeneity. What his fiction does suggest, however, is a restructuring of the traditional rhetoric at work in literary depictions of sickness.

Gilman notes that it 'is the fear of collapse, the sense of dissolution which contaminates the Western image of all diseases... the construction of the image of the patient is thus always a playing out of this desire for demarcation between ourselves and the chaos represented in culture by disease' (Gilman, 1988: 1–4). Thus implicit in all displays of the teratological, be it in confines of the carnival freak show, the penny dreadful or even the more gruesome aspects of Christian hagiography, is a desire to consolidate the normal. In constructing and quarantining images of disease within the confining barriers of art, the mainstream forges its identity through the processes of contradistinction. We know ourselves by what we are not; the more monstrous and raving the 'Other', then, by reverse definition, the more healthy and rational the society which is able to identify it as such. Ironic, therefore, that the institutions in our popular culture which seem most to venerate monstrosity and illness, such as the horror film industry or even the post-punk 'Goth' movement in music and aesthetics, should be associated with the rhetoric of subversion; what could be more orthodox, more conservative than the reinforcement of the line between the normal and the other? '[W]hether we distance ourselves from it or whether we adopt it as our mask', continues Gilman,

> we use the term *bizarre* as a sign of our own completeness. In the first case we demarcate our sense of self from the Other; in the second, we consciously adopt the external label of difference as a means of showing our control over the world. *In both cases we know we are not different.*
>
> (Gilman, 1988: 244)

Within this framework, the rhetorical problems with designating Gothicism 'anarchic', simply because it confronts the alien and the anti-rational, become blatant. Is not anarchy the dissolution, rather than the affirmation, of established categories of definition? It is only when transgression occurs between these categories that one may talk of revolution.

In the first part of this essay I focused on the incongruous fusion of reason and normality in McGrath's diseased narrators; in the second I have argued that the impulse to depict insanity as totally Other and irrational is born from a conservative mentality. Might we then suppose that the refusal to advocate a theory of orthodox difference between the chaotic world of illness and the ordered world of health is revolutionary? A faulty, if attractive, conclusion. While the textual treatment of lunatics and freaks as being outside the normal is canonical and arguably hackneyed, the alternate option of centralising the diseased Other in not particularly unique either. There has been an increasing tendency in recent years, stemming from R.D. Laing's pioneering work in the 1960s and manifested aesthetically in works such as Paul Sayer's *The Comforts of Madness*, to challenge the stereotypical stigma of irreconcilable difference attached to the insane and the malformed, to suggest that those people who would in prior centuries have been confined to an asylum or exhibited at country fairs are, if I may quote from Todd Browning's *Freaks*, 'Gooble gabble, one of us.' This proclivity has also filtered into the ranks of popular culture, manifesting itself particularly in changing attitudes to that most Gothic of twentieth-century figures, the serial killer. A recent article in *The New Yorker* on the notorious cannibal Jeffrey Dahmer notes that

> Media fascination with lurid crimes feeds a seemingly insatiable sensation-hungry public, yet such treatments generally focus upon the criminal as freak, as monster – a 'stranger' in the midst of the presumably normal. What is less known, or acknowledged, is the odd, disturbing connection between extremes of psychopathic behavior and behavior considered 'normal', if not enlightened.
>
> ('A riddle', 1995: 45)

If, as the author suggests, the banality of psychopathic illness is some kind of secret, then it is a poorly kept one indeed, achieving the cultural saturation of such other pseudo-obscure commonplaces as the JFK assassination conspiracy and alien abductions. The urge to view the diseased as variant members of the mainstream is not new, nor is it more radical than the vision of madness as totally Other. Both treatments constitute attempts at establishing categorical homogeneity, of creating a context in which the ferocity of psychopathology may be placed and understood. And it is through the creation of orthodox, distinct ways of seeing that the mainstream subdues the threat of the monstrous.

It is in light of such polar approaches to the literary articulation of illness that the transgressive grotesque of McGrath's style can be properly articulated. At one point in *The Grotesque*, Sir Hugo Coal comments on his miserable physical condition, stating,

> 'This, then, is the "I" who speaks; cocooned in bone, I pupate behind a blank and lizardlike stare, as my body is slowly consumed by its own metabolism ... As for destiny, I have come to believe that to be a grotesque is my destiny. For a man who turns into a vegetable – isn't that a grotesque?'
>
> (McGrath, 1993: 9–10)

Hugo is, of course, using the term in the classical, etymological sense, invoking the Renaissance understanding of the *grottesco* as the fusion of two or more disparate realms. Like Clegg – Haggard too to a certain extent – he is tortured by nightmares of incongruous amalgamation and cojoinment, including one in which he imagines himself to be merging organically with the foundations of his estate. Little wonder these dreams should so horrify him: what could be more terrifying than a world in which the conventions and laws of physical and psychological phenomena are no longer valid, where all traditional boundaries of definition and identity are disregarded? Such a realm is a microcosm of McGrath's approach, not only to the representation of the diseased, but also to the Gothic genre *per se*. Stylistically, in placing conventionally authoritative narratives in the mouths of unconventional and unreliable narrators, and thematically, in constructing the madman as both alien and familiar, his literature belongs firmly to the realm of the grotesque. In the paradoxes and contradictions of his discourse, we find a mordant glee in the failings of taxonomic classification and the futility of all attempts to establish an objective, orthodox version of reality. The *elocutio* of this neo-Gothicism does not stand in insurgent opposition to order and health, but rather uses these abstract principles as vehicles for fusion and transgression.

This essay opened by pondering the ostensibly revolutionary nature of the Gothic. While it is easy, if not necessary, to adopt the vocabulary of radicalism and insurrection when faced with a genre whose corpus seems exclusively devoted to the dark outer limits of man's nature, such terms belie the complexity of Gothic form. Revolutions in time form their own orthodoxies, and orthodoxy is antithetical both to innovation and to the spirit of any art-form interested in mapping the ever-evolving terrain of human fear and insecurity. As long as Gothicism continues to situate itself in the incongruous region between the opposing loci of health and contagion, logic and blind folly, its potency will remain intact. From the sublime paradox posed by the grotesque is born an acknowledgement of the ethereality of all categories of definition and classification.

Works cited

'A Riddle Wrapped in a Mystery Inside an Enigma'. 1995. *The New Yorker*, 9 January, 45–6.

Bayer-Berenbaum, Linda. 1982. *The Gothic Imagination: Expansion in Gothic Literature and Art*. Toronto: Associated University Press.

Fairclough, Peter. 1986. *Three Gothic Novels*. Toronto: Penguin.

Foucault, Michel. 1973. *Madness and Civilization: A History of Insanity in the Age of Reason*. Trans. Richard Howard. New York: Vintage.

Gilman, Sander. 1988. *Disease and Representation*. Ithaca, NY: Cornell University Press.

McGrath, Patrick. 1989a. 'A Childhood in Broadmoor Hospital.' *Granta* 29, 157–62.

McGrath, Patrick. 1989b. *The Grotesque*. New York: Ballantine.

McGrath, Patrick. 1991. *Spider*. New York: Vintage.

McGrath, Patrick. 1993. *Dr Haggard's Disease*. New York: Simon & Schuster.

Winsor, Polly, ed. 1993. *Scientific Revolutions*. Toronto: Canadian Scholar's Press.

Index

abjection, 1, 5–6, 8, 60, 161–4, 166–73, 179–81, 183–5, 188–92, 194–7, 221, 224
Abraham, Nicolas, 1, 6–7, 43, 49, 195–6, 199n.24
Absalom, Absalom! (Faulkner), 56
Acheron, 97
Acton, William, 58–60, 62–3
addiction, 38, 50
Addison, Joseph, 13, 23, 105n.12
Africa, 82, 131–2, 134, 187
After London (Jefferies), 79, 106n.16
aggression, 62, 64
Alford, Bishop, 100
Alien and Sedition Acts, 129–30, 138
Althusser, Louis, 214
Ambrose, Stephen, 128
American constitution, 5, 127–33, 140, 146, 150–2, 154, 158n.8, 158n.11
American Scene, The (James), 165
Americans, native, 129–31
amputation, 147, 165
anarchy, 128–30, 184, 233, 240
Anatomie Titus (Müller), 204
Ancient Mariner, The (Coleridge), 98, 106n.21
Angel in the House, The (Patmore), 209
anti-Semitism, 177, 193
apocalypse, 5, 73, 74–7, 79, 83, 85–6, 98
Apocalypse Now (Coppola), 5, 127, 135
aposiopesis, 167
archaeology, 77, 84
Aristophanes, 204
Armstrong, Isobel, 95, 101
Arnold, Matthew, 76, 89, 101–2, 106n.19
Art of Darkness (Williams), 231n.1
Até, 204–5
atheism, 103, 105n.1
Atlantis, 83
Augustine, St, 74, 81

Austin, J.L., 151, 158n.9
autism, 43, 50
automatism, 14–15, 50

Babylon, 77, 80, 83, 86
Bacon, Francis, 238
Bailyn, Bernard, 143–4
Bakhtin, Mikhail, 67–8
Barber, Paul, 116, 121n.2
Barbier, Dominik, 202
Barnes, Djuna, 57
Bastille, the, 69
Baudelaire, Charles, 82, 93
Baudrillard, Jean, 74–5, 215
Bayer-Berenbaum, Linda, 233, 236
'Beast in the Jungle, The' (James), 167
Beattie, Bernard, 105n.9
Beattie, James, 24
Beckett, Samuel, 49
Beckford, William, 233
Behind a Mask (Alcott), 70
Beloved (Morrison), 56, 70
Belshazzar's Feast (Martin), 85
Benito Cereno (Melville), 5, 56, 127, 132
Benjamin, Walter, 51, 93, 105n.10, 215
Bentham, Jeremy, 157n.5, 214
Bentley, C.F., 108
Berlin, 210
bestiality, 182
Bettelheim, Bruno, 52n.6, 198n.6
Beyond the Pleasure Principle (Freud), 47
Biographia Literaria (Coleridge), 14
Black Sea, the, 95
Blake, William, 41, 73, 81, 93–4, 105n.11
Blood of the Vampire, The (Marryat), 117
bondage, 64
Booth, William, 81, 84
Borderland, 121

245

Daniel, The Book of, 85
Dante, 92, 95, 97
Darwin, Charles, 77, 86, 133, 237
Dawson, Dr, 119
daydream, 98
death, 4, 8, 19, 33, 43, 45–6, 48–9,
  51–2, 65, 75, 89, 92, 95–7,
  99–100, 109, 111–12, 120, 130,
  137–8, 162, 178–81, 185, 190–2,
  194–7, 198n.12, 207–10, 212,
  214, 219–20, 222–3, 228, 230
'Death Drive according to Bernfeld,
  The' (Lacan), 44
Death in Venice (Mann), 220
'Death notice' (Müller), 210
Death on a Pale Horse (Mortimer), 77
de Beauvoir, Simone, 229–30
Debussy, Claude, 189, 199n.17
decadence, 73–7, 80, 86, 177, 183–5,
  198n.12
Declaration of Independence, 150–1,
  158n.8
De Demonialitate (Sinastrasi), 112,
  122n.9
defacement, 92, 168
Degeneration Amongst Londoners, 86
'deject', the, 164
DeKoven, Marianne, 227
Deleuze, Gilles, 37
De Man, Paul, 170
democracy, 5, 127, 129, 131–2, 134,
  140, 145, 156n.1
Democracy in America (de Tocqueville),
  140, 149
denial, 59, 61–2, 66, 222–3
De Quincey, Thomas, 13, 91, 105n.6,
  105n.16
Derrida, Jacques, 1, 6, 8, 21, 33–4,
  34n.2, 37–8, 40, 47, 49, 150–2,
  157n.8, 158n.9, 158n.11, 203
de Sade, Marquis, 233
'Description of a Picture' (Müller), 208
'Desolate' (Thomson), 105n.1
*Despoiled Shore Medeamaterial
  Landscape With Argonauts*
  (Müller), 202, 206
de Tocqueville, Alexis, 140–1, 143–4,
  146, 148–50, 153–4, 156n.1,
  157n.7

devil, the, 104, 110
Dickens, Charles, 51, 83, 92, 96–7,
  105n.15, 109
disease, 103, 115, 130, 147–8, 233–6,
  239–42
Disease and Representation (Gilman),
  236
Don Giovanni (Mozart), 186
'Don't Look Now' (du Maurier), 6,
  219–23, 225–31
'Doom of a City, The' (Thomson), 90,
  95
Dorian Gray, 69, 84–5
doubles, 4, 18–20, 32, 40, 85,
  105n.15, 131, 161, 166–73,
  210–12, 221–2, 226
'Dover Beach' (Arnold), 89
Dracula (Stoker), 11–12, 15–16, 28, 64,
  68–9, 75, 78, 85, 108–10, 115,
  178
Dracula, Count, 5, 15, 32–3, 63, 70,
  79, 84–5, 109–10, 112, 115–16,
  122n.8, 186, 191
Dream Play, A (Strindberg), 205
dreams, 12–14, 17, 42, 45, 56, 64,
  104, 105n.16, 108, 112, 119,
  122n.10, 122n.11, 192, 221, 242
Dreyfus, Alfred, 193
Dr Haggard's Disease (McGrath), 234–5
Dr Jekyll and Mr Hyde (Stevenson), 57,
  63–4, 68, 78, 178, 180
Dryden, John, 23
Dumas, Alexandre, 12
du Maurier, Daphne, 6, 219–23,
  225–31
du Maurier, George, 193
Dürer, Albrecht, 104

Edgar Huntly (Brown), 5, 127–9
Edinburgh, 222
ego, 162–4, 166, 169–72
Ego and the Id, The (Freud), 18
ego psychology, 18
Egypt, 77
electricity, 15
Eliot, T.S., 88, 206, 208
Eller, Eileen, 50
Ellis, Kate Ferguson, 177, 197n.2
Emerson, Ralph Waldo, 96, 106n.17

CPSIA information can be obtained at www.ICGtesting.com
Printed in the USA
LVOW101717171112

307757LV00003BA/2/A